# How to Draw

## David Brody, M.F.A.

THE
GREAT
COURSES®

PUBLISHED BY:

THE GREAT COURSES
Corporate Headquarters
4840 Westfields Boulevard, Suite 500
Chantilly, Virginia 20151-2299
Phone: 1-800-832-2412
Fax: 703-378-3819
www.thegreatcourses.com

# David Brody, M.F.A.
Professor of Painting and Drawing
University of Washington

Professor David Brody has been a Professor of Painting and Drawing at the University of Washington in Seattle since 1996. He did undergraduate work at Columbia University and Bennington College and received his graduate degree in painting from Yale University in 1983. Professor Brody has received numerous awards. He has been a Fulbright Scholar and a Guggenheim Fellow and has received the Basil H. Alkazzi Award for Excellence in Painting, a grant from the Elizabeth Foundation for the Arts, and two fellowships from the Massachusetts Cultural Council. At the University of Washington, he received two Royalty Research Fund grants and three Milliman Endowment for Faculty Excellence awards.

Professor Brody's paintings and drawings have been shown in close to 100 exhibitions in the United States and Europe. These include solo shows at Gallery NAGA in Boston, the Esther Claypool Gallery in Seattle, Gescheidle in Chicago, and Galeria Gilde in Portugal. His group exhibitions include shows at the Chicago Center for the Print; the Frye Art Museum and Prographica Gallery in Seattle; The Museum of Fine Arts at Florida State University; and The Painting Center, The Alternative Museum, and Bridgewater Fine Arts in New York City. His work has also been shown at ARCO Art Fair in Madrid, the RipArte Art Fair in Rome, the Trevi Flash Art Museum, the FAC Art Fair in Lisbon, and Art Chicago in the United States.

Professor Brody's work has been published and written about in two monographs and in many articles and reviews. An exhibit at the Esther Claypool Gallery in Seattle was described by *Seattle Weekly* as "daring, humorous, and superbly executed." According to *Artforum*, "Brody's ... paintings ... provide a stunning visual punch ... [and] are rendered with a bravura that is both compelling and hypnotic." And *Art in America* concluded, "A highly intelligent artist ... Brody is absolutely serious about technique. An emphasis on fine drawing, delicate surfaces and careful considerations of color and light informs all his pictures." In addition, Brody has been written about in many other publications, including *The Boston Globe*, the *New Art Examiner*, the Spanish journal *Lapiz*, and the Lisbon daily *O Público*.

Professor Brody has lectured or been a visiting critic at Carnegie Mellon University, the Massachusetts Institute of Technology, The University of Chicago, Harvard University, Capital Normal University in Beijing, and the China Art Academy in Hangzhou.

Professor Brody has had a parallel career in music. He has published five books on traditional music, including the best-selling *The Fiddler's Fakebook: The Ultimate Sourcebook for the Traditional Fiddler*. He has performed at festivals in the United States, Europe, and Canada; at Avery Fisher Hall and Symphony Space in New York City; and on Garrison Keillor's radio show *A Prairie Home Companion*. He has recorded with the Klezmer Conservatory Band and other artists on the Rounder, Vanguard, and Flying Fish labels. ■

# Table of Contents

# Table of Contents

## SUPPLEMENTAL MATERIAL

# How to Draw

**Scope:**

The 36 lectures in this course are distilled from four decades of study, studio work, and teaching and communicate the most important and useful things to know about drawing—information that will greatly benefit novice artists.

The course presents drawing as a language and, as in many language courses, introduces ideas one at a time to allow you to fully examine each piece of the puzzle. The lectures progress cumulatively in a step-by-step fashion, with each new idea building on the previous ones. We'll start from simple units and move up to ever-greater complexity.

Each lecture or set of lectures deals with a key idea, concept, material, or technique that has been historically important to artists over the long history of drawing. As we'll see, although there have certainly been changes with time and place, there has also been a great degree of continuity in the language of drawing across continents and over the millennia that human beings have been making drawings.

The approach in this course is simple. Each lecture begins by describing and explaining a new concept or technique, which is then situated it in its historical context and illustrated with visual examples. The examples include both masterworks from a range of periods and traditions in art history and student drawings meant to demonstrate that learning to draw is eminently attainable. The lectures themselves run about 18 hours, but working through all the exercises and projects could well keep you occupied for many months.

The course is divided into six sections. The first section, Lectures 1 through 3, introduces the long history of drawing, starting with some lines scratched into a piece of ochre found in a cave in South Africa dating back some 80,000 years or more and bringing us up to the present day. The introductory section presents the course in broad strokes and quickly gets you experimenting with the materials you'll be using throughout.

The second section, Lectures 4 through 14, focuses on the underlying grammar of drawing, referred to as *formal language*. Here, you'll learn to draw with different types of line, including contour, cross-contour, construction line, and gestural line. You'll learn how line creates shapes, both positive and negative, and how you can use simple shapes to draw many complex objects. You'll also see how you can use cross-contour line to transform flat shape into three-dimensional volume.

As we begin to draw more complex groupings of objects, we'll delve into composition. We'll learn how famous artists—spanning the Song dynasty in China, the Italian Renaissance, the French Impressionist period, and beyond—structured their drawings in this regard.

In Lectures 12 through 14, we'll learn how such artists as Leonardo, Dürer, Eakins, and Van Gogh used practical systems to arrive at accurate proportions and a convincing illusion of volume and three-dimensional space. You'll apply these same methods and techniques to your own drawing projects.

In the third section, Lectures 15 through 19, we'll learn about linear perspective. This powerful drawing system, developed during the Renaissance, radically changed the way future generations around the world would draw. It's not only at the heart of what Raphael and his Renaissance contemporaries were able to accomplish but has become ubiquitous in everything from the contemporary works of such artists as Anselm Kiefer, to video games and manga, to animated cartoons, such as *The Simpsons*.

In the fourth section, Lectures 20 through 30, we'll return to complete our examination of formal language, learning to incorporate value, texture, and color into drawings. You'll learn how artists think about palettes of value and how palettes suggest light and mood. You'll also learn to use value as a compositional tool and how you can create the illusion of volume, space, and light through modulations of light and dark. You'll see how you can further affect the feel of a drawing thorough mark-making and the use of texture. And you'll learn about textural approaches to creating value, including hatching, cross-hatching, and other mark-making systems.

We'll conclude the fourth section with an exploration of color. We'll learn about color properties and study the basics of color theory. As with value, we'll see how artists use these ideas and conceive of color in terms of palettes—groupings or limitations of color that help create specific qualities of light and mood. As we did with value, we'll learn how we can use color compositionally to create a visual hierarchy with focal areas and focal points. And you'll apply all these ideas in your own drawings to create different qualities of mood, light, and form.

In the fifth section, we'll focus on the human figure. The approach in this section is geared to help you draw figures from both observation and your imagination. We'll start with an examination of canons of proportion. Here, you'll learn how to build a figure using a set of measures. We'll complement this with a study of artistic anatomy, including both the skeletal and muscular systems. You'll also learn techniques for approaching the foreshortened figure. We'll combine what we learn about the figure with what we learned in our study of linear perspective, giving you the tools you need to draw figures from your imagination in imagined environments. This is just what Leonardo and Dürer did during the Renaissance, and it is the same method many contemporary animators and game designers use to develop their characters and environments.

In the final section, devoted to advanced projects, we'll look at some of the changes that occurred between the late 19th century and the present. We'll see how Renaissance spatial constructs evolved to include a broader understanding of pictorial space and how this related to many movements in art, including Impressionism, Cubism, and abstraction. We'll close with a discussion and a set or projects designed to help you identify the kind of art you want to make and some thoughts on how you can work toward that goal. ■

# Linear Perspective: Advanced Topics
## Lecture 19

In this lecture, we'll conclude our discussion of gesture drawing applied to compositional studies using perspective. You'll also learn how you can relate your knowledge of linear perspective to drawing freehand, from observation. In this course, we separate topics, such as perspective, in order to be able to study them closely. But each artist synthesizes all the pieces we've been learning in his or her own way. Also in this lecture, we'll introduce the basics of two-point perspective, methods for dealing with sloping planes, and three-point perspective.

### Applying Gesture Drawing to Compositional Studies
The goal in using gesture drawing in compositional studies for the constructed space drawing project is to run through a number of different ideas with the goal of finding the best composition. In such small drawings, you don't need much detail, but you should be able to answer several key questions:

- What is the room like? What do the five major planes look like?

- Where is the horizon? Is it high, mid, or low?

- Where's the vanishing point? Is it right, left, or centered?

- What is the drawing's format shape—horizontal, vertical, or square?

- What's the approximate scale of the grid measure at the baseline?

Once you've answered these questions, measure your compositional sketch and scale up the important measures, including the format shape, the position of the horizon, and the vanishing point. Follow the procedures outlined earlier to grid the drawing, and you're ready to make the drawing itself.

If you want to use specific kinds of windows, doors, furniture, or other objects in your drawing, search in books or online for images and data. Then, project what you've learned about the planar nature of the objects into the specific perspectival position and in the specific scale you want.

## Drawing from Observation Using Linear Perspective

For most of this section on linear perspective, we've been plotting things out with triangle and T-square, but we've just seen that we can also incorporate perspectival thinking with gestural drawing from our imaginations. Such thinking can be useful when applied to freehand drawing from observation and for a range of subjects, including still lifes, interiors, and landscapes. It helps you quickly see and understand what's going on in complex visual situations.

A good way to practice this, at first, is to pick subjects that have a clear perspectival recession. Next time you're on a plane or train, take out a sketchbook. Notice how the seats and overhead bins are all united by diagonals moving toward a vanishing point. Or try sketching outdoors, looking down a street. You'll see how the cars parked along the curb relate to the same vanishing point as the curb, sidewalks, and other elements.

Find your eye level in the drawing; that's the horizon. Try to see how all the things around you could be conceived of as blocks, prisms, cylinders, cones, and spheres, all related to a ground plane and the horizon. Locate the vanishing point or points. Draw with horizontals, verticals, and diagonals related to those points. Start with large structures and move from the general to the specific as your basic measures are set.

## Two-Point Perspective

Although one-point perspective is very useful, it has clear limitations. It's great for describing a receding hallway or a room where the back wall is parallel and the side walls are perpendicular to the picture plane. It's equally useful for describing such objects as blocks in a similar spatial orientation, with a face that is parallel to the picture plane and other surfaces that are perpendicular. Vertical lines describe height; horizontals describe width; and diagonals, receding to a common vanishing point on the horizon, describe depth.

But if the object is positioned so that it no longer has a face that is parallel to the picture plane, one-point perspective will not work. Verticals will still express the height of the room or block, but the horizontals are gone. We are left with diagonals shooting back in two different directions: one to a right vanishing point and one to a left vanishing point. In other words, one- and two-point perspective describe objects that are positioned differently relative to the viewer and the picture plane. To start to get a grasp on two-point perspective, we'll repeat an exercise we did for one-point perspective: drawing nine blocks.

## Sloping Planes

Using one-point and two-point perspective, we're able to describe objects with planes that are parallel, perpendicular, or angled to the picture plane. We can also describe an object that is parallel or perpendicular to the ground plane. But if we tip the object at an angle, we need a new set of procedures. The tipped plane of an object is called a *sloping* or *incline plane*.

We've actually already drawn an object with multiple sloping planes, though we didn't speak about it in those terms. This was the open box we drew in an earlier lecture. We'll draw a similar box now, but this time, instead of relying on observation, we'll use what we know about linear perspective and sloping planes to construct the drawing.

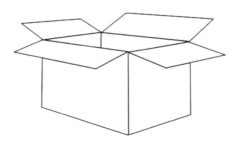

**Three-Point Perspective**

One- and two-point perspective assume that the viewer is looking straight ahead, that his or her centerline of vision is parallel to a flat ground plane. In contrast, three-point perspective assumes that the viewer is tilting his or her head, looking up or down.

As with two-point perspective, in three-point perspective, we have right and left vanishing points to express width or depth. But we also have a third vanishing point expressing height. We'll practice this form of perspective by drawing a block as if we're looking down at it.

## Suggested Reading

Loomis, *Successful Drawing*, "Perspective the Artist Should Know," pp. 29–66.

Mendelowitz, Faber, and Wakeman, *A Guide to Drawing*, "Perspective and Forms in Space," pp. 171–183.

# Linear Perspective: Advanced Topics
## Lecture 19—Transcript

We'll start off here with the conclusion of our discussion regarding applying gesture drawing to compositional studies using perspective, the kinds of studies necessary to make drawings like the student examples we looked at in the previous lecture. You'll also learn how you can relate your knowledge of linear perspective to drawing freehand from observation.

We separate things out, like perspective, in order to be able to study them up close, but each artist synthesizes all the pieces we've been learning about in his or her own way. Lastly, in this lecture, I'll introduce the basics of two-point perspective, how we deal with sloping planes, and give a brief introduction to three-point perspective.

So, let's finish up our discussion of gestural compositional studies for perspective drawings. The idea is to run through a number of different ideas for a drawing with the goal of finding the best composition. In these small drawings you don't need much detail, but you want to answer several key questions: What's the room like? What do the five major planes look like? Where's the horizon located? Is it high, mid, low? Where's that vanishing point? Is it right, left, or in the center? What's the drawing's format shape? Is it horizontal, is it vertical, is it square? What's the approximate scale of the grid measure at the base line? And, of course, you want to determine the subject of your drawing. All the other considerations should relate to this.

Once you've answered these questions, you measure the compositional sketch you made and scale up the important measures. Start with your format shape. Do the same with the positions of the horizon and vanishing point.

Next, you could draw the back wall: Using a ruler, divide the vertical distance between the horizon and the bottom edge of the back wall into units. These units represent the eye height of the viewer in feet. You now have your scale and you can grid the back wall. And, remember, we want to keep the grid light and thin—this is all construction line. It's generally preferable to adjust the back wall's shape so you don't come out with fractional grid units on either axis. Then, you can now project your diagonals forward along the ground plane.

You can assess the first row of grid units from the back. Take into account the square grid on the back wall and the height of the horizon in making the first horizontal. Then, use the rule of diagonals—this time moving forward in space—to find successive rows. It's often preferable to modify the exact placement of the ground line or bottom edge of the format shape to accommodate a final full row of tiles.

Once you have these two planes, project your sidewalls and ceiling, then grid the rest of your drawing. With a completed grid, you're ready to make the drawing itself. If there are specific kinds of windows, doors, or furniture, or other objects you want to use in your drawing, search in books or online for images to get data. Then, project what you learn about the planar nature of the objects into the specific perspectival position and in the specific scale you want.

You now have the tools to dig into this project and create a believable environment from your imagination. You may want to go back and take another look at the student examples for this project. You could even make small gesture studies based on those drawings—it will sharpen your sense about how gesture relates to linear perspective.

For most of this section on linear perspective, we've been plotting things out with triangle and T-square, but we've just seen that we can incorporate perspectival thinking with gestural drawing from our imaginations. And it can also be really useful applied to freehand drawing from observation, and for a range of subjects—still lifes, interiors, landscapes; it's useful for all of this. The knowledge helps you quickly see and understand what's going on in complex visual situations.

A good way to practice this, at first, is to pick subjects that have a clear perspectival recession. Next time you're on a plane or train, take out a sketchbook. You'll see how all the seats and overhead bins are all united by diagonals moving toward a vanishing point. Or try sketching outdoors looking down a street. You'll see how the cars parked along the curb all relate to the same vanishing point as the curb, sidewalks, and other elements.

Find your eye level in the drawing—that's the horizon. Try to see how all the things around you could be conceived of as blocks, prisms, cylinders, cones, and spheres, all related to a ground plane and the horizon. Locate the vanishing point or points; draw with horizontals, verticals, and diagonals related to those points. Start with large structures and move from the general to the specific as your basic measures are set.

You'll remember, earlier, I briefly introduced linear perspective as the final tool that would help us understand proportions. Well, let's take one of the observational drawings we did and see how we could have applied linear perspective to do just that.

In an earlier lecture we drew a deep room using Alberti's *velo* using grid coordinates. We could equally have approached this using one-point perspective.

This is one of the hallways I use for this project at the University of Washington. It's on the third floor of the art building, right outside the classroom where I teach. If we used linear perspective to draw this, our first goal would be to locate the vanishing point and the horizon, and that's easy enough—any two receding diagonals will yield this information.

Here's how. Using our clock hands tool, we can measure a diagonal receding in space. Then, either by eyeballing or using a standard unit of measure, we can place the angle in our drawing. We'll make sure to extend it back beyond the end of the wall, because that's where this angle will reveal the vanishing point's location.

Using the same method we'll add a second diagonal. Where the two diagonals intersect is the vanishing point, and that reveals the horizon's height. We can check for accuracy by holding a pencil horizontally in front of our eyes with one eye closed, we'll look at the alignment of the horizon in the drawing, and compare it with what we see in the hallway. Looking at the negative shape that occurs between the horizon and the two diagonals is a good test, too.

The vanishing point will reveal all the angles of the receding diagonals on the right wall. To draw them, all we have to do is locate their point of origin along the right edge of the drawing's format. To do that, we could eyeball the distances in relation to the horizon, or we could use a standard unit of measure.

We'd also need to locate the back edge of the right wall. That will fix the termination of the diagonals. Alternately, we could have drawn the vertical of the back wall first, then measured to find the relative positions of the terminations of the diagonals and, lining these points up with the vanishing point, bring lines forward to the format's edge.

Once we have one wall, we could use level lines to identify the placement of events along the vertical axis of the second wall. The vanishing point, in combination with points of origin or termination, will give us the information we need to draw the receding diagonals. We can proceed the same way to locate the lights on the ceiling, and the tiles on the ceiling, and even the reflections of the lights on the floor, and the reflection of the walls on the floor, too. So, this one little point offers up a wealth of data.

I think you'll enjoy applying one-point perspective to an observational drawing. Redrawing the room you did using the grid could be a good place to start. Another good subject is a road, either in the country or a city, going back into space. You can tackle any subject that has a strong one-point perspectival view. This will really solidify your ability to use perspective in a wide variety of ways.

While one-point perspective is very useful, it has clear limitations. It's great for describing spaces like a receding hallway or room where the back wall is parallel to the picture plane and the walls are perpendicular to the picture plane, and it's equally useful for describing objects like these boxes. Like the room, they each have a face parallel to the picture plane and other surfaces perpendicular, all at right angles. Vertical lines describe their height, horizontals their width, and diagonals receding to a common vanishing point on the horizon their depth.

But, let's rotate the block on the left. In contrast to the block on the right, there's no longer a face parallel to the picture plane, and we won't be able to draw it using one-point perspective. Verticals still express the block's height, so that's the same, but the horizontals are gone—now we just have diagonals shooting back in two different directions. Let's see where they go.

One set of diagonals, three in all, vanish back to the right. That would be the right vanishing point. The other three go back to the left. That would be the left vanishing point. And this, as you've likely guessed, is two-point perspective. We use it to describe planes that are angled to the picture plane. Both of the vanishing points are located on the already existing horizon, and that's no surprise. Remember, the horizon's not a place; it's a function of eye height. Another thing to note is that we're seeing one- and two-point perspective objects at the same time, and that's perfectly normal. We have two boxes in different orientations: One is showing a face, the other an edge.

We experience this all the time. You walk into someone's office for a meeting, you're looking straight ahead at them at their desk, you see the base of the desk as a rectangle; it's in one-point perspective. If the chair you're going to sit in is angled to the desk, it's in two-point perspective. If you're looking straight at your refrigerator so its face is a rectangle, it's in one-point perspective. Someone comes along and opens the refrigerator door—while the refrigerator remains in one-point, the door is now in two-point.

One- and two-point perspective simply describe objects that are positioned differently relative to the picture plane. With one-point perspective, there's a single fixed rotational position for our box; with two-point, the possible rotational positions are infinite.

Right now we're seeing an equal amount of both the right and left sides of the box. Let's rotate it slowly to the left. As we do, you'll note that we're seeing less and less of the right face. And, as this happens, the diagonals and the two vanishing points are being pulled to the left along the horizon. If we keep going, the right plane disappears and we're back in one-point perspective.

Rotate the other way, around to the right, and we'll see the inverse. We see less and less of the left face. The diagonals and vanishing points move to the right along the horizon and, finally, the left face disappears and we've returned to one-point perspective.

There's a factor I should mention that affects where the vanishing points will be. As you move closer to an object the vanishing points move in toward the object; as you move farther away, the opposite.

Let's take a look at the room we're in. It's a one-point perspective room. The room and the two boxes all share a common vanishing point: All the vertical edges are parallel, all the horizontal edges are parallel, and all the diagonals receding to the vanishing point represent edges that are parallel.

Now, let's rotate both the room and the box on the right to the left, and we'll keep them parallel as they rotate. You'll note that they share right and left vanishing points, and here's the principle: Objects that are parallel in nature will share the same vanishing point or points. This is true in both one- and two-point perspective.

Let's leave the room where it is but begin to rotate the box to the left. Now its diagonals and vanishing point move to the left—we see less of its right plane and it's no longer parallel to the walls in the room.

Finally, let's take the box on the left and rotate it so that we see more of its right plane and less of its left plane. Now, none of the objects are parallel— each is angled differently and each object has its own set of two vanishing points. If we reposition the boxes so that they're parallel to the walls, all will share the same two points.

Here, in two-point perspective, what we'll see of an object related to its location—vis-à-vis the horizon—is much like what we encountered in one-point. Here, we have two boxes below the horizon and we see a top plane and two side planes. Throw another two identical boxes above the horizon and now we see the bottom planes instead of the tops. Throw two more on the horizon and all we see are the side planes.

So far we've been seeing the boxes as opaque structures. Let's make them transparent and see what's going on inside. A box or block has 12 edges—four describe its width, four its height, and four its depth. Drawing with line, we need 12 line segments to describe a transparent block. In one-point perspective, vertical lines describe height, horizontals width, and diagonals depth. And this is just what we see in Leonardo's *Last Supper*.

In two-point, verticals still describe height, but diagonals converging to a vanishing point on the right describe depth or width on the right side of that object; diagonals converging to a point on the left, depth or width on that side. And that accounts for most of the furniture in Van Gogh's *The Night Café*.

The key to remember is that edges that are parallel in nature converge to the same vanishing point. Let's repeat what we did in one-point here, but in two-point. We'll draw nine transparent blocks: three above the horizon, three straddling the horizon, and three below.

Put a new sheet of paper on your drawing board in the landscape position. First, we'll draw a centered horizon line. In one-point perspective, the vanishing point is generally located within the format shape. In two-point, it's common for one or both points to be located outside the format shape. If the points are too close together, you get distortion. This can mean doing a smaller drawing in a larger page so that you can locate the vanishing points outside the format shape. Another strategy is to attach several sheets on a long drawing board or on a wall.

For this exercise, we'll place the right and left vanishing points at the far right and left edges of the horizon, at the vertical edges of the page. In two-point perspective, the closest part of a block to the picture plane is its edge, so we'll start by drawing three vertical lines on the horizon to represent three edges. Make each an inch and a half tall. We'll put the first one right in the center at the 12-inch mark. We'll put the other two five inches away on either side. And we'll add three more verticals two inches above these, then another two inches below. Lightly, one and one-quarter inches to the right and left of each of these three stacked verticals, we'll draw a long vertical construction line.

Let's start with the vertical on the lower right. Turn this into a block. From both the top and bottom, we'll draw diagonals back toward the right vanishing point and stop at the vertical construction line. Then, draw the vertical. Now, we'll repeat these steps going to the left vanishing point: top to vanishing point, bottom to vanishing point, and define the depth with a vertical. From the top of the second vertical, we'll draw a line back toward the right vanishing point, and from the far right vertical we'll draw one going back to the left vanishing point and intersect the line we made in the last step. We have an opaque block.

Let's turn it transparent. Remember to draw the interior with a lighter and thinner line. From the right lower corner, we'll draw a line back toward the left vanishing point. From the far left corner, we'll draw a line back to the right vanishing point. If we've been accurate, a vertical extended from their intersection should connect to the back corner of the block. With that introduction, you're ready to draw the remaining blocks yourself. This is what it should look like.

Using one- and two-point perspective, we're able to describe an object with planes that are parallel, perpendicular, or angled to the picture plane. We can also describe objects that are parallel or perpendicular to the ground plane. Now, that's a bit abstract, so let's take a look at an animated sheet of plywood and see what this means.

Face forward, it's parallel to the picture plane and parallel and perpendicular to the ground plane: We're in one-point. Rotate it 45 degrees on its axis. Now, we're at an angle to the picture plane but still parallel and perpendicular to the ground plane: We're in two-point. Rotate another 45 and we're back in one-point. Rotate and stop anywhere and we'll be in either one- or two-point. We could also lay it flat on the ground, rotate it in any which way, and it will be in either one- or two-point perspective.

So, we're able to use one- and two-point perspective to draw many different orientations of form in space, but the moment we tip the plywood up at an angle, or down for that matter, we need a new set of procedures. We call these kinds of planes sloping or incline planes. We encounter them as streets going uphill or downhill, or pitched roofs, or ramps. These are all examples of sloping planes.

So, let's take that piece of plywood lying on the ground—it's in two-point perspective. We can see its vanishing points on the horizon, right and left. Let's leave the left front edge of the plywood on the ground but lift the rear right edge up a bit. It becomes an ascending incline plane—it's sloping upward to the right. Since it ascends to the right its sides will now vanish to a point along a vertical line extending straight up from the right vanishing point. This line's called a vertical trace. The point where the lines meet is called the vertical trace point or vertical vanishing point. The back edge of the sheet of plywood will still be defined by the left vanishing point.

As we lift the sheet of plywood further off the ground, the point where its sides converge on the vertical trace moves higher and higher, and this changes the diagonals of the edges of the plywood sheet. This will continue until the sheet is perpendicular to the ground plane and we're no longer sloping—until we're back in unadorned two-point perspective. If we continue past the vertical, we begin to descend—we're sloping down. We're far from the ground plane, so the sides of the panel will converge to a point on the vertical trace way below the horizon. As the panel returns closer to the ground, the vertical trace point climbs up the vertical trace until we return to the ground plane and all vanishing points return to the horizon.

If we were to lift the rear left edge, the panel would now be sloping upwards toward the left and its edges would converge on a vertical trace going through the left vanishing point. As we continue to lift and then rotate the panel, we see the same relationships play out here as we did when we inclined the plane to the right.

You've actually already drawn an object with multiple sloping planes, though we didn't speak about it in those terms. It was the open box we drew in the lecture that centered on proportion. Let's try something similar here. This is what we'll draw, but this time, instead of relying on observation, we'll use linear perspective to construct the drawing.

Start with your page in the landscape position and draw a horizon line seven inches from the bottom of the page. Then, add right and left vanishing points about a quarter of an inch from the right and left edges.

First we'll draw the block shape of the box. Start with a two-inch vertical line one and three-quarter inches below the horizon line. One and a half inches to the right of this, draw a vertical to represent the width of the box on this side. From both the top and bottom of the central two-inch line, draw a line back toward the right vanishing point. Stop at the vertical. Erase anything you don't need.

Two and one-eighth inches to the left of the centerline, draw another vertical. Then, from the centerline, draw the top and bottom edges of the left side of the box receding toward the left vanishing point and stop at the vertical. Erase anything extra. From the far right corner, vanish left. From the far left corner, vanish right. And, again, erase anything you don't need. To complete the box's base, add a vertical in the box's interior.

Now for our sloping planes. First we'll draw vertical traces above the right and left vanishing points. Let's start with the flap in the rear on the left. Place a vertical trace point six inches above the left vanishing point. Then, draw from the rear left corners toward that point. We can eyeball the width and draw a line to the right vanishing point to complete the flap.

Let's move to the front right flap. Add a vertical trace point three inches above the left vanishing point and project lines out to the left from the box's corners. Again, eyeball the width and draw a line to the right vanishing point to define this. Note here that if we were to lift this flap up above the edge of the box, it would vanish to a point on the vertical trace below the horizon. Similarly, if we were to lower the rear flap below the box's edge, it would also vanish to a point below the horizon.

Let's move to the rear right flap. I think you get the idea. Add a vertical trace point eight inches above the right vanishing point and draw that flap. Add another four inches above the right vanishing point and draw the final one. Erase where the flaps overlap the box and you're done.

If you want rigorous results, drawing the horizon, the vertical traces, and all the horizontal and vertical vanishing points will do the trick. But, once you've done this a couple times, you'll likely have a reasonable grasp of the underlying principles governing these kind of planes, and for many purposes, you can dispense with all the ruled construction lines. As you begin to get a feel for this, you can eyeball where given edges should vanish. For many kinds of drawing this will work just fine.

You could practice this by setting up a still life of two to three boxes with open flaps so you have a good number of sloping planes, make a couple compositional sketches, decide on a point of view and format shape, then make the drawing itself. Start with empirical perspective to get the essentials located. Then, apply what we've just covered, but this time don't actually draw all the construction lines, just try to imagine where they'd be, and draw the edge of the boxes in relation to these imagined lines.

You'll remember that one- and two-point perspective assume that the viewer's looking straight ahead, that the viewer's center line of vision is parallel to a flat ground plane. Three-point perspective assumes we're tilting our head looking up or looking down. Like in this early Superman cover. Here, it's as if we're tilting our heads down, looking down from above. You'll find that three-point's a staple of superhero comics.

Three-point won't be totally foreign to you—in fact, you've already drawn an object in three-point perspective, though I didn't describe it that way. It's the box we drew in the lecture on proportion. We were looking down to get a lot of complex angles. As with two-point perspective, we have a right and left vanishing point to express width or depth, but we'd also have a third vanishing point expressing height. In this case, the box's vertical edges appear to angle down toward a common point way below.

We only have time for a brief introduction to three-point, but let's draw a block as if we're looking down. Start with the page in the landscape position. The first part of this will be just like drawing a block in two-point perspective.

We'll draw a horizon one inch from the top of the page. Then, add vanishing points about a quarter of an inch from the page's edges. We'll make a small mark two and a half inches below the horizon, centered in the page. This will be the top front corner of the block.

From this point we'll draw a two-inch vertical line straight down. This will represent the box's height. One and a half inches on either side of this, we'll draw a light vertical construction line. From the block's top front corner, we'll draw diagonals back toward both the right and left vanishing points, stopping at the vertical construction lines. Then, erase your construction lines. From the line on the right we'll draw a diagonal toward the left vanishing point and from the left to the right vanishing point.

Next, from the center bottom of the block, we'll draw lines back to the right and left vanishing points. Now we need our third point. We'll locate this vanishing point one quarter of an inch from the bottom of the page and centered in its width. From each corner we'll draw a diagonal down toward the third vanishing point, stopping where we intersect the lower diagonal. You're done. And if you rotate your page 180 degrees, you'll have an example of three-point perspective, but this time looking up.

You could take some time to play with this page. Try blocks to the right and left and, of course you could turn them into buildings or other objects. You can, of course, create the sensation of looking up or down using one- or two-point perspective and place things above or below the horizon. And, historically, that's what many artists have done. In fact, I don't know of any drawings by Leonardo, Raphael, Dürer, Canaletto, Ingres, or Eakins that use three-point perspective. And there are some pretty dramatic uses of one-point perspective to achieve this, like this 17th century ceiling fresco in Florence's Pitti Palace by Agostino Mitelli.

You've now done three major perspective drawings: the quad, the gridded room, and your constructed room. After doing the first two you learned how to draw curvilinear forms and pattern in perspective. In this lecture, you added two-point perspective and sloping planes. No reason not to work into all three drawings to apply your new knowledge—it should be a good bit of fun.

This lecture concludes our investigation of line and you've learned a tremendous amount about its complexities, but I'm sure you're anxious to learn about value, and light, and shade, and that's just where we're going to turn next.

# Value: How Artists Use Value
## Lecture 20

All the drawings we've done thus far have been line drawings, primarily because it's easier to learn about proportion, measurement, composition, and linear perspective when we're just dealing with line. But now, we're ready to draw into all the areas between the lines. We'll do this first with value, followed by mark making, texture, optical value, and color. Many people, when they think about value, think primarily about shading. Although shading is one of the things that value is used for, it's only one among many. In this lecture, we'll take a comprehensive look at the ways artists think about and use value.

### A Nine-Step Value Scale

*Value* refers to neutral or achromatic tone. *Chroma* means "color"; thus, *achromatic* means "no color." These achromatic tones extend from the brightest white, through intermediary grays, to black. The word *value* is also used to describe the relative lightness or darkness of a color.

We know what black and white are. Gray, though, is a much "grayer" subject area. Although we might describe something as light gray or dark gray, we don't usually get much more specific than that. Artists, however, quantify gray by using a value scale, such as the nine-step scale shown below:

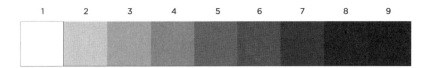

### Value Palettes and Mood

Using the concept of a value scale, we can think about a drawing as existing in a specific range of value—a *value palette*. Drawings with values on the light end of the scale are said to have *high-key* value; those with values on the dark end are said to have *low-key* value; and those with values in the central range have *mid-key* value. Of course, some drawings also use a full range of value.

The choice of a tonal palette literally sets the tone for the drawing. It creates the governing mood, sense of light, and time of day. It's at the heart of how we experience the drawing on an emotional level.

The greater the value range in a drawing's palette, the greater the opportunity for high contrast. A palette of white and black will generally feel strong and aggressive. The tighter the value range, the lower the opportunity for contrast. A palette of four dark grays will feel much more subdued. A drawing with white, black, and many of the steps in between can result in some high contrast areas balanced by others that have much more gentle transitions.

### Compositional Value
Although most non-artists are aware of shading, they're generally unaware of the importance of value as a key compositional tool. Value can divide the page into large constituent compositional shapes. We can control the viewer's eye and create focal points and focal areas through value contrast. All else being equal, viewers will focus on the area of highest contrast first. As you draw, determine what's important in your work and use the tools of drawing, including value contrast, to lead the viewer through your composition. In other words, let your use of value reiterate what you've done through placement, direction, choice of subject matter, and narrative intent.

### Relative Value and Simultaneous Contrast
In looking at the value scale, you may have noticed that each square appears to be a little darker on its left edge and a little lighter on its right edge.

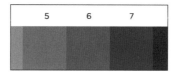

This is an optical illusion and an instance of what is referred to as *simultaneous contrast*. The left edge appears darker because it's next to something lighter;

the right edge appears lighter because it's next to something darker. White will also appear brighter as its ground becomes darker and brightest when set against black. Black will appear darker as its ground gets lighter and darkest when set against white.

We experience value relatively, which means that we won't know how any value really appears until we see it in context—next to all abutting values. Imagine that you're drawing a still life of two bottles on a table in front of a wall. Beginners will tend to finish the objects first, then add the cast shadows, and finally, the wall and table. But given the relative nature of value, it makes much more sense to look at the central area, where we see the interior sides of the bottles and where those two sides meet the intersection of the wall and table. If you can give an indication of what happens at this set of intersections, you'll be able to understand how the different values affect one another.

Developing such a key area can give you a clear idea of the overall value range or value palette in a drawing. Based on this, you can lay in general values for the back wall, table, and bottles. In this way, you see all the value relatively and can move toward greater detail and specificity from a solid base.

Another good practice is to work from the back to the front in a drawing because whatever is behind the main subject or objects—such as a wall—must be overlapped to truly feel as if it is behind. The same thing is true for whatever is underneath the main subject or objects, such as a table; it must be overlapped to feel underneath the objects. This means that the actual graphite or charcoal marks and smudges that the bottles are drawn with should overlap the graphite or charcoal of the wall, not vice versa. Beginners who don't do this often wind up with a halo of light around their objects. They finish the objects first, then they try to draw what's behind them. But because they're afraid to mar the edges of what they've drawn, they stop the value of the wall or table short of the object's edge. This makes the wall and the spatial environment feel unbelievable and discontinuous.

In most cases, if you develop the habit of working from back to front, the overlaps of edge will work to your advantage. Once you've found the general value palette by putting value into a juncture where key edges meet, go to the largest plane in deep space, such as the wall, then address the tabletop, and finally, the bottles. If they're physically drawn on top, they'll feel in front. In addition, the walls, tables, floors, and similar large planes often account for the largest shapes in the drawing, and it's much easier to attend to their values first.

## Space: Atmospheric Perspective

In an earlier lecture, we spoke about atmospheric or aerial perspective. We saw how, on a light to mid ground, dark marks and shapes tend to advance in space, while lighter, fainter marks and shapes tend to recede from the picture plane. Another way to say this is that events of greater value contrast will tend to project forward in space. Those of lesser contrast will tend to recede. As with line, much of the art here involves balancing a compositional or hierarchical use of value with a spatial one.

## The Effects of Light on Nominal Value

We've spoken about many of the "big picture" uses of value in drawing and can now turn to value as it relates to objects. When we look at things around us, we identify some as lighter and others as darker. We'd likely agree that a white shirt is lighter than a black shirt. This is true under what might be termed "normal" light conditions. An object's value under these conditions is called its *nominal value*.

However, light affects nominal value. Put the same black shirt in front of a strong light, and the planes receiving the light will become light gray. If the shirt has a somewhat reflective surface, some planes or parts of planes may even appear close to white. Thus, although objects have a given nominal value, their actual value is a function of light, and that's compounded by the object's surface qualities. Because of this dependence on light, the range of values that a given object might display is infinite. The primary factors contributing to perceived value in this regard are the strength of the light source, its distance from the object, and its angle and direction.

## The Direction of Light

One of the factors affecting whether an object appears flat or three-dimensional is light. Ambient and diffuse lighting reveals little planar change. Similarly, a light source directly behind a subject produces a silhouette—another fairly flat view. And placing the light source directly in front of the subject also tends to minimize the appearance of planar changes and result in relative flatness.

To bring out three-dimensional form, we generally light from the side. This breaks the object into distinct planes: light ones facing the light and darker ones turned away from the light. Light coming from the side produces *chiaroscuro* ("light-dark"). When objects have both light and dark planes, we experience them as being three-dimensional. Thus, moving from light to dark to imitate the effect of light is a dependable way to create the illusion of three-dimensionality in a drawing.

Artists generally describe the passage of light over form in steps, such as the nine listed below:

- Highlight: the brightest area

- Light: a broader light area surrounding the highlight

- Mid-tone, or halftone: precedes the true shadow side of the object

- Penumbra: the beginning (lighter part) of the form shadow

- Core of the shadow, or umbra: darkest part of the form shadow

- Reflected light: occurs when light hits a surface and bounces back onto the object

- Reflected shadow: the cast shadow of the object reflected back onto itself

- Cast shadow: occurs when the object blocks light rays from reaching a plane behind it

- Light reflected from the object into the shadow.

Artists don't always use nine steps of value. Some use fewer, and some use even more gradations. However, thinking about these nine steps gives us a reasonable reference for analyzing what's going on with light on objects in nature. It's also a useful template for analyzing value and light in drawings and paintings. And it's extremely useful conceptually when drawing from your imagination.

When we draw observationally, we won't always see light and shadow divided up into these nine steps. That will depend on the light source or sources and the nominal value and reflectivity of the surfaces involved.

Cast shadows can be extremely varied. In strong sunlight, for instance, shadows appear uniformly dark, but in very diffuse light, shadows can be dim. The appearance and quality of cast shadow also depend on the height of the light source, its direction, its intensity, and its proximity to the object.

We've seen how light plays out on a sphere, an object with a continuous surface. In contrast, a block is discontinuous, giving us clear edges at each plane change. Note that each of the planes has a much greater uniformity of value than the continuous plane of the sphere, though the side plane evidences a clear shift from lighter to darker as it recedes from the light source.

© David Brody.

### Steps of Light in Drawings and Paintings

If we understand the way light moves over a continuously curving surface and the way it moves over a faceted surface, we have the basics to apply to most of the things we see around us. Spheres and spheroid objects, such as eggs, bowls, and breasts, take light in a graduated way. When we draw these kinds of forms, we modulate the value with greater continuity. In contrast, blocks and block-like forms, such as tables, walls, and the heads of people with chiseled features, retain a much greater consistency of value within each plane. Many artists actively use these kinds of geometric forms as a means of conceiving of the way light affects the things they want to draw.

### Suggested Reading

Boyer, http://www.artinstructionblog.com/drawing-lesson-a-theory-of-light-and-shade.

Pumphrey, *The Elements of Art*, "Value and Color," pp. 147–161.

# Value: How Artists Use Value
## Lecture 20—Transcript

Congratulations, you've made it to Lecture 20 and now have a solid grounding in many of the most important aspects of drawing, things like proportion, measurement, composition, and linear perspective. And you've also had a great deal of experience using line. In fact, all the drawings we've done so far have been line drawings. That's because in these first stages of learning to draw, we're trying to understand many things—everything we've covered so far—and it's easy to do this with line. Much simpler to move a couple lines around than large, dark masses of charcoal or areas of color. But now you're ready to draw into all the areas between the lines. We'll do this first with value; then with mark making, texture, and optical value; and, finally, with color.

Many people, when they think about value, think primarily about shading. And while shading's one of the things value's used for, it's only one among many. In this lecture, we'll take a comprehensive look at the ways artists think about using value.

So, let's define the term. Value refers to neutral or achromatic tone. Chroma means color. So, achromatic means no color. These achromatic tones extend from the brightest white, through intermediary grays, to the darkest black. The word value's also used to describe the relative lightness or darkness of a color. For example, a yellow lemon has a relatively light value; a purple eggplant, a dark one.

We all know what black and white are. Gray though is, well, a much grayer subject. While we might describe something as light gray or dark gray, we don't usually get much more specific than that. But artists quantify the gray. They do this using a value scale, like this one. We have two givens, our end points: white and black. There's nothing lighter and nothing darker. Our grays exist between these two limits. In this example, we have seven equal steps, nine steps of value in all.

If you've studied music, the idea of a scale will be familiar. We could start on a C and arrive at a C one octave up in many different ways. We could traverse the distance in 7 notes—a diatonic scale—or in 12 tones—a chromatic scale—or even 24 tones, a quarter-tone scale.

Similarly, there are different value scales. I've seen 7-step scales and 12-step scales, among others. All will work. But I've found that 7 steps is a little limiting, and drawing 12 steps can be difficult at first, so I've used a 9-step scale for many years. Right now, it's enough to grasp the concept of a value scale. Later, we'll draw one.

Using the concept of a value scale, we can think about a drawing as existing in a specific range of value, a specific value palette. We could make a drawing using just black and white; or white, black, and a mid-gray; or just the values on the light end of the scale. We call this high key value.

This drawing by William Bailey is a good example—all very light. By removing the color, we realize that the lightest value—the value of the wall above the objects—is between a one and a two on our value scale. And the darkest value, the shadow side of the fifth object from the left, is a four. So, this drawing's constructed using three-and-a-half steps of value on the light end: high key.

Conversely, we could imagine the same drawing using values on the dark end of the scale. That would be an example of low key value. Or, we could stay mostly on the dark end, but with an event or two of light, like this drawing by Seurat. This drawing's also on toned paper, so the value on the light end is limited here, too. We could also make a drawing using only the values in the central range. That would be called mid key value. Or, we could use a full range of value, like in the Lundin.

The choice of the tonal palette literally sets the tone for the drawing. It creates the governing mood, sense of light, and time of day. It's at the heart of how we experience the drawing on an emotional level. If you begin to pay attention to this, you'll see this principle used in everything from greeting cards to advertising to movies. The musical corollary extends here, too. If I compose a piece of music using a major scale, it will have one emotional quality. Use a minor scale, another. High in the treble clef, one quality; low in the bass, another.

We'll discuss this aspect of value at greater length down the road. Here, I'd like you to note that the same subject and composition, even a simple block, will feel markedly different in different tonal palettes. The greater the value range in the drawing's palette, the greater the opportunity for high contrast. A palette of white and black will generally feel strong and aggressive. The tighter the value range, the lower the opportunity for contrast—a palette of four dark grays will feel much more subdued. A drawing with white, black, and many of the steps in between can result in a drawing with some high-contrast areas balanced by others that have more gentle transitions.

This means shading individual elements has to be considered contextually within a given palette. And as we'll see next, to make visual sense, this has to happen in relation to the focal hierarchy of the drawing. While most non-artists are aware of shading, they're generally unaware of the importance of value as a key compositional tool. Let's see how this works, how value divides a page into large constituent compositional shapes.

Squint for a moment at this Rembrandt. The touch of the brush is beautiful and there are many subtle changes of value in the landscape and sky. But there are two large shapes of value that structure the drawing, more or less like an envelope—a light one above, a darker one below. We control the viewer's eye and create focal points and focal areas through value contrast. All else being equal, we'll focus on the area of highest contrast first. The primary focal area in this drawing is located where the light shape meets the dark one—where the trees meet the sky.

Here's a drawing by Francois Boucher. It's called *Les Crêpes*—that's what the woman's cooking. There's a lot going on here compositionally. We have a long format with stresses at the vertical thirds. There's a stress at the horizontal half, at the top of the woman's head; another at the vertical half, moving down from the cupboard through the two female figures. We also have three depths of space, with the figures located in that central depth. The figures are grouped in a modified triangle. This hugs those all-important center diagonals that cross at the main character's—the woman's—head: dead center.

We have three high-contrast value areas. These are the places where we see the lightest and darkest values placed edge-to-edge. We see this in the window on the left, in the fireplace on the right. These serve as left/right counterweights. The third high-contrast zone is the figure grouping. This last is dominant because the value contrast is compounded by other factors: It's in the center, both topographically and in spatial depth; it also gets those active diagonals; and, last, these are figures. All else being equal, we'll pay more attention to people than windows.

So, we have four compositional factors making us go to the figures first, and this is a good way to start thinking about using value compositionally. Determine what's most important and use the tools of drawing, including value contrast, to lead the viewer through your composition. Let your use of value reiterate what you've done through placement, direction, choice of subject matter, and narrative intent.

Let's take a look at the curtain and cupboard at the back of the room. Plenty of form there—the drape feels three-dimensional, and there's a complex still life on the cupboard's shelves, but this is all low contrast. These are all close steps of value in the mid-range, no ones and nines. Most of this is in the four to seven range.

By using value contrast hierarchically, we can lead the viewer through a drawing: to see one thing first, something else second, something third, and so on. This is the same principle you applied to line weight and line contrast earlier in the course.

While looking at the value scale earlier, you may have noticed that each square appears to be a little lighter on its right edge and a little darker on its left. This is an optical illusion—it's an effect called simultaneous contrast. The left edge appears darker because it's next to something lighter. On the right, it appears lighter because it's next to something darker. White will appear brighter as its ground becomes darker, and brightest when set against black. Black will appear darker as its ground gets lighter, and darkest when set against white. We experience value relatively. We won't really know how any value appears until we see it in context, until we see it next to all abutting values.

Let's say we're drawing a still life: two bottles on a table in front of a wall. Beginners tend to finish the objects first, then add the cast shadows, then finally the wall and table—if these are attended to at all. That's a bad idea. Given value's relative nature, it makes much more sense to look at the central area where we see the left side of the bottle on the right, the right side of the bottle on the left, and where these two edges meet the intersection of the wall and the table.

If you can give yourself an indication of what happens at this set of intersections, you'll be able to understand how the different values affect one another. Developing a key area like this can give you a clear idea of the overall value range or value palette in the drawing. Based on this, you can lay in general values for the back wall, table, and bottles. Now you're seeing all the value relatively and can move toward greater detail and specificity from a solid base.

Another good practice is to work from the back, forward. That's because the thing behind the objects, the wall, has to be overlapped to really feel behind the objects; same for the table to feel underneath the bottles. This means that the actual graphite or charcoal marks and smudges that the bottles are drawn with should overlap the graphite or charcoal of the wall, not vice-versa.

Beginners who don't do this often wind up with a halo of light around their objects because they finish the objects, then they try to draw what's behind them, but they're afraid to mess-up the edges of what they've drawn, so they stop the value of the wall or table short of the object's edge. This makes the wall and the spatial environment feel unbelievable and discontinuous.

In most cases, if you develop the habit of working from back to front, the overlaps of edge will work to your advantage. Once you've found the general value palette by putting value into a juncture where key edges meet, go to the largest plane in deep space—in this example, the wall. Then address the tabletop, and finally the bottles. If they're physically drawn on top, they'll feel in front. The walls, tables, floors, and similar large planes often account for the largest shapes in the drawing, too. Value's relative, so attend to their value first, much easier that way.

In an earlier lecture, we spoke about atmospheric or aerial perspective. We saw how, on a light to mid-ground, dark marks and shapes tend to advance in space, while lighter, fainter marks and shapes tend to recede from the picture plane.

We looked at Xià Guī's 13th-century ink painting and Monet's 19th-century *View of Rouen* in this regard. Though separated by 600 years, and based in very different cultures, both Xià Guī and Monet employ the same idea: Use greater value contrasts and clearer edges in the foreground, progressively diminish the value contrasts and clarity of edge as the space recedes.

As with line, a lot of the art here involves balancing a compositional or hierarchical use of value with a spatial one. And, remember, a light form like a sphere will tend to advance in illusionistic space, especially on a mid to dark ground. We could sum up this principle this way: higher contrast, closer; lower contrast, farther away. But, if I have three depths of space and focus in the mid-ground, it will have greater contrast than the foreground.

We've spoken about many of the big picture uses of value in drawing and can begin to focus on value as it relates to objects. When we look at things around us, we identify some as lighter and others as darker. We'd likely agree that a white shirt is lighter than a black shirt. And this is true under what might be termed "normal" light conditions. We'll call this the object's nominal value. But, that same white shirt will appear dark in a dark room. And in a pitch-black closet, the white shirt will be indiscernible from the dark surrounding it. Put the black shirt in front of a strong light, and the planes receiving the light will become light gray. If a black shirt has a somewhat reflective surface, some planes or parts of planes may even appear close to white.

So, while objects have a given nominal value, their actual value's a function of light, and that's compounded by the object's surface qualities. This is a photo of a white sphere on a white tabletop in front of a white wall. But, almost nothing is white. The range of values that a given object might display is infinite. It's all dependent on light. The primary factors are the strength of the light source, its distance from the object, and its angle and direction.

Let's start with direction. Fashion designer's drawings are generally pretty flat. Their drawings reveal a much greater interest in the shape of a garment, its silhouette, than its three-dimensional volume. It's likely one of the reasons many designers prefer stick-thin models; they don't want you to see the shape of a body, they want you to see the outline shape of the dress they've designed.

In much fashion photography the subjects feel relatively flat, like the designer's drawings. The photos bring out shape over volume. One of the factors affecting this is light—here, ambient and diffuse. Lighting like this reveals little planar change. Similarly, a light source directly behind a subject produces a silhouette, another fairly flat view. And placing the light source directly in front of the subject will also tend to minimize the appearance of planar changes—hence, relative flatness.

To bring out three-dimensional form, we light from the side. This breaks the object into distinct planes: light ones facing the light, darker ones turned away from the light. Walk into the drawing and painting studios at most universities and this is just how you'll find the still lives and models set up. There'll be a floodlight somewhere to the right or left of the setup. This produces what's called chiaroscuro. It's often associated with artists like Caravaggio. The word's Italian—*chiaro* is like our word clear, *oscuro* like our word obscure. Chiaroscuro simply means light-dark.

With the light at a 90-degree angle to the set up, the objects will break more or less half-and-half—light and dark. From the quarter positions, you get a 75/25 split. And, of course, the light could be put anyplace in between. The essential point's that when objects have both light and dark planes, we experience them as being three-dimensional. So, moving to light to darks to imitate the effect of light is a dependable way to create the illusion of three-dimensionality in a drawing.

Let's see how this works using a simple object: a white sphere on a white tabletop in front of a white wall. It's side-lit from above with a single directional light. Since everything's white, we get a clear sense of light's contribution to shifts in value. The basics are clear: planes or portions of planes closer to and facing the light receive more light—they'll be lighter;

planes or portions of planes farther away and turned away from the light get less light—darker.

You can see how this affects the ground planes. The light's directed downwards, so the tabletop gets more light than the wall. Overall, it's lighter. And, being closer to the light source, both planes get more light on the right. This gradually diminishes as we move to the left. Both planes get progressively darker.

Now, I'd like you to squint at the sphere on the table. Squinting eliminates small differences in value. When trying to figure out what's going on in a given form value-wise, squinting can help you see the major shapes or groupings.

Artists generally describe the passage of light over form in steps. I use nine. The first step, step one, is the highlight: the brightest area on the sphere. Here, it's in the interior of the sphere. In drawing a spherical object, if you locate the lightest light along the edge, it can have a flattening effect. On a sphere, the highlight's generally that part of the sphere closest to the light source.

Step two is the light. This represents a broader light area surrounding the highlight. Step three is a mid-tone, also referred to as a halftone. It precedes the true shadow side of the object.

The next two steps, four and five, are on the shadow side of the object. This is referred to as the object's form shadow. That's to distinguish it from the cast shadow. Step four is the beginning of the form shadow, called the penumbra. Pen is the anglicized Latin for almost; umbra means shadow. So, this is the almost shadow, the lighter part of the form shadow. Five is the darkest part: it's called the core of the shadow, or simply the umbra. These first five steps are produced directly by the light source, and we refer to them as the effects of direct light.

Our next two steps are effects of indirect light. The first, step six, is reflected light. This occurs when light hits a surface—here, the table—and bounces back onto the object. This is most pronounced when the surfaces are reflective. If we put the same sphere on a black surface, we may get reflected dark. On a green surface, reflected green. When we speak about color, we'll learn more about how color reflects all around us all the time.

You may have noticed that the light doesn't move in a purely gradual way across the sphere—there's a high contrast edge, sometimes called the terminator or the hump, where the penumbra transitions to the core of the shadow. That's partly an effect of the reflected light softening the shadow internally, making this edge the zone of highest contrast on the sphere. The effects of simultaneous contrast exaggerate the effect. Eliminating most of the reflected light by placing the sphere on a dark ground makes the transition from penumbra to core of shadow gauzier, more gradual, and the zone of highest contrast shifts to the right edge of the sphere in relation to the black ground.

The next step of indirect light, step seven, is reflected shadow. As the name suggests, this is the cast shadow of the object reflected back onto the object. You won't always see reflected light or reflected shadow, it depends on the strength of the light source, the presence of any secondary light sources that could diminish the effect, and the reflective quality of the surfaces involved.

Next, step eight, is cast shadow. This is nothing more than the object blocking light rays from reaching a plane behind it. Depending on light conditions, cast shadows can appear divided into regions of different value. When this occurs, the darkest part, and the part closest to the object, is termed the umbra; the lighter middle section, the penumbra. These are the same terms used for the similar areas in the object shadow. The light tail of the shadow disappearing into the surface is called the antumbra—ante meaning before—so, this is a section before we get into the real cast shadow.

We won't always see a shadow divided up like this. In strong sunlight, for instance, shadows will appear uniformly dark. And in very diffuse light, shadows can be non-existent to dim.

Shadow length depends on the light source's height. If we start with a light source at the object's height, we get a long shadow. As we raise the light source, the shadow's length diminishes and reaches its smallest size when the light source is directly overhead. If the light source continues in an arc over the object, the shadow begins to lengthen, this time in the opposite direction. This is the same progression we note when we look at the sun's passage in relation to a sundial.

The angle of the shadow is a function of the light's direction: light coming directly from the side creates a shadow at 90 degrees to the object; from directly in front, a shadow receding directly behind the object; from oblique angles in the front, shadows receding along diagonals; from directly behind, a shadow projecting in front of the object; from oblique angles in the rear, shadows projecting forward along diagonals.

The light source's intensity and proximity to the object will affect the quality of the cast shadow. Cast shadows can be very gentle and hardly visible, powerful and stark, and anything in between. An intense and close light source will create deep shadows with clear edges. A more distant and less powerful light source will create a less intense shadow with less defined edges. If there's a secondary ambient light source, the shadows will be diminished in strength.

Our final step of light, step nine, occurs when light from the object is reflected into the cast shadow as it is here. We've just seen how light plays out on a sphere, an object with a continuous surface. Though we can have a hump, there are really no sharp breaks. That imitates the form of the sphere itself.

In contrast, let's take a look at a white block. The block's discontinuous, so we get clear edges at each plane change, and each of the planes has a much greater uniformity of value than the continuous plane of the sphere, though the side plane evidences a clear shift from light to dark as it recedes from the light source.

If we understand the way light moves over a continuously curving surface and the way it moves over a faceted surface, we have the basics to apply to most of the things we see around us. Spheres and spheroid objects like eggs, bowls, and breasts take light in a graduated way. When we draw these kinds of forms, we modulate the value with greater continuity. In contrast, blocks and block-like forms like tables, walls, and the heads of people with chiseled features retain a much greater consistency of value within each plane. Others take part of both. A banana or a human arm can seem at once cylindrical and faceted.

Many artists actively use these kinds of geometric forms as a means of conceiving of the way light affects all the things they want to draw, even the figure, and we'll apply this in a later lesson. But, now, let's see how what we've just learned actually plays out in a number of drawings and paintings.

In analyzing the sphere, we listed nine steps of value, but artists don't always use nine—some use fewer, and some use even more gradations. But, thinking about these nine steps gives us a reasonable reference for analyzing what's going on with light on objects in nature. It's also a useful template for analyzing value and light in drawings and paintings, and it's extremely useful conceptually when drawing from your imagination.

At the most basic, to create the illusion of dimension, all we really need are two values: one to play the role of the light, one to play the role of the dark. Exactly how light or dark they are is, in one sense, immaterial. A mid-gray could serve as a dark in relation to a lighter gray or as a light in relationship to a darker gray—all relative.

Here's a drawing by Daumier. While there's some minor variations, it's essentially a two-value drawing. The color of the paper serves as the light, the *chiaro*; the charcoal the dark, the *oscuro*. The color of the paper is about a four on our value scale, and the darkest dark like a number eight.

The light's coming from above on the left. So, in the standing figure, we get a plane break, light to dark, between the top of the chest, abdomen, and legs, and their under planes. And this figure's head throws a cast shadow over his shoulder. His forward leg does the same on the rear leg.

In Lundin's *Model Standing Before a Blackboard*, we get a much more extensive use of steps of value in the figure. In many ways, the head, neck, rib cage, and arms are treated like cylinders, and the breasts like hemispheres. In the lecture on flatness, volume, and space, we noted how the changes in value in this drawing create the illusion of volume or space. With our new knowledge, we can get more specific in our analysis of what's going on here.

The upper arm on the right, moving from right to left, shows a light tone, about a three on the value scale. As we move in toward the center of the arm, we get a bit lighter. At the center, we get the lightest tone, between a one and a two. Then we get a mid-tone, about a four. The core of the shadow sinks to about a seven. Then reflected light, light bouncing off the model's ribcage and back onto her arm, varies between a five and a six. Finally, we get a sliver of cast shadow falling over the breast and rib cage. This goes to about an eight. So, here we have about seven steps of value taking us around the form. Looking at the breast on the left, we see a similar passage, but executed in a broader range of value.

There are many other common step structures used to modulate form including a three-step progression using a light, a mid- or half-tone, and a dark. Or, you could move across a form in six steps: a lighter-light or highlight, a darker-light, a light half-tone, a darker half-tone, a lighter-dark, and a darker-dark. And if we added a mid-tone between each of these pairs—lighter-light, mid-light, darker-light, etc.—we'd have a nine-step passage over the form.

In addition to formal concerns, we have many cultural associations with both light and dark. In the west, ideas associated with these opposites have included good and bad, Apollonian/Dionysian, Heaven and Hell, the known/the unknown, order and chaos, pure and impure, life and death, and day and night. But it's not all so, well, black and white. We also read dark as elegant—think sleek black limo or tux and black cocktail dress. And, of course darkness can conjure the mysterious and romantic.

And, we have to remember, much of this is culture specific. In one of the most ancient Chinese texts, the *I Ching (Yijīng)*, or Book of Changes, black is associated with Heaven, while more broadly in Chinese culture, white is associated with death.

In the next lecture, we'll revisit materials with a focus on drawing areas of value.

# Value: Drawing Materials for Value
## Lecture 21

To draw with value, we'll need to expand on our use of materials. This lecture reviews some of the materials we've been using, including graphite, charcoal, and erasers, and covers additional materials needed, such as fixative, dip pens, portfolios, and lighting. We'll also look at paper in detail and learn how to make test sheets to understand how different papers, materials, and techniques interact.

## Graphite

You can make areas of value with the point or sharp edge of a wedge-sharpened pencil, but if you want more even gradation, use the flat face of the wedge. If you have a set of 18 to 22 pencils, sharpen the first to a wedge, the next to a point, and so on. This will give you a good range of tools for both line and value.

As mentioned earlier, graphite also comes in solid sticks. Most are soft, in the range of 2B to 6B. Such sticks can be sharpened into wedge or square shapes to to make different kinds of lines or areas of value.

When using your sanding block, save the graphite powder. You can apply it with a brush or other tool to create smooth areas of value in your drawings.

## Charcoal

Vine charcoal will not create a deep black; for this, you need compressed charcoal, which is made by mixing charcoal powder with varying amounts of binder and clay. Some manufacturers add black or dark pigments to enhance the color. The proportion of binder and clay to powder determines the charcoal's hardness—more clay for harder charcoal and less clay for softer. Compressed charcoal is commonly labeled soft, medium, and hard or with a system similar to that used for pencils. As with pencils, the grading of charcoal varies from one manufacturer to the next.

Charcoal pencils are useful for more detailed work. These pencils are made of compressed charcoal encased in wood. Some manufacturers label them extra soft, soft, medium, and hard. Others label them similar to graphite pencils, with grades ranging from 6B to 2H. You can sharpen charcoal pencils with a sharpener or a knife and sandpaper, but be gentle. These pencils are more brittle than graphite. A near relative of the charcoal pencil is the carbon pencil. It, too, gives deeper blacks than vine or willow charcoal, but like compressed charcoal, it is harder to erase.

Again, save the powder you produce when sharpening your charcoal.

### Blending, Spreading, and Applying Value

A number of tools can be used to blend, spread, and apply material, including a chamois cloth for large areas and tortillons and blending stumps for small areas. Tortillons and blending stumps are both pencil-shaped tools made of rolled paper. Tortillons are small and pointed at one end; stumps vary in size, are denser, and are pointed at both ends. Brushes—from stiff bristle brushes to softer ones—are also useful for blending. Many artists also use their fingers for blending and get fine results. Note, however, that the oils in your skin can mix with graphite or charcoal and discolor it. These oils may also make the material difficult to erase.

### Erasers

It's a good idea to experiment with different erasers to see how they work with your various drawing tools. For example, kneaded erasers tend to smear the darkest materials, such as charcoal and charcoal pencil when they've been applied heavily.

As you explore value more, you'll find that an eraser can also be used as a tool to draw light lines, marks, or shapes into areas of value. To make a thin, light line, try the Pink Pearl or pencil-type erasers against a straightedge.

Some artists use a tool called an erasing shield. This is about the size of a credit card and made of thin metal. It has a number of punched-out openings of different shapes and sizes. You can place the shield over a part of your drawing and erase through the opening to control the erasure.

## Fixative

Fixative is a spray varnish that artists use to protect their drawings. It comes in two basic types, workable and final. Use workable if you intend to continue working on a drawing after you spray. Use final when your drawing is finished. Once you've sprayed a drawing with either workable or final fixative, you won't be able to change what you've sprayed, so make sure you've done any blending or erasing you might want before spraying. When you spray, aim for a light, even coat. A single spray is often enough for light to medium graphite. For heavy pencil and charcoal, you may need two to three coats. For successive coats, alternate the direction of application and make sure to wait until each coat is fully dry before spraying again.

Fixative can darken tonal values if oversprayed, and it can change value, chroma, and saturation, especially with delicate pastels. It's always a good idea to do some test sprays before fixing a drawing using a new material or paper. Similarly, if you pick up a new brand of fixative, do several tests.

Note, too, that there are some safety concerns with fixative. Follow the instructions on the can and the material safety data sheet (MSDS) before using.

## Pen and Ink

Dip, or nib, pens are excellent drawing tools. Dip pens consist of a nib and holder. Nibs vary in size and shape, from very small crow quills to larger, more robust shapes. Some are pointed; others are round, flat, oval, or oblong. To start, get one flexible pointed nib and a couple others of differing sizes and shapes. Also, get one holder for each nib.

Some manufacturers use a protective coating on nibs to prevent rust, but the coating can impede ink flow. To remove it, scrub new nibs gently with an old toothbrush, warm water, and dish soap. Make sure to rinse and dry your nibs after each use, as well.

Getting rid of ink is much more difficult than getting rid of charcoal. Some manufacturers make ink erasers, although these work best for small areas. You can also try scraping away ink with a utility knife. Again, this won't work on large areas or with lightweight papers.

**Paper**

As we begin to explore value, texture, and color, paper choice becomes increasingly important. A number of variables and specialized terms are associated with drawing papers.

Perhaps the most obvious variable is color. Papers run the full range of color and value. Most of the time, we draw on white paper, but even papers classified as "white" exhibit differences. Notably, some whites are warmer, while others are cooler. Such differences can have a real effect on the way a drawing feels. For example, a portrait of a doctor drawn on warm white paper might convey caring and empathy, while one done on cool white paper might feel more analytical and clinical.

Probably the second most obvious paper characteristic is texture or surface. Papers can be very smooth, very rough, or anywhere in between. Different manufacturers use a host of terms to denote surface quality; some of these are listed in the table below:

| Very Smooth | Smooth | Light- to Medium- Textured | Medium | Rough |
|---|---|---|---|---|
| Ultra smooth | Smooth surface | Fine tooth | Medium surface | Rough surface |
| Plate surface | Hard finish | Laid finish | Regular surface | Coarse surface |
| True plate | | Textured surface | Semi-tooth | |
| High surface | Hot pressed (HP) | | Vellum surface | High tooth |
| | | | Kid surface | |
| | | | Cold press (CP) | |

Another factor affecting surface in some papers is grain direction, though not all papers have a pronounced grain. When the grain is parallel to the long dimension of the paper, it's referred to as *long grain*. When parallel to the short dimension, it's *short grain.*

Some papers also have a starch, glue, or similar synthetic material applied to the surface, referred to as *size* or *sizing*. This coating creates a barrier between the paper's surface and its fibers, helping to prevent unwanted bleeding when using wet media. It can also make a paper more easily erasable.

Another important paper factor is thickness. The thickness of a piece of paper is referred to as its *caliper*. This is generally measured in thousandths of an inch or in millimeters. Another measure of thickness is *ply*. One thickness or one sheet is one-ply. Two-ply means that two sheets have been glued together to create a thicker sheet. The word *bristol* is also used to refer to multi-ply papers.

Papers are also classified and often named by weight. The weight referred to is known as the *basis weight*. That's the weight of a ream of a given paper at its *basis size*. Note that the basis size is not always the same as the sheet size. For example, the 20-pound paper for your printer is 8½ x 11 inches, but the industry basis size for this kind of paper is 17 x 22 inches. This means that a ream of this paper, with sheets measuring 17 x 20 inches, would weigh in at 20 pounds. The basis size for most watercolor papers is 22 x 30 inches, and for drawing papers, 24 x 36 inches.

The best artist-grade papers are made of cotton linter. These are the short fibers that cling to the cotton seed as it's ginned. Hemp and wood pulp are also commonly used to make papers.

Another important consideration with paper is permanence, and the enemy of permanence is acidity. For this reason, many papermakers add alkaline substances, such as calcium carbonate, as a buffer. Acidity and alkalinity are measured on the pH scale, which runs from 0 to 14. Low pH is acidic; high pH is alkaline; and 7 is neutral. Archival papers generally score in the 7.5 to 9.5 range.

As you attempt more ambitious drawing projects, you should experiment with better-quality papers. Buy single sheets of 10 different papers, cut each into 6 pieces, and label each piece on the back with the paper's name. With 5 of each of the 6 pieces, make yourself a small sketchbook. With the remaining 10 pieces, make some test sheets using a variety of different materials, including soft and hard pencils, graphite sticks, different types of charcoal, pens, and brushes and ink. Try blending and erasing on these test sheets. You'll learn a tremendous amount through this activity. As you touch each of your materials to each sheet of paper, you'll immediately feel the distinctive interaction of a given material with a specific paper.

Although papers are labeled for different uses and materials, such as drawing, charcoal, pastel, watercolor, etching, and so on, any paper can be used for any purpose, though, the labeling is not meaningless. For clear, articulated line drawings, a smoother, harder paper is generally desirable. Charcoal and pastel papers tend to have more tooth, or texture. Watercolor papers tend to be stiffer and more textured, while printmaking papers tend to be smoother.

**Portfolios**

Portfolios range from simple, inexpensive cardboard types to more high-end versions with zippers and other enhancements. For storage at home, the inexpensive cardboard ones are fine. If you're carrying your drawings around, something more protective and durable may serve you better over time. Make sure to bring a portfolio when you go out to buy paper and leave the paper in the portfolio for storage.

**Lights**

Finally, for a number of the projects done from observation using value, you will need a light for your still-life table. Either a floodlight on a stand or a clamp light attached to the vertical support of a floor lamp will work well.

## Suggested Reading

Chaet, *The Art of Drawing*, chapter 4, "Media and Materials."

Guptill, *Rendering in Pen and Ink*, chapters 1–3.

Mendelowitz, Faber, and Wakeman, *A Guide to Drawing*, "Wet Media," pp. 208–227.

# Value: Drawing Materials for Value
## Lecture 21—Transcript

To draw with value, we'll need to expand on our use of materials. Let's start with graphite. We can make areas of value with the point or sharp edge of a wedge-sharpened pencil, but if you want a more even gradation, use the flat face of the wedge. I have lots of pencils, but if you only have one set with 18 to 22 pencils, sharpen the first to a wedge, the next to a point. Continue alternating sharpening style—wedge, point, et cetera—across the set. This way, you'll have a good range of tools for both line and value.

Graphite also comes in solid sticks. Most are on the soft side: 2B to 6B. This is a round sharpened to the wedge shape. You can make linear value with the edge and a more even tone using the wedge. This piece is a square shape; you can draw with the edge or flat face. You can also sharpen it to a wedge. You'll get more linear value using the edge and more even value with the wedge.

Save the graphite powder when using your sanding block. You can apply it with a brush or other tool to create smooth areas of value. You can also buy jars of graphite powder. So, take some time to create value using your graphite tools.

Next, charcoal. We've been using the point. We can also use the side to get an area of value. In addition to cylindrical sticks, charcoal comes in thicker rounds and rectangular pieces. Vine won't create a deep black—for rich blacks we need compressed charcoal. It's made by mixing charcoal powder with varying amounts of binder and clay. This gets compressed into round or rectangular shapes. Some manufacturers add black or dark pigments to enhance the color. The proportion of binder and clay to powder determines the charcoal's hardness.

You'll commonly find compressed in soft, medium, and hard—or HB, 2B, 3B, 4B, and sometimes you'll find 6B. As with pencils, the grading varies from one manufacturer to the next, so get a couple different grades from the same manufacturer and you'll begin to find out what you like.

Here's a soft square shape, makes a rich black. Like the graphite sticks, you can draw with the edge or flat face. This is a harder round sharpened to a point. The point's great for line and smaller areas of value. You can use the side for larger areas.

For more detailed work, charcoal pencils are very useful. They're made of compressed charcoal encased in wood. Some manufacturers label them extra soft, soft, medium, and hard, others label them like graphite pencils with grades ranging from 6B to 2H. You can sharpen these with a sharpener or knife and sandpaper, but you want to be gentle, they're much more brittle than graphite. The twisting motion of a dull sharpener can crack them, and you want to avoid dropping them on the ground, that can shatter the material inside.

Some charcoal pencils are encased in paper. Here, you want to unwrap the paper to expose the charcoal. If the wrapping tears, make a small incision with a utility knife and it'll continue to unravel. The exposed charcoal can then be sharpened with your knife and sandpaper. This is an extra soft charcoal pencil. I'll make a line, then an area of value. This is an extra hard—I'll do the same. When charcoal pencils get too small, we can use pencil extenders here, too.

A near relative of the charcoal pencil is the carbon pencil, and you may want to try these out as well. Again, here, I'll make a line and an area of value. This is a soft, very similar to the charcoal pencil.

Compressed charcoal, and charcoal and carbon pencils, give us deeper blacks than vine or willow. The downside is that they're harder to erase. You want to save the powder you produce when shaping your charcoal. Some artists keep vine and compressed powder separate, others mix them. You'll see what works best for you. I'll apply an area of powder here with a brush. As with graphite, charcoal powder's also available commercially.

Our next tools are those we use to blend, spread, and apply material. Each one's a bit different. We'll talk about a couple now and return to this when we discuss texture.

The chamois or shammy cloth is a common large blending tool. I have one for graphite and another for charcoal. It does a good job blending and spreading graphite but with vine it can act like an eraser, removing a lot of the material. Even with compressed, it removes a fair amount of the material.

Once you have material on the chamois you can use it to apply value. You can also pick up material from a test sheet and apply it in a drawing. Or, rub a material on the chamois, or vice-versa, and apply.

For smaller areas, artists use tortillons and blending stumps. Both are made of wound paper. Tortillons are small and pointed at one end; stumps vary in size, are denser, and are pointed at both ends. I'll use a tortillon on the graphite—for the charcoal, a stump. Both the tortillon and stump produce darker values than the chamois. Like the chamois, you can use the tortillon and stump to apply material, too.

Brushes are also great blenders. Try all kinds from stiff-bristle brushes to softer ones. I'll use a stiff one on the graphite, creates a smoother value than the tortillon, and I'll use a soft bristle on the charcoal, it removes more material than the stump.

Haven't yet mentioned the most obvious tool—fingers. Many artists use their fingers all the time and get fine results, and I'm going to use mine here, but some artists caution against this—it's common for the oils in our skin to mix with graphite or charcoal and discolor it, and the oil can make the material difficult to erase or blend, so you want to see what will work well for you.

You'll note that each of these swatches look somewhat different. As we begin to work with value, blending, and smudging, the range of possibilities opens up exponentially. So, take some time to experiment with blending, spreading, and applying areas of value.

Let's take another look at erasers. Try erasing some of the graphite with the kneaded, then the vine: no problem. Erasing the compressed charcoal and charcoal pencil's more difficult. The kneaded won't do much good with the darkest materials, tends to smear them. The Pink Pearl and pencil-type erasers will do a better job.

As you get into value, you'll find that the eraser's not only an erasing tool, it's also a drawing tool—it's how we draw light into dark. Try the Pink Pearl against a straight edge to make a thin, light line. Then try your pencil-type erasers to make light lines and shapes.

Another tool you can use with your eraser is the erasing shield. Now, I don't use these much, but some people find them useful. Most are about the size of a credit card and made of thin metal. They have a number of punched-out openings of different shapes and sizes. You place the shield over a part of your drawing and erase through the opening, and that controls the erasure. You could, of course, make your own using a utility knife and a piece of thin cardboard and any cutout shape you want.

We now have a sheet of paper covered with value. It's been manipulated, erased, smeared, and blended, and all that stuff is delicate. The lines and marks could be smeared if you touched it accidentally. To prevent this, artists spray their drawings with fixative, a protective spray varnish. There are two basic types: workable and final. Use workable if you intend to draw after spraying; use final when you're drawing's finished.

There are a number of reasons why people fix drawings mid-process. One is that they need to transport the drawing, as my students do, back and forth from class. Another common reason is that the artist has roughed out the drawing and wants to work in further detail, but doesn't want to risk disturbing what's already done.

When working with color, pastel for example, you might want to apply one color over another. Ordinarily, the two colors would mix together, but let's say you don't want actual mixing, you want the second color to appear transparently over the first, what we call optical mixing. Then you'd use workable fixative.

Once you've sprayed a drawing with either workable or final fixative, you won't be able to change what you've sprayed, so make sure you've blended or erased anything you might want before spraying. Fixative is available in different finishes: transparent, matte, and gloss. Transparent's the default, it shouldn't change the surface in any visible way.

There are safety concerns with fixative. Ask for the MSDS, that's the Material Safety Data Sheet, for the product you buy. Read it, along with the instructions on the can, before you start spraying. Generally, these are the concerns: Fixative's highly flammable, so you don't want to use it while smoking, near a heat source, or open flame. It's also toxic. You only want to spray your drawings in a well-ventilated place. Outdoors, away from other people, is good. And, of course, you want to avoid inhaling the fumes. Some instructions suggest wearing a protective respirator. This should also be listed in the MSDS for the product you buy.

So, try spraying your test sheet. First, clean the surface of any erasure crumbs and loose graphite or charcoal dust. Then, take your drawing to a well-ventilated place. Make sure the area's clean, dust-free, and the humidity's relatively low. Shake the can for a couple of minutes to mix the can's contents. Set your drawing upright and slightly tilted against the wall or other support. Hold the can about 12 inches from the drawing and start just off to the side—you want to make sure you get the whole page—and finish off to the other side. Then return in the other direction.

The goal's a light, even coat—your drawing shouldn't look wet. If you go too slowly, you'll get liquid dripping down the surface; move too fast and you won't get adequate coverage. After spraying, let the drawing dry. It'll take about three to five minutes.

A single spray is often enough for light to medium graphite. For heavy pencil and charcoal, you may need two to three coats. Test your drawing—touch it with a clean piece of tissue paper or your finger. If you're picking up material, give your drawing a second coat then test again. For successive coats, alternate the direction of application, and make sure and wait until the drawing is fully dry each time before spraying again.

When you're done, clear the nozzle—turn the can upside down, point the nozzle away from you, and spray for four to six seconds. After the first couple seconds, you'll only get propellant coming out of the nozzle. This helps clear sticky residue that might cause a clog.

Fixative can darken tonal values if oversprayed, and fixing delicate pastels can be tricky, it can change a color's value and saturation, so it's always a good idea to do some test sprays before fixing a drawing using a new material or paper. Similarly, if you pick up a brand of fixative, do several tests.

Let's turn to ink. In addition to your small round-pointed brush, you'll want a medium-sized brush for washes and larger areas. You should also try some dip, or nib, pens. The earliest versions go back many centuries. In his book, *Rendering in Pen and Ink*, Arthur Guptill wrote, "Bronze pens were excavated at Pompeii, and we have other instances of their Roman use."

Dip pens consist of a nib and holder. They're not all interchangeable, so make sure you get the right holder for your nib. Nibs vary in size and shape, from very small crow quills to larger more robust shapes. Some are pointed; others round, flat, oval, or oblong. To start, get one flexible pointed nib and a couple others of different sizes and shapes. Also, get one holder for each nib—changing inky nibs while drawing's a real hassle. Some manufacturers coat nibs with a protective coating to prevent rust. The coating can impede ink flow, so rinse your new nibs with warm water and dish soap. Scrubbing them with an old toothbrush can also help remove the coating.

Some nibs are made of a single piece of metal; others are made of two pieces. The latter are made so that there's a reservoir between the two pieces. When you dip the pen, this is where the ink gets stored. It'll flow to the tip as pressure's exerted. Now careful calligraphers, fearful of a large blot, don't dip their pens. Instead, they load the reservoir with an eyedropper or small round-pointed brush. You could try this, too, though most artists I've seen dip their nibs directly in the ink.

So, take out your pens and nibs. Starting with a simple pointed nib, make the thinnest line possible. Then, adding pressure, make the thickest. Then, move from one to the other. Try making other kinds of marks—fast and slow, continuous and skipping, and whatever else comes to mind. Then, try any other nibs you have, making similar experiments. When you're done, rinse the nibs and dry them to prevent rusting. These tools are related to fountain pens and technical fountain pens. If you have any of these, you may want to experiment with them, too, to see how they contrast with the dip pens.

Now, getting rid of ink is much more difficult than getting rid of charcoal, but there're a couple things worth mentioning. There are ink erasers, like these, and they'll work on thin, light lines. You can also try scraping with a utility knife. Using both the knife and an eraser can help you get rid of lines and marks that are a bit heavier. Best to try this on thicker paper, you can easily tear through a lightweight one.

As we get into value, texture, and color, paper choice will become more and more important for a whole set of reasons. At the most basic, if you try to erase a large area of compressed charcoal on a standard sheet of 18 × 24-inch white bond paper, it's not hard to rip or wear a hole in the surface. So, you may want something more robust and durable, but there are quite a number of factors to consider when choosing a paper.

Paper's an endlessly useful material. It's worth noting how recently it came into our lives. Our word paper derives from the Ancient Greek word for papyrus. First Dynasty Egyptians were making writing surfaces out of this plant as early as about 5,000 years ago. They'd split the stem into lengths, lay these flat next to each other, then put a second layer on top. The split stems were wet and sticky, so you could smash them together to form a single sheet like a laminate, kind of like plywood. The sheets would be dried and polished and, voilà, one sheet of papyrus. It didn't have the most uniform surface but it held up well enough in dry Egypt, but it didn't do so well in more humid climes.

In many places, the ancient surface of choice was parchment or velum, which was basically a stretched and dried sheep, goat, or cow skin. While this was very sturdy, it was expensive.

The invention of paper is credited to a Han dynasty Chinese official, a eunuch named Cài Lún. We even have a date for his invention: 105 C.E. We know this because he made a formal report to the emperor about his discovery. Before paper, officials in China wrote on bone or strips of bamboo—it was clumsy. Silk was also used but silk was expensive, so paper was an extraordinary and welcome discovery.

To make paper, you break your material down into its fibers and mix it up with water. Cài Lún reportedly used tree bark, rags, hemp, old fish nets, and mulberry. This oatmeal-like mash gets laid out into flat sheets and dried. Now, scholars dispute Cài Lún's claim to his invention because paper dating back to about 250 years before his purported discovery was found in Gansu, China. But, it's a great story.

Whatever the case, Cài Lún didn't enjoy his fame for long. He got involved in court intrigue and the emperor sentenced him to prison. When he learned of his fate, he took a bath, dressed in an elegant silk robe, and drank a cup of poison. But, that didn't prevent the court from valuing the discovery— far from it. Papermaking was considered a state secret. The knowledge was highly protected and the Chinese did a good job of preventing leaks. It took about 500 years for the knowledge to make its way east to Japan via Korea.

And paper didn't even begin to make its way west until 751 C.E. That's when the Tang Chinese, expanding westward, fought the Arab Abbasid Caliphate in the Battle of Talas. The precise location isn't known but it was probably around the border area of what's now Kazakhstan and Kyrgyzstan. In any event, the Tang army was defeated and Chinese prisoners were taken. The story goes that among them were a couple skilled papermakers. Shortly thereafter, papermaking was flourishing in Samarkand, a central location along the Silk Road. The knowledge soon spread through the Middle East, from Baghdad to Damascus to Egypt.

By the 11th century, paper was being made in the Iberian Peninsula. Over the next 400 years, the knowledge would spread over much of Christian Europe. Its use would be firmly established by the mid-15th century, reams stacked and ready for Guttenberg's press.

There are a number of variables and some vocabulary associated with drawing papers. Perhaps the most obvious variable is color. Papers run the full range of color and value. Most of the time, we draw on white paper, but even among white papers there are real differences between the whites available. Notably, some whites are warmer, more toward the orange-yellow; while others are cooler, more toward the blue. And these differences can have a real effect on the way a drawing feels.

Imagine you're drawing a landscape, it's a warm summer day. Warm white would be a good choice. Now imagine drawing a cold, snowy day. Well, the cool white would likely be a better choice. Or, imagine you're doing a portrait of a doctor in her office. Choose the warm white, she'll likely feel more caring and empathetic; choose the cool, and she'll feel more analytic and clinical.

Perhaps the second most obvious paper characteristic is texture or surface. Papers can be very smooth, very rough, or anyplace in between, and there are a host of terms used by different manufacturers to denote surface quality.

Broadly speaking, very smooth papers are generally labeled ultra smooth, plate surface, true plate, or high surface. Smooth papers are labeled smooth surface, hard finish, and hot pressed, or HP. This last, hot pressed paper, is rolled through heated cylinders which, like a hot iron on a shirt, take out the wrinkles. Light to medium textured papers are often labeled: fine tooth—tooth here means texture; laid finish—this type of paper has horizontal and vertical lines impressed in the sheet; and textured surface. Medium surfaces are generally labeled medium surface, regular surface, semi-tooth, vellum surface, kid surface, and cold pressed, or CP.

Another factor affecting surface in some papers is grain direction, though not all papers have a pronounced grain. When the grain is parallel to the long dimension of the paper, it's referred to as long grain. When parallel to the short dimension, you guessed it, short grain.

Some papers also have a starch, glue, or a similar synthetic material applied across the surface. This is referred to as size or sizing. It creates a barrier between the paper's surface and the paper's fiber. This helps prevent unwanted bleeding when you're using wet media. It can also make a paper more easily erasable. Some papers have the same kind of starch or glue mixed into the pulp. This is called internal sizing and it can improve the longevity and strength of the paper.

As you begin to use different papers, you'll find that some are harder and some softer. All else being equal, the softer the paper, the less well it will take erasure. You'll notice that many good quality papers have uneven edges.

These are called deckled edges. This light feathering occurs as the pulp is pressed and it's spread out.

Many manufacturers put their name or logo on each sheet through the use of an embossed watermark along the edge or in the corner of the sheet. Holding the sheet up to the light makes the watermark easily visible. When the letters of the watermark are in their proper orientation, it means you're looking at the top, or felt side, of the sheet. When the letters are reversed, you're looking at the underside, or wire side, of the sheet.

Another important paper factor is thickness and weight. The thickness of a piece of paper is referred to as its caliper. That's generally measured in thousandths of an inch or in millimeters. Another measure of thickness is ply. One thickness or one sheet is one-ply. Two-ply means that two sheets have been glued together to create a thicker sheet. The word bristol is also used to refer to these multi-ply papers.

Papers are also classified, and often named, by weight. The weight referred to is known as basis weight. That's the weight of a ream, or 500 sheets, of a given paper at its basis size. Now, this can be a bit confusing because the basis size is not always the same as the sheet size. For example, the 20 pound paper for your printer is 8½ by 11, but the industry basis size for this kind of paper is $17 \times 22$. This means that a ream, or 500 sheets of this paper, measuring $17 \times 20$ would weigh in at 20 pounds. The basis size for most watercolor papers is $22 \times 30$; for drawing papers $24 \times 36$. While some manufacturers refer to weight in pounds others refer to weight in grams per square meter. That's often labeled $g/m^2$.

Since the time of Cài Lún, people have been making paper out of all kinds of fibers. The best artist-grade papers are made of cotton linter. These are the short fibers which cling to the cotton seed as its ginned. Hemp and wood pulp are also commonly used to make papers. Newsprint, for instance, is made of wood pulp.

Another important factor is permanence. The enemy of permanence is acidity, so many papermakers add alkaline substances like calcium carbonate as a buffer. Acidity and alkalinity are measured on the pH scale, which runs from 0 to 14. Low pH is acid, high pH is alkaline. Seven is neutral. Archival papers generally score in the 7.5 to 9.5 range.

When companies label their papers as archival, they're assuring you that their papers are safely alkaline. As noted, the best papers are made of cotton. Papers made from wood pulp or a mix of wood pulp and cotton can be archival if the pulp has been properly buffered. Newsprint's highly impermanent because it's made of untreated wood pulp.

Soon we'll be getting into some ambitious drawing projects with value. I'd suggest using better quality papers for these projects—most are sold in single sheets. To begin to acquaint yourself with the range of paper, and what's available, I'd suggest buying 10 different papers to start off.

You'll see paper labeled as drawing paper, charcoal paper, pastel paper, watercolor paper, etching paper, et cetera, et cetera, but any paper can be used for any purpose, though the label's not meaningless.

For clear, articulated line drawings, a smoother, harder paper is generally desirable. Charcoal and pastel papers tend to have more tooth or texture— that's what causes the charcoal or pastel to abrade and deposit itself on the surface. The texture also keeps the material on the surface. Watercolor papers tend to be stiffer and more textured. Printmaking papers tend to be smoother.

To get started, buy a selection of these different kinds of papers. Make sure some are smooth, others textured, some hard, some soft, some thick, and some thin. Cut each sheet into six pieces. If the paper's 22 × 30, a common size, you'll get six pieces that are 10 × 11 inches each. Label each one so you'll know what it is. Set one of each aside and put the other 50 sheets together. Now you have a sketchbook of interesting papers to experiment with.

But before you do, take the 10 pieces you put aside and make tests on each one like I've done here. I imagined a grid with eight divisions in the page. In each one I tested a different material.

In unit one, I tested my softest pencil, a 10B, line above and an area of value below. The value's darkest on the far left and mid-tone for the rest. Then I blended both line and value on the right, and erased through the center. In unit two, I tried my hardest pencil, a 10H. In three, a graphite stick. In four, five, and six, vine charcoal, compressed charcoal, and a charcoal pencil. In each, I made the same tests I did in unit one. In seven, I tried two nib pens: one thin, one thick. In eight, I used brush and ink—first line, then a wash. I repeated this on each paper.

You'll learn a tremendous amount doing this. As you touch your pencil to each sheet of paper, you'll immediately feel the distinctive qualities of each surface. You'll find that the hardest pencil will be all but invisible on some papers, clearly visible on others. Some papers will suck in wet media, others will let it pool on the surface. And save those test sheets—you'll begin to create an invaluable library.

When buying paper, you want to make sure you get it home without folding, denting, or otherwise bruising it, so it's best to bring a clean, rigid portfolio for transport. Then, leave the paper in the portfolio in a dry, safe place until you're ready to use it. I advise my students to store their paper and drawings flat under their beds.

It's useful to have several portfolios on hand for storing paper and drawings. Portfolios range from simple, inexpensive cardboard folding-types to more high-end versions with zippers and other enhancements. For storage at home, the inexpensive cardboard ones are fine. If you're carrying your drawings around a lot, something more protective and durable will serve better over time.

You'll also want a light for your still life table. A floodlight on a stand's great but a clamp light attached to a vertical support or a floor lamp can work, too—anything that'll approve strong directional light.

# Value: Black and White and a Value Scale
## Lecture 22

In an earlier lecture, we learned how artists use value to create mood, space, and the illusion of light on form. Artists also consider the way the overall arrangement of light and dark creates pattern or rhythm at an abstract level. This is true no matter what the value palette is—whether it's white and black or a full value scale. Values are not simply copied from observation but are considered holistically in their interactions. This is related to the way we think about shape. Although a given shape may relate to the shape of an object, it should also relate to the negative shapes with which it connects. Together, the positives and negatives combine to create the shape of the drawing. In this lecture, we'll learn how to create both positive and negative shapes of value.

### Yin and Yang

The Japanese word *notan* literally means "shade" and "light." It refers to principles of design governing the interaction and patterning of dark and light shapes. The idea is that the dark completes the light and the light completes the dark. Together, they create the whole. The Chinese *yīnyáng* symbol demonstrates this principle and translates similarly. Yīn means "overcast" or "shady," the negative principle. *Yáng* is the "sun," the positive principle. Together, the dark negative and light positive shapes forge the whole, with nothing left over.

© MariaTkach/iStock/Thinkstock.

We see this at play in many paintings and drawings. In many cases, the light tones are not drawn but created by surrounding dark tones. For this reason, we need to learn how to create both positive and negative shapes of value. Creating the dark ones feels natural. The light ones are a bit more challenging because we draw them indirectly—by creating dark negatives around them.

### Defining Edges with Value

As we've seen, line does a great deal of work for us. Among the first things we noted about line is that it can create shape by defining the edge of something, such as a circle or a bottle. It can also define the edge where two planes meet, such as a tabletop or floor meeting a wall. In addition to using line, we also want to be able to define edges with value.

In the value scale, you'll note that there are no lines—just value shapes. We read the tones as shapes because where they meet, the values are different; these differences establish the edges of the shapes. We can do the same thing in a drawing, that is, establish edges with changes in value, doing the same work that we might have done earlier with line.

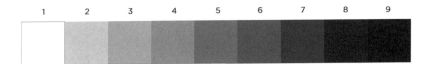

### Creating Volume and Light with Black and White

After you have practiced drawing positive and negative shapes with value instead of line, the next step is to create three-dimensional form in light using black and white shapes. We'll do this first by imagining some basic forms in light, then working from direct observation. Working only in black and white can help you think about using value compositionally—that *notan* notion of the play of lights and darks across the surface—while also creating the illusion of light. Keep these steps in mind when working from observation:

- Use your viewfinder to find a point of view, composition, and format shape that interests you.

- Pay particular attention to the large positive and negative shapes and how they fit into the format you've chosen.

- Also pay attention to the large groupings of light and dark caused by planar changes and cast shadows.

- As you did with single objects drawn from your imagination, rule out the format on your paper with a light pencil. Then, translate all the values you see into either white or black shapes. You want to make this translation or reduction based on choices that will maximize the illusion of depth and volume.

### Returning to the Value Scale

We've now seen that we don't have to copy every value to get a convincing sensation of light, space, and volume. In fact, we can translate those values into just two: black and white. But now, we're ready to use a fuller range. One exercise to help you begin thinking about the range of values is to create your own nine-step value scale using charcoal. For this exercise, don't try to copy the values from the scale shown above. Start on the outside and work toward the center, imagining and adjusting the values as you go.

After you complete the exercise, ask yourself:

- Is 5 accurately gauged as the midpoint between 1 and 9?

- Are 3 and 7 accurate as midpoints between 1 and 5 and 5 and 9, respectively?

- Are 2, 4, 6, and 8 gauged accurately as midpoints between their neighboring values?

- Are there any sub-groupings? Are there any squares that feel as if they group more with some than others?

### Gestural Value Sketches

Before we move onto more complex value drawings, it's a good idea to incorporate value into your quick gestural compositional studies. As we saw earlier with line, it can be helpful to try out several different compositional strategies before committing to a drawing. And as we get into value, completing a drawing can demand an even greater investment of time. You can save time and frustration by doing some preliminary value sketches.

Using any materials you like, make some quick drawings that use different value palettes compositionally, allowing them to structure the hierarchy in your drawings. Start with some simple forms from your imagination and three values, a light, a mid-tone, and a dark. Then, try different value palettes.

Next, set up some still-life objects and repeat the exercise. Experiment with the light source, too, varying its direction, height, and distance from the objects. Then, try making gestural value sketches using an interior or a landscape as your observational source.

## Suggested Reading

Bothwell and Mayfield, *Notan*.

Mendelowitz, Faber, and Wakeman, *A Guide to Drawing*, chapter 6, "Value and Color," pp. 96–114 .

# Value: Black and White and a Value Scale
## Lecture 22—Transcript

In an earlier lecture, we learned how artists use value to create mood, space, and the illusion of light on form to create volume. Artists also consider the way overall arrangement of light and dark creates pattern or rhythm at an abstract level, and this no matter what the value palette, whether it's white and black or a full value scale. Values aren't simply copied from observation but they're considered holistically in their interactions.

This is related to the way we think about shape. While a given shape may relate to the shape of an object, it should also relate to the negative shapes it connects with because, together, the positives and negatives combine to create the shape of the drawing.

There's a Japanese term, *notan*. Literally, it means shade and light. It refers to principles of design governing the action and patterning of dark and light shapes. The idea is that the dark completes the light and the light completes the dark. Together, they create the whole. The Chinese *yīnyáng* symbol demonstrates the principle, and translates similarly. *Yīn* means overcast or shady, the negative principle, and *yang* is the sun, the positive principle. Together, the dark negative and the light positive shapes forge the whole— nothing extra, nothing left over.

We see this at play in the Boucher. The values fit together like puzzle pieces. Look at the lightest tones of the fire: They're not drawn—it's the surrounding dark that creates them. We see the same thing in the woman's right shoulder and left breast—it's the surrounding dark negatives that create the light positives. We see a similar treatment in this Poussin—the pillars in both the center and right buildings are created by the abutting dark shapes. The figures are constructed similarly.

And we see the same thing in this Picasso. The central nude is created by the dark shapes that surround her. The small light window framing the woman at the easel's head is created by the large dark shape that surrounds it. In fact, this drawing's like a visual essay on the way we can draw something as dark against a light, like the woman's face against the window and the horse and vase above her. Or as light against a dark, like the central woman, the light vase behind her, and the tabletop on which it sits.

So, in working with value, we have to learn how to create both positive and negative shapes of value. Creating the dark ones feels natural. The light ones are a bit more challenging because we draw them indirectly; we draw them by creating dark negatives around them.

And this brings us to the importance of edges. As you've learned, line does a lot of work for us. Among the first things we noted about line is that it can create shape by defining the edge of something, like a circle or a bottle. It can also define the edge where two planes meet, like a block's front plane meeting its side plane, or a tabletop or floor meeting a wall.

Now, we want to be able to do this with value. In the value scale you'll note there's no line, just value shapes. We read them as shapes, as squares, because where they meet the values are different.

We find the same thing in the Lundin—no outlines. Even the literal chalk lines on the blackboard aren't really lines, they're drawings of lines, and making a drawing of a line is different from drawing a line. These lines are rendered to have the specific shape and character of chalkboard lines in a specific light situation. Note the change in value where they fall under the wall's shadow. In this sense, they're thin shapes that have been modulated in value and texture.

All the other edges in the drawing are formed by one value meeting another—there are no outlines. The light from the window on the blackboard is created by a value meeting a distinct and different value at an edge. The same applies for the model in relation to the board. It also applies to her hip on our left overlapping her arm, and to the arm on our right overlapping her hip. In each case, a value meets another—another different value—and this establishes the edge of the form. This does what we would have done earlier with a line.

Also note that not all edges are the same. Contrast the far right shadow on the blackboard with its diagonal continuation on the lower left. On the right, the edges between the shadow on the blackboard and the light on the blackboard are softer and the value contrast is softer—softer light. On the left, the edges between that shadow on the blackboard and the light are harder and the value contrast greater—harder light. So, with value, the edges of a shape are doing what contour did previously. And there are internal edges as well, and these are doing what cross contour did in the world of line.

The edges of the woman's watch act like a cross contour, making the wrist feel three-dimensional. On both arms, the long vertical edges where the darker value meets a lighter one behave like cross contours to bring out the form, as does the shadow meeting the light on the breast on the left. The light areas are shapes defined by edges, the gray areas are shapes defined by edges, and the dark areas follow suit.

So, let's start out by making some shapes with value. Like Boucher, Poussin, and Picasso, let's use: brush and ink; we'll also need some printer paper or a sketchbook; viewfinders; a 2H pencil; some white still life objects; and both a light and a dark ground or drape for the still life we set up.

Many people, when they start using value, assume that they should outline everything first and then fill in the value. While this can work, it's only one way to go about things. Often, making a shape directly, without outlining and filling in, can feel less stiff, less colored in. In fact, in both the Poussin and the Picasso, the ink is brushed in directly creating shape—anything but fussy. The brush is a great tool—by applying pressure, you can get the full length of the soft bristles onto the page: This creates a shape. By pulling the brush, you can control the shape.

Let's make some basic shapes first; let's draw a circle. Instead of starting with an outline, we'll start with shape moving out from the center of the shape to its edges. Then a rectangle, then a triangle, and a trapezoid, and last a diamond.

Now, let's draw negatives—rectangles with cutouts. Again, no outline, and we want to produce these same shapes. We can also try a pattern, alternating black and white shapes. Let's try a checkerboard, just rectangles, then triangles, and diamonds.

Let's up the complexity with compounded shapes like an hourglass, then the negative of an hourglass, and a simple house shape, then its negative.

Now, let's try a more complex positive/negative situation. We'll start with a single bottle made of three constituent shapes: a rectangle with a curving base, a hemisphere, and a rectangle for the bottle's neck. Then another bottle, same height but different shape, spaced to the right of the first. We'll make this out of four constituent shapes: a trapezoid with a curving base, then two more trapezoids—the first tapering down, the second up—and a small rectangle for a cap.

Now we'll draw a border around the bottles so there's space on the right and left but the border will touch both the tops and bottoms of both objects. Now, let's break down the complicated negatives into simpler building block shapes. Then, redraw the two bottles starting with the negatives to construct them as light objects on a dark ground.

Play out other variations on your own. Construct other objects like the ones you first made up when we started drawing with line and shape: candlesticks, bowls, wine glasses, et cetera. Do them singly as positives, then as negatives, and then do two or three together like we just did with the two bottles, and do this a number of times, varying the objects. Once you begin to feel comfortable creating a variety of shapes with the brush, try this from observation. The steps will be very similar to those we used when doing the first negative shape drawings earlier in the course.

Place two objects of similar height on your still life table. The shapes will appear clearest if you have white objects and place them on a dark ground—you could use a dark drape or black foam core. Frame them in your viewfinder so that there's space on both the right and left, but let the viewfinder touch both the top and the bottoms of your objects. Trace the format shape lightly in the center of your page and draw the shape of the objects with your brush. Now, on a new sheet of paper, retrace the format shape and this time draw the negatives.

Next, open up the viewfinder so that you have an amount of space above and below the objects and add this to the drawing. Remember, both complex positives and negatives can be constructed using constituent shapes. Try this a couple times with different objects. Then, try starting with the viewfinder in the open position so that you have some space all around the objects. Draw the positives first then make another drawing of the negatives.

Now you should have a handle on drawing positive and negative shapes with value. Let's take it another step and create three-dimensional form in light using black and white shapes. For this drawing everything has to be either black or white—no grays. This can really help us think about value compositionally, that *notan* notion of the play of lights and darks across the surface, while also creating the illusion of light.

It also helps us simplify. Many beginners try to copy every instance of shift in value they see, but sometimes the changes have to do with local color, surface texture, or even a stain or spot of dirt. None of these will help us bring out a sensation of three-dimensional form, and often they'll lead to the direct opposite and the form collapses. We want to think like Poussin, Boucher, or Daumier: Find the large groupings of value that will be significant in creating the illusion of three-dimensional form in light. For this drawing, we'll start with line, just to get the idea—the others we'll do directly with shape.

Let's imagine a table and wall seen straight on. Compose this in a longish horizontal rectangle; make a horizontal line and you've got a tabletop and wall. On the table, in our central line of vision, we'll imagine a block in one-point perspective. We see its front plane; it will be a rectangle. Place it so its right edge is about at the vertical half. We'll draw the front face so that it extends up above the edge where the table and wall meet. We're looking down, so we'll also see the block's top plane: a trapezoid.

Now you're ready to think about light. I'd like you to imagine that the light is coming from above left. That means the tabletop will get more light than the wall. The tabletop will be lighter; the wall, darker. Everything has to be either black or white, no grays, so the tabletop stays white, the wall goes black.

As we've noted before, table and wall are nothing more than an inside-out version of a block. The block has a top plane parallel with the tabletop. Like the tabletop, it receives more light, it stays white. The block's front face is parallel to the wall; it gets less light than the top plane and has to go black, and we let the black of the block flow into the black of the wall. Since the light is coming from the left, we'll have a cast shadow moving out to the right. It will of course be black to the tabletop's white.

Take a look at your drawing. How many shapes are there? Well, it's somewhat open to interpretation. We could say three: one large black shape and two whites. We could say four: the black ground shape, the black face of the block and its shadow, and the two white shapes. We could also say five: three black and two white. However you count it, it's a lot like a still life version of the *yīnyáng* symbol—a black half and a white half with a white shape in the black and a black shape in the white.

Now, try redrawing this but without line. Try shape with your brush as we did in the prior exercise. Start by making the back wall but leave the negative of the top plane of the box. Then, add the front plane of the block with its shadow.

Now, let's try an open box in two-point perspective sitting on a table in front of this wall, but this time we'll start with value shapes. We'll imagine it lit from the left, but not from 90 degrees; we'll imagine the light source as being a bit more frontal. Here's where we'll end up.

We'll start with the back wall with the negative of the box's silhouette. Next, we'll add the box's side plane that's in shadow, then the cast shadow, and finally the left inside plane of the box, also in shadow. We'll leave a sliver of white for the thickness of the top edge.

Now let's try a cup. This time we'll imagine the light coming from the right. The cup will resemble the box but will be curvilinear. Start with the ground shape, then the shadowed side plane, leaving a bit of white for a reflected light, then the cast shadow, and the small inner plane that's also in shadow.

Let's try a cone. We'll start with the wall, then the shadow side of the cone. Leave a sliver of white for the reflected light, then the cast shadow.

Now, get several simple objects and your light and try this from observation. Best if everything's white: the object, the tabletop, and the wall. Put a single object on your still life table. Start by lighting the object from above and from the side or a side angle. This should give you clear chiaroscuro and a cast shadow.

When you begin drawing, you have to make broad generalizations about light and dark. Think about which planes are getting more light and which one are being deprived of light. You want to see past all the small gradations, and you want to connect what you observe about light on the object, table, and wall to composition, to the overall organization of shape and value in the format shape. Use your viewfinder to help determine the format. Then lightly trace this with pencil on your paper before starting the drawing.

After you've tried a number of individual objects from observation, put some objects together to form a still life. Here are some examples from my students at the University of Washington.

Let's look at the large planar structure first, those large ground shapes that create the shape of the drawing itself. Here we get a large white shape for the corner of the tabletop, then a horizontal boot-like shape for the space beyond.

Here, we have horizontal stripes: a thin black one for the table's front plane, a white one for the tabletop, and a black one for the wall.

This composition uses the guillotine strategy for the two ground shapes. That's where the two ground shapes meet on a diagonal—excellent planar analysis in the pitcher.

Here, it's worth noting how the shadow of the box helps to define the front plane of the tall pyramid.

There's a similar play here, with the shadow of the pitcher helping to define the right edge of the object in the center. The central object's shadow then helps to define the block on the left.

As you did with the single objects you just drew, lighting is key. Spend some time getting the objects and light to work together to bring out the planes and form. Follow these steps to do your own version of this exercise: Use your viewfinder to find a point of view, composition, and format shape that interests you. Pay particular attention to the large positive and negative shapes and how they fit into the format you've chosen. Pay close attention to the large groupings of light and dark caused by planar changes and cast shadows. As you did with the single objects, rule out the format on your paper with a light pencil. Then translate all the values you see into either white or black shapes. You want to make this translation or reduction based on choices that will maximize the illusion of depth and volume.

Once you've had some experience with this method of working with white and black, you can try it with a variety of subjects from landscape to the figure.

You've now seen that we don't have to copy every value to get a convincing sensation of light, space, and volume—we can translate it. In the last set of drawings, you took what you were seeing in a full range of values and boiled it down to two: black and white. Now we're ready to open things up to a fuller range. To get you up to speed in creating these values, we'll start by drawing a nine-step value scale like the one we looked at in the last lecture. This exercise will really help you develop a conceptual map for thinking about value and it will give you hands-on practice creating the distinct values you'll need. I think you'll find this an interesting and challenging project.

I'd suggest doing this first with charcoal; you'll be using it a lot in your value drawings. Doing the value scale will help you get a better sense of how to work with this material. You'll need a sheet of white paper, at least 18 × 24. The brighter the white, the better—it will give the scale a greater value range. You want to create even areas of value, so best to avoid papers with any prominent texture. Centered in the sheet, rule out a rectangle 2 inches by 18 inches with a pointed piece of vine charcoal.

Now, many people are tempted to use a graphite or charcoal pencil to rule this out—don't. At the end we want to see nine distinct shapes of value without any line circumscribing or dividing them. If you use graphite or charcoal pencil, you'll never be able to get rid of the line, it'll always be visible, and that's going to spoil the scale.

So get a good point on a piece of medium or hard vine charcoal. Draw as thinly and lightly as possible to outline the two-inch by 18-inch rectangle. Next, draw a series of very light vertical lines to divide the rectangle into nine two-inch-by-two-inch squares. Above the squares, lightly number them one through nine.

I've asked you to put this two-inch by 18-inch rectangle in the center of your page. That's so you'll have the challenge of keeping the rest of the page white while you work with charcoal in this central area. I'm not trying to torture you here, but we often want to preserve the white of our page in some areas while working in others with charcoal, so this is good practice.

The basic method is to start on the outside and work towards the center. One is an absolute—it's white and that's a given; it's the original value of the paper. Nine is also an absolute—it's the darkest dark we can make. We'll get our darkest dark with compressed charcoal, so, using the compressed charcoal, make square nine the deepest black possible. Make sure you extend to the edges and keep the value even across the whole of the square. Now, put aside the compressed charcoal—we'll be using vine for the next set of steps.

The center square, square five, is next. Try to imagine the gray that would be halfway between your black and white. And a note here: Go through this without looking back at the value scale I've used as an illustration. You'll get more out of it if you try to imagine the values and then adjust them as you move forward. Trying to copy the gray on your monitor will defeat the purpose; you want to develop your eye in judging values relatively. Copying a value won't help much in this regard. So, in square five, create an even value, edge to edge, of a central gray.

Once you've got this, go to square three. It's halfway between one and five. Try to imagine what this gray would look like, then create a value halfway between white, step one, and mid-gray, step five. Next, in square seven, create a value halfway between mid-gray, step five, and black, step nine.

With the darker values you may need to use a mix of vine and compressed charcoal. Once you've finished seven, eyeball your four values and make any changes you think are necessary, then turn your attention to steps two, four, six, and eight. Gauge them as half steps between the values on either side of them.

Once you've got all this blocked in, check to make sure that all the squares meet clearly edge-to-edge, value to value. You shouldn't see any lines anywhere, and you shouldn't see any white except in square number one.

Ask yourself, is five accurately gauged as the midpoint between one and nine? Are three and seven accurate as midpoints between one and five, and five and nine, respectively? Are two, four, six, and eight gauged accurately as midpoints between their neighboring values?

Let's take a look at a couple of examples from some past students. This is a very good first shot; it'll give you a sense of some things to look for. Ask yourself, are there any subgroupings? Are there any squares that feel like they group more with some than others? Another way of asking is this: Do you get a break anyplace?

In this first example you'll note one, two, three, and four group together, then five, six, and seven, though six and seven break off a bit from five, and eight and nine form a final subgroup. What this tells us is that there's too great a jump at these steps. Some of the darkness has to be shared down the scale.

Here's another very good scale, though you'll note here that four and five form a subgroup, as do seven, eight, and nine.

You'll likely find some subgroups in your own drawing, so use both charcoal and erasure to adjust the values—the malleable kneaded works well here.

It's often easier to see a problem after a break, so put your drawing aside for a couple days and take another look, then make any adjustments needed. Then, after doing some of the value drawings described in the next lecture, take another look at your value scale. You'll likely see discrepancies you hadn't noticed before, and that's not a bad thing at all, it's a mark of enhanced perceptual skill.

It's a great idea to try this with pencil, too. You'll want to get good wedge shapes on your pencils before trying this—it's the best way to get an even gradient. Start with your very darkest pencil to get step nine; work with a wide range of pencils to get the other values. But, once you've finished this first value scale, you're ready to begin to put a wide range of value to work.

Before we get into the complex value drawing projects we'll be doing it'll be a good idea to incorporate value in your quick gestural compositional studies. As we saw with line, it helps to try out several different compositional strategies before committing to a drawing. And, as we get into value, completing a drawing can be a real investment of time, so you can save on time and frustration by doing some preliminary value sketches.

We've already seen some examples of quick compositional studies done in value—the Daumier is one. The subject's the death of the Greek mathematician and engineer, Archimedes. He was killed by a Roman soldier during the siege of Syracuse in 212 B.C.E.

As we've noted, we have two basic values in this drawing. They provide a general compositional map for the drawing. We get large alternating shapes of light and dark in the ground. The arm and sword of the Roman soldier are light and stand out in contrast to the dark ground behind. The soldier, centered in the page, splits light and dark. This creates a focal area here, and Archimedes head, like the sword, is contrasted against a dark ground. So, the organization of light and dark contrasts tells us what to pay attention to—it advances the narrative.

The Poussin also shares this quality, though here there are four values: the color of the paper, a lightish tone, a mid-tone, and a dark tone. The figures get the greatest contrast; the paper's against the dark tone. The buildings get less contrast; by and large, they don't go darker than the mid-tone. We pay most attention to the highest contrast, so we'll pay most attention to the figures.

These drawings have a similar quality to the studies we did in black and white. In both the Daumier and Poussin, there's little detail—no fancy shading. It's all about hierarchy, shape, plane, and light.

Rembrandt did hundreds of quick compositional drawings. This was probably done in a matter of minutes. The screaming kid's the star; the woman holding him is second in importance. He's central and the shadow he casts on the woman represents the largest high contrast area in the drawing. The woman gets the next highest contrast, the older woman behind her the next, the architecture and the two kids in the doorway follow.

Here's a Degas—obviously, quickly done. We get a stress at both the vertical and horizontal halves. The woman and the man ride one diagonal. As a counterbalance, the table straddles the diagonal that formats central horizontal quarters, creating two mirrored wedge shapes: top and bottom. Value contrast tells us that the woman's head and neck are the focal point, and that her body is the focal area.

So, give this a shot. Use any materials you like: pencils, charcoal pencils, pen and ink, brush and ink, ballpoint pen, felt tip marker. Keep the drawings on the small end—you want to be able to move through them quickly. Try putting some of these ideas together. You want to make quick drawings that use different value palettes compositionally to structure a hierarchy in the drawings.

First draw some simple forms from your imagination as we did earlier. Use blocks, cones, cylinders, and spheres—imagine them as still lifes. Make sure you're using value holistically, and don't ignore the wall and tabletop. Start with three values: a light, a mid-tone, and a dark. Then try two lights, two mid-tones, and two darks. You can think of this as a six-step scale, a third of which is light, a third mid-tone, and a third dark.

Then use your still life objects; three to four would be fine. Experiment with your light source—vary the direction, the height of the light, and its distance from the objects. Then try a range of subjects: interiors, cityscapes, and landscapes are all great. If a family member's watching TV or sleeping, that's a great opportunity to draw the figure. Likewise, coffee shops, public transportation, and libraries are all great places to draw figures in environments. Concerts and sporting events work well too. Knowing that people could move at any moment will push you to draw quickly.

# Value: Eight Complex Drawing Projects
## Lecture 23

We've now looked into the ways in which artists think about value. And you've gotten some hands-on practice creating value shapes, the illusion of light and volume with black and white, and steps of value. In this lecture, we'll outline eight drawing projects that are designed to get you started using value with a range of subjects. We will also briefly recap some of the major topics we've covered in order to relate them to the new projects using value.

**Review**

Let's briefly recap some of the major topics we've covered:

- First, we can use gestural line, quickly and incisively, to do the work of contour, cross-contour, and construction line, and we can add value to gestural line drawings. Such drawings are helpful for finding the best composition for a complex project.

- We can construct many things we want to draw using contour and basic shapes as building blocks, often using construction lines as an aid.

- Oblique shapes and cross-contour lines can make the things we draw feel three-dimensional. When working with value, contour and cross-contour lines can appear as edges where one value meets another.

- It's important to think compositionally and organize disparate objects into large aggregate shapes related to the ground shapes. These aggregate shapes generally create the shape of the drawing itself.

- The shape of the drawing has an underlying abstract structure. Earlier, we saw how we could create strong compositions by relating negative shapes to positives. We've now seen that those negatives and positives can be created out of value shapes, and these can be organized to form visual pattern within the format.

- We studied 12 methods for arriving at accurate proportions and another 12 principles that can be applied to create the illusion of volume and space on a two-dimensional surface.

- We also learned about linear perspective. We're aware that which planes and how much of any given plane we see depend on eye height and point of view.

- In recent lectures, we learned that we can think about value as occurring in steps from white to black. And we've seen how we can create mood by being selective in our choice of value palette.

- By controlling contrasts, we can create a visual hierarchy with cascading zones of focus. And we can create volume and space within the palette and within the hierarchy by showing the effects of light as it moves across a three-dimensional form and by modulating value to create atmospheric perspective.

**Tips for Value Drawings**
Here are some suggestions that apply globally to the projects in this lecture:

- First, analyze the value situation you see. Squint at the scene in front of you to cut down on the amount of detail you're able to discern. An effect of this is to diminish many of the smaller value changes so that you see the larger changes that have the greatest impact.

- Make small, quick compositional studies with broad generalizations about value. Find the large value groupings first.

- If you want to analyze a particular instance of value, try this trick: Cut a small hole in the center of a mid-gray piece of cardstock.

Look out at your subject so that the value or color fills the hole you've made, and read the value against the viewer.

- When you're looking at the effects of light, try to understand what's causing the specific effect. Is it the result of direct light or reflected light? It's much easier to draw something if you understand why it looks the way it does.

- A common pitfall is to try to copy every detail of light and shade without understanding what's producing those details. The result can be an incoherent pattern that doesn't succeed in representing what you're trying to draw.

- Analyzing what you're seeing is important, but remember, nothing has a fixed value. The value of an object depends on our focus. If you copy the value of everything you see while you focus on it, you will inflate all the value contrasts. Try focusing your eyes on the most important place, the focal point. Note how you see all the other visual events while focusing on this point. They'll have less contrast and their edges won't be as well-defined.

- Think hierarchically. Don't copy value; organize it. In a still life, you generally want less contrast between the wall and tabletop and more associated with the objects in relation to one another and to their environment.

- Work from the general to the specific. When applied to value, this means putting in large areas that approximate the overall values in the drawing. This approach allows you to see the drawing whole at an early stage. Then, lighten and darken within the approximation as needed.

- A practical way to begin a drawing that will have a fairly full range of values is to use a light tone, a mid-tone, and a dark tone. But note that the light shouldn't be white and the dark shouldn't be black.

- It's not a hard-and-fast rule, but if you reserve the occurrence of the darkest dark against the lightest light for the intended focal point, you'll be well on your way to having it assert itself as such.

- When drawing with charcoal use vine or willow to find proportions and block in general value. Once this has gelled, use compressed charcoal and charcoal pencils to deepen the darks and work in greater detail.

- You may want to try one or more of these projects as a *reductive drawing*. This type of drawing involves lightly outlining the format shape on the page with vine charcoal, then creating an even mid-tone to fill the shape. You shouldn't see any outline—just a rectangle of mid-gray for the format shape. Erase the mid-tone to create lights and darken it to create darks.

- Choose one of the suggested projects for this experiment: Try interpreting the same subject, lit in the same way, as an overall light drawing (high key) and an overall dark drawing (low key). Then create a version restricted to mid-values. This exercise will give you a sense of how much freedom you have to modulate a subject in different tonal keys and how these keys pay off in terms of mood and emotion.

- Take time and care setting up and lighting your subjects. Use your viewfinder. Evaluate your subject from a variety of points of view. If you think compositionally when setting up and in locating the best point of view and format shape, the drawing will make sense much more readily.

- Keep some white foam core on hand to reflect light back onto your subject. This can enhance the reflected light on the subject's surface and help make it feel more three-dimensional.

- Finally, give yourself different light situations. Try different intensities of bulbs or set up a still life by the light of a window on a bright day, a cloudy day, and at night. If you draw outside on a day when the sun is strong, you'll note strongly delineated shadows. Return to the same scene on an overcast day, and you'll see that the shadows are much more minimal.

## Working with Colored Objects

Although we are not yet drawing with color, below are some tips for drawing objects that have color:

- Color has three attributes: hue (the attribute that gives the color its name), saturation (the color's level of purity), and value (the lightness or darkness of the color).

- For the projects in this lecture, focus on the color's value. The idea here is to learn to see the value as distinct from the color's hue and saturation. You want to be able to see the world as if you were a black-and-white camera.

- As we've already noted, you want to establish a mood, a hierarchy, and the sensation of light and space. Essentially, you have to translate color into value, keeping all this in mind.

- When setting up a still life, if you want the objects to dominate, make sure the two ground colors have less contrast, one to the other, than the objects have to the ground and to one another.

- Start with three or four objects at the most. In choosing them, think about how they'll affect one another hierarchically. Two darkish objects placed against a dark ground will group together with the ground. Imagine, for example, two bottles of red wine against a violet drape of similar value. There's not much contrast in that scene. If you add a light, cream-colored vase upstage, you will get color and value working together compositionally. The cream-colored vase will be the focal point.

- You might also try starting off with colors that are closely related. For example, you could choose objects and grounds that are all in the yellow-orange family. Start with lighter, more neutral tones for the ground; then, use a couple of objects that are somewhat darker and more saturated but still light. They will read as more important than the ground. Light the scene from the side to produce chiaroscuro, and all the objects will gain in contrast. Finally, add a red object as the focal point. This object will be the darkest thing in an otherwise light environment and will have the greatest light/dark contrast.

## Suggested Reading

Aristides, *Classical Drawing Atelier*, chapter 4, "Value," pp. 52–65, and "Sphere Drawing," pp. 124–125.

Loomis, *Successful Drawing*, "Complex Forms in Light," pp. 89–95.

Smagula, *Creative Drawing*, chapter 5, "Value," pp. 108–131.

# Value: Eight Complex Drawing Projects
## Lecture 23—Transcript

You now know about many of the ways artists think about value. And you've also gotten some hands-on practice creating value shapes, creating the illusion of light and volume with black and white, and in creating steps of value.

In this lecture I'll discuss eight drawing projects that are designed to get you started using value with a range of subjects. But before we do, I'd like to recap some of the major topics we've covered to date. There are quite a few of them. And you want to hold onto them and relate them to the new projects using value.

First, we can use gestural line quickly and incisively to do the work of contour, cross-contour, and construction line. And we can add value to our quick drawings. We want to use these quick compositional drawings to help us find the best composition for a complex project.

We can construct many things we want to draw using contour and basic shapes as building blocks, often using construction lines as an aid. We saw how oblique shapes and cross-contour can make the things we draw feel three-dimensional. When working with value, those contour and cross-contour lines will now appear as one value meeting another along an edge.

We want to remember to think compositionally and organize disparate objects into large aggregate shapes related to the ground shapes. These large aggregate shapes will generally create the shape of the drawing itself.

The shape of the drawing has an underlying abstract structure. Earlier, we saw how we could create strong compositions by relating negative shapes to the positive. We've seen that those negatives and positives can be created out of value shapes. And that these can be organized to form visual pattern within the format.

We studied 12 different methods for arriving at accurate proportions. And another 12 principles that we can apply to create the illusion of volume and space on a two-dimensional surface. We want to use everything we now know about illusionistic space including what we learned about linear perspective. We're aware of eye height and point of view and how we're actually seeing an object.

In recent lectures, we learned that we can think about value as occurring in steps from white to black, and we've seen how we can create mood by being selective in our choice of value palette. By controlling contrasts, we can create a visual hierarchy with cascading zones of focus. And we've learned that we can create volume and space within the palette and within the hierarchy by showing the effects of light as it moves across a three-dimensional form and by modulating value to create atmospheric perspective.

Here are some suggestions that apply globally to these projects. First, analyze the value situation you see. It can really help to squint at what you're looking at. Squinting cuts the amount of detail you're able to see. An effect of this is to diminish many of the smaller value changes so you see the larger, greater impact changes. Make small quick compositional studies with broad generalizations about the value. Find the big groupings first.

If you want to analyze a particular instance of value, here's a trick. Take a mid-gray piece of cardstock. Cut a small hole in the center. Look out at your subject so that the value or color fills the hole you've made. Read the value against the viewer.

When you're looking at the effects of light, try to understand what's causing the specific effect. Is it the effect of direct light or reflected light? And what's its source? It makes it much easier to draw something if you understand why it looks the way it does.

A common pitfall is to try to copy every detail without understanding what's producing these details. The effect can be an incoherent pattern that doesn't succeed in representing what you're trying to draw. Analyzing what you're seeing is very important, but remember, nothing has a fixed value. The value of an object depends on our focus. As we saw in an earlier lecture, when the camera focuses on me, my contrast is high. But when the camera focuses on Jaimee—my producer behind me—my contrasts diminish.

If you copy the value of everything you see while you focus on it, you'll be inflating all the value contrasts. Try focusing your eye on the most important place—the focal point. And note how you're seeing all the other visual events while focusing on this point. They'll have less contrast and less well-defined edges.

Think hierarchically. Don't copy value. Organize it. In a still-life, you generally want less contrast between the wall and tabletop and more associated with the objects in relationship to one another and to their environment.

Work from the general to the specific. When applied to value, this means putting in large areas that approximate the overall values in the drawing. This allows you to see the drawing whole at an early stage. See how all the parts are relating. Then, lighten and darken within the approximation as needed. The problem of working detail to detail is that you won't see how the parts relate until late in the game. And things can get considerably off.

A practical way to begin a drawing that will have a fairly full range of values is to use a light, a mid-tone and a dark to begin with. But the light shouldn't be white, and the dark shouldn't be black. Reserve the white and black. Why? Leon Battista Alberti tells us why in his Renaissance treatise, De Pictura:

> You have to remember that no surface should be made so white that you cannot make it a great deal whiter still. Even in representing snow-white clothing you should stop well on this side of the brightest white. For the painter has no other means than white to express the brightest gleams of the most polished surfaces, and only black to represent the deepest shadows of the night.

And that's echoed by John Ruskin in his 1857 book, *The Elements of Drawing*. He wrote "However white an object may be, there is always some small point of it whiter than the rest. You must therefore have a slight tone of grey over everything in your picture except on the extreme high lights."

While not a rule, if you reserve the occurrence of the darkest dark against the lightest light for the intended focal point, you'll be well on your way to having it assert itself as such. Use the vine or willow to find proportions and block-in general value. Turn to compressed charcoal and charcoal pencils once this has been achieved because they're harder to erase.

You may want to try one or more of these projects as a reductive drawing. This entails lightly outlining the format shape on the page with your vine charcoal. Then, create an even mid-tone to fill that shape. You shouldn't see any outline, just a rectangle of mid-gray for the format shape.

Start the drawing using three tones: a light, a mid, and dark. The mid-tone that what's already there covering the format, so you erase to create your lights—all the planes or parts of planes that are generally light. Leave the mid-tones where they should be, and darken to create your dark tones.

An additional idea you could apply to any of these projects that follow is to interpret the same subject lit the same way as an overall light drawing high key, then as an overall dark drawing low key. And then a version restricted to mid-values. This will give you a real sense of how much freedom you have to modulate a subject in different tonal keys. And it will give you a handle on how this pays off in terms of mood and emotion.

There's a real parallel to music here. We can take a given melody which starts on middle C and reconstruct it starting on different pitch—say A above middle C. We keep the internal relationships consistent and wind up with a modulated version of the original melody. We can shift the whole drawing up or down on the value scale. And we could also compress the range or expand it.

Take time and care setting up and lighting your subjects. Use your viewfinder. Evaluate your subject from a variety of points of view. If you think compositionally when setting up and in locating the best point-of-view and format shape, the drawing will make sense much more readily.

Have some white foam core on hand, and that can really be useful. You can use it to reflect light onto your subject to create particular light effects. Reflected lights can really help make things feel three-dimensional. And lighting considerations go beyond the formal. Now that you're engaged with this, pay attention to how professionals do this in film and on TV.

An oft used trope in horror films is to light from below. This rearranges normal readings of light and shadow. For instance, it can result in large shadows cast upward onto walls. And all of this is unusual so it helps to contribute to the sensation of anxiety or fear.

If you're a theater or opera fan, lighting plays a big part here too. So much of what we experience as in mood and emotion is related to the use of lighting in these art forms. And it plays a large role in many of the visuals we see in advertising.

Give yourself different light situations. Try different intensities of bulbs. Try setting up a still life by the light of a window too. And try bright days and cloudy days, and also at night.

Draw outside on a day when the sun is strong. You'll note strongly delineated shadows. Return to the same scene on an overcast day. The shadows will be much more minimal. Back indoors if you want something like a corner to pose still-life objects in—a cardboard box is a good solution. Cut away the top and two sides and you've got a corner. You can paint these a range of values or colors. And this will give you a variety of grounds for your still lives.

So let's talk about the projects. The first has two parts. Part one is to draw a white sphere on a white table top in front of a white wall. The second, a white block. Same situation. We want everything white so that the effects of light are not obscured by other factors. This will give you clear insight into the way value and light play on a curvilinear and rectilinear surface respectively.

If you don't have a white sphere or box, you could use any ball or box sprayed white. If the wall or tabletop is not white cover them with paper or foamcore.

The goal in these drawings is to use steps of value to create the illusion of the steps of light that we learned about in the first lecture on value. So, light the object and environment carefully to bring out as many of these nine steps as you can. Let's go through them: The first one was highlight, then the light, then our half-tone, then the penumbra, then the umbra, then the reflected light and a reflected shadow, then the cast shadow, and the reflected light from the object into the shadow.

Do this drawing with charcoal on white paper. Repeating this project with pencil will help you learn to create gradations with graphite.

Next, try a still life of white objects in a white environment. Three to five are fine. Again, take time to set up and light it. Be attentive to the hierarchy of value shapes. Do as much as you can to organize things compositionally in the set-up.

You'll note in this example that there's a visual hierarchy. The central chalice is pretty dominant. Why? It's central. It's not overlapped or cropped. It has among the highest value contrasts, and it has high contrast of shape. It's the curvilinear thing among the mostly rectilinear things.

You could do a first version using the actual values. Then try another version using only steps one through five, and another using only steps five through nine, or use one through five with one event of nine, or five through nine with one event of white. Once you've completed a white still life, you're ready for color. I don't mean drawing with color. That's up ahead. But, we're going to draw things that have color using a range of value.

So, let's talk a bit about the relationship of color to value. For present purposes it's important to understand that every color can be understood as having three attributes or qualities.

The first is hue. This refers to the attribute of the color that gives the color its name. Its redness or blueness. The next attribute is saturation. This refers to the color's level of purity. For instance, we have versions of blue all along a spectrum stretching from very gray at the achromatic end to the most intense blue at the saturated end. The third attribute is the color's value. The same blue could be made lighter or darker. These variants represent three values of the same color.

For now, we want to focus on this last attribute. We need to learn to see a color's value as distinct from its hue and saturation. We want to be able to see the world as if we were black and white cameras. Here are four clearly different colors: a red, a blue, a green, and an orange/brown. If I were to take a black and white photo of the red it would look like this. The blue would come out the same as would the green and the brown.

Now, imagine I'm doing a charcoal drawing of a lime in a red bowl on a brown table in front of a blue wall. And the colors are like the colors in the example, and it's very evenly lit. If I draw the values accurately, I wouldn't have much contrast. My drawing wouldn't capture the very real obvious differences among the four colors. So, copying values can be a problem. We use what we see, but we also have to structure the value in each drawing.

As we've already noted, you want to establish a mood, a hierarchy, and the sensation of light and space. Essentially, you have to translate color into value keeping all this in mind. Now, there are no hard and fast rules here. It's about making judgments in relation to the formal and content concerns of the drawing. The art's in balancing all this.

A couple basic principles: If you want the objects to dominate, make sure your two ground colors have less contrast—one to the other—than the objects have to the ground and to one another. And start with three or four objects tops. In choosing them think how they'll affect one another hierarchically.

Two darkish objects placed against a dark ground will group together. I'm thinking like two bottles of red wine against a violet drape of similar value. Not a lot of contrast. Put a light, cream-colored vase upstage, and you've got color and value working together compositionally. The light vase will dominate.

Another way of starting off is to try colors that are closely related, say objects and grounds that are in the yellow-orange family. Start with lighter more neutral tones for the ground, then a couple still light but somewhat darker more saturated objects. They'll read as more important than the ground. If you light from the side you'll get chiaroscuro, and all the objects will gain in contrast.

Finally, add a red object as the focal point. All else being equal, the red will dominate. It'll get the attention. It's special. And it'll be the darkest thing in an otherwise light environment and have the greatest light-dark contrast.

Or you could do the inverse; ground dark red. Most of the objects similar red or orange, not too different. And one light yellow object. It will be the focal point. At the outset, it will help a great deal to think about these formal relationships as you select, pose, and light your objects.

Having understood something about the complexities of translating color to value, you're ready to draw a wide range of subjects. The next five projects will call on this knowledge. The first project is an interior. It's a form that doesn't always get its due, though it presents many interesting opportunities.

For this project, I send my intro drawing students to the architecture building—Gould Hall—on campus. It has a clear planar structure. But any room can be made interesting if you find a compelling point of view, the right format shape, and a strong value structure.

In drawing like this, you'll want to use your eraser as a drawing tool, particularly where you have light shapes in front of darker ones. For instance, look at the light handrail in front of the dark steps. It's generally preferable to draw the steps first. Then erase into them to create the handrail.

If you try to draw the steps just meeting the handrails edges, you can run into two common problems. First, they don't feel overlapped so they come forward in space. Second, they'll often feel discontinuous. The right side won't really relate to the other along a continuous edge.

The pencil type erasers are particularly good for this. As are the sharp edges of the pink and white pearls, they can be used against a straight edge to great effect.

We can apply the same kind of thinking to a landscape or cityscape. As you go about your day, look at the places you routinely go with a view to finding great places to draw.

We're used to thinking about natural pristine landscapes and seascapes or bustling city streets as appropriate subject matter for drawings. And sure, they can provide great material. But any place can be made interesting if the visual structure of the drawing is compelling. So don't rule out a simple backyard, a residential street, or even a strip mall.

One of the major differences between a still life and a landscape is that when we're drawing in nature or a city things will change. The light will likely change over the hours and clouds, birds, cows, people and vehicles will all move. So it's even more important to think about the large structural divisions first. Place things that are unchanging.

Van Gogh was very good at finding points of view with compelling large shape structures to hold the details in his drawings and paintings. Here, the horizontal format is divided into two simple shapes that contain everything else—a large lower rectangle and a smaller upper rectangle.

These are divided into sub-shapes. In the large bottom shape, most of the divisions make use of linear perspective that he worked so hard to master. You can see how he's lining up his road and several of the fences with a vanishing point toward the right edge of the format on the horizon. Other fences vanish off to the left.

He understands the principle involved. He doesn't have to use linear perspective rigidly ruling out lines. But armed with the concept, he can organize the shapes and space in the drawing. So, it's a good idea to start with these kinds of large structural elements; the ones that don't move.

You'll note that the Van Gogh is composed of three main values: a light, a mid-value, and a dark. And most of the contrasts are fairly subtle. Also, each shape has a value identity—light, mid, or dark.

Some subjects—like the path—have a pretty consistent value. Others like some of the thin trees on the left, they vary. You'll notice that lower down, they're light shapes against the darker ground of the fence. As they rise up they become dark first against a lighter fence, then against the light sky.

Other elements—the ones that move and change like the cast shadows or the clouds in the sky or the figures and the bird—are much easier to add once the large structure has been drawn and been established. And you can relate these kinds of elements to the larger structure as you decide what to include and how to include them.

Another project involves combining an interior with an outdoor space. Choose an interior with a window looking out at a something that you can relate compositionally to what's occurring inside the room. Once the basic architecture of the drawing is laid out, it's interesting to proceed from the depth of space forward. Helps in generating clear overlaps. It's also a great opportunity to work with atmospheric perspective. Really leaning on the contrasts and the qualities of edges to stretch the sensation of depth.

Next, try a self-portrait or a portrait of a friend or family member. Try this several different ways. First, try dramatic lighting. Here's one example: a drawing of a head moving out of the darkness into the light.

Remember to think about planes when drawing the head. The human head shares qualities with both the block and the sphere. It has a top plane, front plane, two side planes, a rear plane, and a bottom plane. The last would be the underside of the chin and jaw. The plane changes are like something between the delineated angles of a block and the continuous curve of a sphere or cylinder.

We looked at this planar head in an earlier lecture. The plane changes are accentuated to help students conceptualize the three-dimensional form. When you're drawing the head and figure, push yourself to make a planar analysis of the form. This is particularly important when drawing the visual events on the front plane of the head. Many people who've studied drawing revert to childlike symbols here.

A nose—like the head itself—has a top plane, side planes, and a bottom plane. It's a lot like a block or prism. Noses would also share roundness with cylinders or spheres. Chins and cheeks can be thought of in the same way. The eye sockets are like concave spheres. The eyes—like convex ones—sunken into concavities.

The lips have planes too. Generally, the upper lip angles down toward the lower lip, and the lower lip generally has a visible top plane and front plane. In most cases, the center of the lips sit on the front plane of the head, but the right and left extremes curve onto the side planes. When you look at the meeting of your upper and lower lips, ask yourself which one is overlapping the other at any given point.

Everything depends on a cogent analysis of the form. This drawing has a quiet mood, and that suits the subject—a woman reading in her bed at night. Notice the compositional use of value. Highest contrasts in the head. Next in the body and cast shadow. Next in the bed. Then the painting on the wall. And, last, the walls themselves.

The light comes from below left. It creates clear plane breaks in the head, arm, chest and legs. But the modulations occur within the value palette for that area.

Here's another drawing where we have value being used hierarchically, compositionally, and to modulate the form. We see the greatest contrast in the head. Then, the body. Then, the still-life on the table. Then, the rest of the room. Different parts of the drawing are handled in different palettes— different ranges of value.

Think about how you can include other objects in a figure drawing to create space and drama. Notice how we move back in space from the bottle to its reflection to the young woman, then the lamp, the cast shadow and the window. The sequence of overlaps helps to define the space. This progression is also linked to the diagonal of the format.

Looking for interesting reflective surfaces can be a great way to approach a self-portrait. One of my students used a window at night. He found lots of dramatic reflections in the glass and interesting scale changes in the night landscape; has a very strong mood.

Here, the figure on the right is balanced by the light switch on the left.

Absent the figure, the value palette here is all high key—about one through three or four on the value scale. But in the figure, we get the full range—one to nine. This creates a clear focal hierarchy.

There's great planar analysis in both the light switch and head. The planar analysis of the switch and nose are very similar. Also, note how the eraser is being used as a drawing tool particularly in the hair.

In this next example, take a look at how the figure on the right is balanced by the umbrella, the fire extinguisher and its reflection on the left. Note how the contrasts in the figure dominate. Nothing else in the drawing comes close.

The framing of the light shape of the head in the dark of the hair makes this the focal area. The high contrast and level of detail in the eyes make them the focal point. Lastly, notice how the value in the floor is put down directionally so that it sits in this plane.

Make sure you try a full-figure portrait or self-portrait too. This goes well beyond drawing a head or a head and shoulders which will generally be right up against the picture plane. Drawing the full figure lets you locate the figure in a depth of space. Here, we have a foreground defined by the edge of the bed. We have a middle ground where the figure's located. And last, a background defined by the drape and wall.

And let's take a look at how this is composed. The ground consists of two rectangles—an upper and lower one. The upper one is then divided along a vertical, very abstract. The woman, book, and pillow form an aggregate shape—a triangle. Very good articulation of the large planes in this drawing.

The planes of the walls convincingly pivot due to the change of value. The light's coming from the right. The small side plane of the wall gets a fair amount of light. The wall at 90° to this goes darker. The 90° turn puts us parallel to the first wall so this section again receives some light. But as we move away from the light source, the light diminishes.

We find this same progression of light along the floor. And note how the light on the floor is reflected up onto the underside of the woman's thigh. The way the floorboards are drawn converging toward a vanishing point really help the floor sit down and have a convincing spatial orientation.

There's very good control here of value palettes. We see the light plane of the woman's head against the dark of the table behind her. This gives us a very high contrast event here; helps to cement the head as the focal point.

While we have some real lights on the right side of the drawing in the wall, they're not associated with strong darks. Also, note how the pictures on the wall and on the table are drawn as if in peripheral vision. The edges are blurred and the contrasts less pronounced.

Here's a last example. The figure really sits convincingly in a mid-spatial depth. The head is the focal area because of its dominant value contrasts and edge clarity. Within the head, the eye on the left is the focal point—bright white against black.

As we move into the hoody, pants, and sandals, the contrasts become more muted and the edge definition less crisp. Move out into the room and the contrasts diminish further.

This last group of projects all called on you to translate color to value. The final project I'll mention here centers in on this. It involves translating a painting into a value drawing. We did this once before with line. Here, you'd follow the same basic steps, though you'd map out the value as discussed earlier in this lecture.

It's a great exercise that'll help you understand how an artist you admire uses value. It will also give you great practice in thinking strategically about translating color into value.

# Value: Side Light and Cast Shadow
## Lecture 24

In the past few lectures, we've concentrated on the use of value in drawings done from observation, but we also want to use value in drawing from the imagination. Learning something about projecting cast shadows will help you gain greater confidence in doing this. As we've done with many problems, we'll build from simple geometric forms. The goal is to wed your knowledge of geometric solids and perspective to ideas about value to create believable objects in light and shade drawn from your imagination. Because this topic is really part of linear perspective, it's often termed the *perspective of shadows*. It involves step-by-step schematic procedures, but like the rest of linear perspective, once you understand the underlying principles, you can apply it freely, basically eyeballing how you want to construct light and shade in your drawings.

### Cast Shadow Variables

As we've already seen, a number of variables affect the way we see the form of an object and the cast shadow it produces. The strength of the light source is a primary factor. All else being equal, the sun will dwarf a 300-watt bulb, and a 300-watt bulb will dwarf a match. The type of light is another factor. Sunlight is different from moonlight, which is different from an incandescent ceiling fixture, which is different from a fluorescent one, which is different from a flashlight or a campfire. And the shadows created by a strong, focused light—say, bright sun on a cloudless day—are different from those created by diffuse light on a gray and overcast day.

The position of the light source relative to the object—both its distance and its angle—is another important variable. Imagine that you're looking directly at an object. Light could come from any direction in relationship to that object. If it came from directly in front, the result would be a partially or fully obscured shadow because the shadow will be overlapped by the object itself. Light coming from directly behind the object leaves it in silhouette; here, the cast shadow projects out toward the viewer. Light could also come from the right or left side and from any of the oblique angles in between these first four positions. With a concentrated light source coming from either the right or left side or from a right or left oblique angle, we'll get the effects of chiaroscuro, as well as defined cast shadows. This is why many naturalistic works are lit in this way. This lighting brings out the form of the object, and the cast shadows help define the spatial orientation of the ground or other large planes.

Further, the shape and spatial orientation of the object producing the shadow have a measurable effect on the cast shadow. Similarly, the planar orientation of the surface receiving the shadow influences the shape of the cast shadow.

All these factors combine to increase the complexity of drawing cast shadows. However, as we've done in the past, we'll start with a simple situation and build from there. First, we'll look at a stripped-down side-lit situation. We'll build from this base and learn how to project cast shadows of blocks and curvilinear solids in one- and two-point perspective. Then, we'll learn about compound surfaces receiving shadows and inclined planes throwing them. In the next lecture, we'll look into light coming from oblique angles, both in front of and behind the object. We'll also take a look at artificial light.

**Important Principles of Side Light**
As we move through the drawing exercises in this lecture, keep these principles in mind:

- In linear perspective, we consider all light rays coming from the sun as being parallel.

- To draw the shadow of a vertical that's perpendicular to the ground plane, extend a horizontal from the base of the vertical to meet the ray of light.

- With side light, the shadow of a horizontal edge recedes to the same vanishing point as the edge itself.

As you're working through variations on the drawing exercises in this lecture, try changing the variables. For example, try a given situation with a low horizon, then a high horizon. Keep in mind that the lower the horizon, the more oblique the shadow, and the higher the horizon, the wider the shadow. You might also try different locations and angles for the light source, which will translate to different shadow lengths. If you go through the exercises methodically several times, you'll begin to develop an instinctive feel for how the shadows should relate to one another, to the point of view, and to the time of day.

## Suggested Reading

Auvil, *Perspective Drawing*, chapter 8, "Cast Shadow," pp. 59–74.

Norling, *Perspective Made Easy*, chapter 16, "Shade and Shadow," pp. 155–166.

# Value: Side Light and Cast Shadow

## Lecture 24—Transcript

So far, we've concentrated on the use of value in drawings done from observation. We want to build on this so that you'll be able to draw from our imagination, too. There's a piece that will help you gain greater confidence in drawing from your imagination with value. And, that's learning something about projecting cast shadows.

As we've done with many problems, we'll start with simple geometric forms and build on this. The goal is to wed your knowledge of geometric solids and perspective to ideas about value, to create believable objects in light and shade drawn from your imagination.

Since this is really part of linear perspective, it's often termed the perspective of shadows. It involves step-by-step schematic procedures. But, like the rest of linear perspective, once you understand the underlying principles you can apply it very freely. Basically, eyeballing how you want to construct light and shade in your drawing.

As we've already seen, there are a number of variables that affect the way we see the form of an object and the cast shadow it produces.

The strength of the light source is a primary one. All else being equal, the sun will dwarf a 300-watt bulb. And a 300-watt bulb will dwarf a match. The type of light is another. Sunlight's different from moonlight, which is different from an incandescent ceiling fixture, which is different from a fluorescent one, which is different again from a flashlight or a campfire. And the shadows created by a strong focused light—say, bright sun on a cloudless day—is different from diffuse light—say, the shadows we'd see on a gray and overcast day. The position of the light source relative to the object is another important variable. Both its distance and angle.

So, let's imagine we're looking directly at an object. Light could come from any direction in relation to that object. It could come from directly in front. In this case, the object this would produce a partially, or fully, obscured shadow because the shadow will be overlapped by the object itself. Light could come from directly behind the object. This leaves the object in shadow, in silhouette. And, the cast shadow will project out towards us. Light could also come from the right or left side, and from any of the oblique angles in between these first four positions.

With a concentrated light source coming from either the right or left sides, or from right or left oblique angles, we'll get the effects of chiaroscuro, as well as defined cast shadows. This is why many naturalistic works are lit in this way. It brings out the form of the object. And, the cast shadows help define the spatial orientation of the ground or other large planes.

Next, the shape and spatial orientation of the object producing the shadow has a measurable effect on the cast shadow.

Similarly, the planar orientation of the surface receiving the shadow will likewise, influence the cast shadow's shape. So, with all these factors it can get complex. But, as we've done before, we'll start with a simple situation and build from there.

First, we'll look at a stripped-down, side-lit situation. We'll build from this base and learn how to project cast shadows of blocks and curvilinear solids in one and two-point perspective. Then, we'll learn about compound surfaces receiving shadows and inclined planes throwing them. In the next lecture, we'll look into light coming from oblique angles, both from in front and from behind the object. We'll also take a look at artificial light. Like a light bulb hanging from the ceiling.

In linear perspective, we consider all light rays coming from the sun as being parallel. For drawing purposes, the sun's so far away that any slight differences aren't germane. That's different from the way we conceive of a naked bulb in a room. There, as we'll see, we conceive of the light rays as radiating out from a central point. But, for our purposes here, it all stays simple. And this is our first principle: All light rays from the sun are treated as parallel.

Let's imagine a pole in the ground. The sun rises in the east. At first, with the sun at a low elevation, the cast shadow is quite long. But, as the sun continues to rise, the shadow progressively shortens until we get to midday when the shadow disappears. Past noon the shadow begins to extend in the opposite direction. At first, the angle of the light ray is almost vertical and the shadow is short. But as we progress through the afternoon, the shadow lengthens. As the sun sets we, once again, get very long shadows. Of course, this is what we experience—long dramatic shadows at dawn and dusk, minimal shadows at midday. We get shadows pointing west in the morning, east in the afternoon. If the viewer is looking north, shadows go left before noon and right after.

So, you can draw whatever length of cast shadow you want, whatever suits your expressive purpose. A key point is that when you're drawing from your imagination you can inflect time of day and mood through shadow length and direction.

Draw along with me here. Even though this involves linear perspective, you could follow along that way approximating the angles—a pencil and a sketchbook's fine, but if you're more comfortable with a straight edge and your 18 × 24-inch paper that's fine too.

So, we're out in the desert. We have a horizon. And we have a post stuck in the ground. It's a sunny afternoon. One of the sun's parallel light rays glances the top of the pole and extends down toward the ground plane. To draw the shadow of the pole, we extend a horizontal out from the pole's base to meet the ray. And, that's our second principle: With side light, to draw the shadow of a vertical that's perpendicular to the ground plane we extend a horizontal from the base of the vertical to meet the ray of light. We'll use this idea over and over again. It's the basic concept behind projecting all kinds of more complex cast shadows.

Now, let's imagine we have a second pole. It's the same height as the first pole. But it's located back, behind the first one. First, we place the point where the second pole meets the ground plane. Then we extend a diagonal from the base of the first pole to the base point of the second. And, we continue to the horizon. And, that's our vanishing point. From this vanishing point, we draw a diagonal to intersect the top of the first pole. Then, extend a vertical line from the base of the second pole to meet the diagonal. Now we have two poles of equal height. And we can get rid of some of the construction lines. To construct the shadow of the second pole we'll repeat what we did earlier. All light rays coming from the sun are parallel. So, we'll draw a ray of light that's parallel to the first ray, then a horizontal from the base of the pole to intersect the ray. We've got our shadow.

But let's imagine we're really building a wall here. Line-up the two poles, top and bottom. Draw the lines connecting them. That's the wall. These diagonals will also line-up with the vanishing point. Now, we need the wall's shadow. As you've likely guessed, all we have to do is connect the ends of the two posts' shadows. You may have noticed that this diagonal also lines-up with the vanishing point. And that's our third principle: With side light, the shadow of a horizontal edge recedes to the same vanishing point as the edge itself. At this point, you could shade it in if you'd like.

Now, let's imagine we're not just building a wall, but we're building a block in one-point perspective. Draw the front face of our block. And we already have its shadow. For a block that's straddling the horizon in one-point perspective in 90-degree light, the shadow of the block will be the same as the shadow of the block's side plane.

Let's do another. But this time we'll start by drawing a block, a transparent one. And we'll put it below the horizon. And we'll make it closer to us in space. Start with the front face on the right side of the page. Take a line from each corner of the rectangle back toward the vanishing point. We'll use the same one we used for the other block, draw the back face and we've got our block. I've asked you to draw this transparently because we'll need the internal structure to generate the block's cast shadow. The block's vertical edges will function like the vertical posts we drew in the last drawing. Parallel light rays will glance their tops and continue to the ground plane. To mix things up a bit, we'll change the ray's angle more towards the vertical. Make it a little earlier in the afternoon. As we did before, we'll extend horizontals from the verticals' bases to create the cast shadows of these edges.

Next, we'll connect these with a diagonal to create the shadow of the top right receding edge of the block. Then, erase the rays and the three lines representing the block's interior. Since this is a solid block, we'll only see the triangular portion of the shadow emerging to the right of the block's right edge, so erase the part of the shadow we wouldn't see. Here's what it would look like shaded-in. But, don't do this yet in your drawing. The point here is that, depending on the point of view, we may need to draw through the object. See it as if we had x-ray vision, and construct the whole cast shadow. Then, erase the parts we wouldn't see.

You may have guessed that there was a less complicated way to get this. We could have drawn one ray of light glancing off the far right vertical edge. Drawn the shadow of that edge—a horizontal out to meet the ray—and then drawn a line from that intersection back toward the vanishing point. That represents the shadow of the receding top edge of the block. That's our third principle at work. The shadow of an edge vanishes to same vanishing point as the edge itself.

But let's take this in another direction. Get into some additional complexity.

Take what you have and erase three things: the triangular cast shadow, the front bottom horizontal, and the left bottom receding diagonal.

We'll imagine this as a surface suspended on four posts. Like a table or a carport. So we'll add the rear right leg. You can also shade-in the top plane if you like.

Now for the cast shadow. For each post we draw a ray of light, all parallel from the bases, horizontals to intersect. This gives us the posts' cast shadows. Now, we need the tabletop's shadow. We connect the ends of the shadows of the two posts on the right, then the same thing on the left. These diagonals represent the shadows of the two receding edges of the tabletop—they lineup with the vanishing point, no surprise, third principle. The shadow of an edge vanishes to same vanishing point as the edge itself.

We have the shadows of the table legs and the receding top edges. We're missing parts of the shadows of the horizontal edges of the tabletop. These partially overlap the cast shadow of the legs on the right. We just need to fill in the gaps. We'll draw in a line, starting at the cast shadow of the left edge of the tabletop, toward the right leg both in the front and the rear. Shade it in to up the illusion.

Take out a new sheet of paper and we'll do this in two-point perspective. Draw a horizon. Then, locate right and left vanishing points at the page's edges. Start with a single post or table leg. Lightly carry both top and bottom back toward the vanishing points. Next, add a right and left leg. From the left leg, we'll recede to the right, from the right to the left. At their intersection, draw the rear leg. Connect these to construct the top plane of the table. Now for the shadow. We'll start with four parallel rays of light, imagining late afternoon, rays with acute angles to the ground plane producing relatively long shadows, and then intersecting horizontals from each of the legs. We'll connect the front leg's shadow to the shadow directly behind it. This line represents the shadow of the tabletop's right front edge. Then draw a line from this point to the rear table leg's shadow. This is the shadow of the table's back edge. You've got the idea now. From here, connect to the shadow of the table's far left leg. And, back to where we began.

If we assign value to the cast shadow's shape, it helps complete the illusion. I've used a mid-gray. This allows for a slightly darker gray for the right table leg creating a compound shadow. We could equally allow the table leg's shadow to be subsumed in the shadow of the tabletop. Whether we'd see this or not would depend primarily on the strength of the light source. Once again, the shadows of the tabletop's edges recede to the same vanishing points as the edges themselves—principle number three. The long edges of the table and their shadows vanish to the right, the short edges, and their shadows to the left. Good to remember this, it's a good check if you get confused.

If this table were a solid block, we'd need to project the cast shadows of the three right-most vertical edges.

Start with a transparent block. Project light rays glancing the tops of the three right vertical edges. Draw intersecting horizontals from the bases. Connect the ends of the horizontal shadows. Now to edit get rid of the light rays. Then the internal structure of the block, and the parts of shadows we wouldn't see. Add some value, and you're done.

I'd suggest repeating everything we've done a number of times for practice. It will really help you make this your own. Use both one- and two-point perspective. Change the variables in your drawings. Try a low horizon then a high horizon, the lower the horizon the more oblique the shadow, the higher, the fatter. Try locating the light source on the right. Try different angles of light. These translate to different shadow lengths. Try different types of blocks, some tall, and some squat.

Then up the complexity. If the table we drew were an actual table, the legs would have planes as well. Each table leg is really an elongated block. You'd figure the shadow of each leg the same way we did for the block itself—blocks within blocks. Then try a stack of boxes. Try it freehand, approximating the angles.

For most purposes, you'll want to be able to adapt the core principles to freehand drawing. As you do this more and more it will become very natural, part of the way you see and think visually. You'll be able to draw more quickly. And it'll help you see how you could apply this to your sketching from your imagination.

Let's try some curvilinear solids. We'll start with a transparent cone sitting on a table in front of a wall. This time light from the right. Draw a ray glancing the cone's point. We can sketch a trapezoid around the cone's elliptical base. Cross diagonals to find the perspectival center. Then a horizontal line out to intersect the light ray. Erase any extra line. Draw diagonals to this point from the close and far edges of the base. Erase the construction lines and those in the cone's interior. Edit as needed. Reduce the line's strength. Then, add value to the tabletop and wall. And to the cone and cast shadow. Next a cylinder. Now for a sphere. We'll add parallel light rays glancing the widest points on each side. Then a horizontal line connecting these where the sphere touches the ground plane. We'll draw an ellipse on the centerline and you've got your shadow. Again, edit. Erase back the line. And treat everything with value.

You might ask, "How did you determine how wide to make the ellipse?" The short answer is "I made it up." So, here's the long answer. We don't know how fat the ellipse of the shadow should be because we haven't established eyelevel.

When we look at a block, a cone, or a cylinder, what we see of each of these forms is dependent on eyelevel. If we see a block or a cylinder from high above, we'll see a lot of its top plane. As our eyelevel is lowered, we see less and less. If we imagine these solids as transparent, the same would hold true for their bases—wider shapes from high above diminishing to a line at eyelevel. When we drew the blocks, the cone, and the cylinder, one plane of each of these objects was sitting on the ground plane. The width of that shape indicated eyelevel. And, we projected the cast shadow from the width of that shape. Drawing lines out from points where the form met the ground plane—front back, left and right. Using this system, a block seen from high above will produce a wider shadow, one closer to eyelevel, a thinner one. It's built into the system. The spatial orientation of the object was captured by its base and translated to the cast shadow.

Spheres are special. They have no plane that coincides with the ground plane. They look identical from any point of view. So when we draw a sphere from our imagination, it, in and of itself, tells us nothing about its spatial orientation. So we have to make this up.

Here's a sphere with a cast shadow seen from three different heights. Higher, the shadow wider, lower, thinner, lower yet, thinner yet. But the shape of the sphere is identical in each case.

So, when we draw the shadow of a sphere we need to set eyelevel. If there are other objects in the drawing, block-like things for instance, use their shadows as a guide. If not, and you want greater specificity, draw the cube the sphere would inhabit and use its bottom plane as an indication.

Another point here. This isn't just, or even primarily, a technical problem. When artists draw from their imagination, they think about the expressive difference between long thin shadows that dissipate slowly and short hard shadows that end at an abrupt edge. Generally, we want the technical to follow the underlying expressive intent.

Up next, cast shadows on compound surfaces. And this is a good bit of fun. You'll need a new sheet of paper. Start with a post in the desert, with a wall to the right. Then a ray of light glancing the post's top. Draw a horizontal toward the ray of light. But, where it hits the wall, climb up vertically until it hits the light ray. Erase the ray. As the sun sets, the shadow lengthens and climbs farther up the wall. Lower light, longer—or in this case—taller shadow. Let's apply this to a tallish one-point block. Draw one freehand. Then add a wall to the right. Draw angled rays of light glancing the block's top right corners. From the right vertical edges of the block draw horizontals out toward the light rays but stop at the wall. Then head-up vertically to intersect the rays, and connect the top points. This last diagonal line lines-up with the vanishing point. That's principle 3 once again. With side light, the shadow of a horizontal edge recedes to same vanishing point as the edge itself. Add some value and you've got the cast shadow.

Let's try this in two-point—a little more complicated but, really, much the same idea. Start with a transparent two-point block. Next a wall behind it. Add light rays glancing the tops of the three right-most vertical edges, and horizontals moving out from their bases. The first will extend fully to the ray of light. The other two will end at the wall. From the ends of each of the latter, draw a vertical to intersect the ray.

Now, for the shadow's outline. Start with the line representing the block's long top edge's shadow. Do this by drawing a line from the end of the shadow of the first vertical edge to intersect with the ray glancing the far right vertical. Stop at the wall. From here, draw a line to the point of intersection of the far right edge with its light ray. This is the same point we'd intersect if the shadow were flat on the ground. Then connect this point to the final vertical edge's shadow and ray intersection. Now, erase the internal structure of the block, the light rays, other construction lines, and the part of the shadow outline we wouldn't see. Erase back the outline, add some value, and you've drawn the cast shadow.

Let's do this now with our curvilinear volumes. Draw a tallish transparent cone like this one. Then the trapezoid suggested by the cone's base. Cross diagonals to find its center. And draw a horizontal from the center out to the left. This will help us place the wall we'll draw next. Vanish the trapezoid back to find the vanishing point and horizon. From the vanishing point, we'll draw a wall to the left of the cone, then a light ray. From the point where the horizontal we drew earlier meets the wall we'll draw a vertical to intersect the ray on the wall's surface.

From both the front and back of the elliptical base of the cone, we'll draw lines toward the intersection of the ray with the cone's centerline on the ground plane. And we'll stop at their intersection with the wall. From these two points, we'll draw diagonals to meet the intersection point on the wall. You can erase the construction lines, edit as needed, and add value at your leisure.

Next up—draw a transparent cylinder. Then, draw the trapezoid of the cylinder's base. Cross diagonals to find its center. And draw a horizontal from the center out to the right, project lines to find the vanishing point and horizon. Using the vanishing point draw a wall to the cylinder's right. Next, a central light ray from the cylinder's lip. Now, a vertical up to intersect the light. Two more light rays from the widest parts of the top ellipse. Then the horizontals from the wide points of the base out to meet them. But, stop at the wall.

Draw verticals up to intersect the light rays. And, a curve to connect the three points of intersection. Erase and edit, and add some value to all the planes. Next, draw a sphere like this one. We'll imagine light from the right and draw two light rays and a long cast shadow, then a trapezoid for the shadow's shape. Project a vanishing point and the horizon.

Let's locate a separate vanishing point on the horizon for the wall. And draw the wall. From the center of the base of the sphere, we'll draw a horizontal toward the light ray and stop at the wall. Then draw a vertical to intersect the light ray on the wall. Where the contours of the cast shadow hit the wall we'll draw a curve arching up to the point of light ray intersection on the wall. Again, erase and edit. And you can treat the drawing with value.

Our last topic concerns the cast shadows of incline planes. Start by drawing an incline plane like the one I have here. Again, drawing freehand is fine. Next, draw two light rays glancing the top corners.

Now, we'll need to draw horizontals out from the base of the vertical heights of the corners. So, we have to extend a vertical line down from the top corners of the incline plane to the ground plane. But, we don't know where the ground plane should be. In other words, we need to know where the incline plane would lie if it were lowered down to the ground.

There are a number of ways to do this. If we want real accuracy, we'd start by drawing the plane on the ground in two-point perspective. Then using a vertical trace and a trace point above one of the left vanishing point, we'd draw the incline plane. Then, simply drop the verticals down to meet the receding diagonals to find the vertical height from the ground. A variation is to start by constructing a triangular prism that would produce a similar incline plane. The third way is to eyeball the ground plane—imagine the prism's structure, its vanishing point and trace point. For most purposes, eyeballing will work just fine, especially if you've constructed a few of these the long way. You'll begin to develop a sense of what looks right.

So, one way or the other, we have verticals dropping to the ground. From their bases, draw horizontals out to meet the rays of light.

Now for the cast shadow. First, draw a line from the lower left corner of the plane to meet the lower horizontal line. This represents the shadow of the plane's left edge. Next, a diagonal line from this point to the horizontal above it. This represents the shadow of the top edge of the plane. And a final line from this point to the plane's lower right corner. This is the inclined right edge's shadow. Erase the rays and construction lines to reveal the shadow's shape. Erase the portion we wouldn't see. And you can treat the shadow shape with value.

Try this a couple more times. Try different kinds of incline planes, different directions of plane, and directions of light. Like most of the things we've done, getting a grasp of this comes with repetition and variation.

When most artists draw from their imaginations, they don't plot all this out with a ruler. Though, of course, some do. But, they use the principles and procedures to ballpark things so they'll be convincing.

As with many things in drawing, you'll begin to develop a feel for what these kinds of cast shadows should look like if you go through this methodically several times. You'll begin to have an instinctual feel for how the shadows should relate to one another, to the point of view, and to time of day.

# Value: Oblique Light and Cast Shadow

## Lecture 25

In this lecture, we'll complete our discussion of cast shadows. We'll cover oblique light coming from both the front and the rear of objects, artificial light, multiple light sources, and a method for determining shadows of irregular forms. We'll then discuss a number of drawing projects that will allow you to apply the knowledge you've gained about value and about constructing cast shadow.

### Oblique Light

With oblique light coming from the front, cast shadows will recede into space. With oblique light coming from the rear, cast shadows will project forward into space. In this lecture, we'll walk through several exercises that explore how we project cast shadows in oblique light. Key points to remember include the following:

- A cast shadow has two major components: angle, or direction, and length. The light ray's intersection with the angle, or direction, of the shadow determines length.

- To project the shadow of an object in oblique light, we need a new kind of vanishing point: a *shadow vanishing point*.

- We also need a *shadow trace point*. This is a point where light rays intersect a 90-degree vertical passing through the shadow vanishing point.

- All shadow directions from a given light source converge toward the same point, the shadow vanishing point.

- All shadow lengths are defined by rays of light converging toward the shadow trace point, where they intersect shadow directional lines.

- With light coming from the front, as we move laterally away from the shadow vanishing and trace points, the cast shadows get longer and the angle of the shadow to the vertical edge becomes more obtuse. As we move closer, the shadows get shorter and the angle becomes more acute.

- With light coming from the back, as we move laterally away from the shadow vanishing and trace points, the cast shadows get longer, but the angle of the shadow to the vertical edge becomes more acute with distance. As we move closer, the shadows get shorter, and the angle becomes more obtuse.

- When drawing from the imagination, the angle of the shadow and shadow length can be important compositional choices.

**Artificial Light**

In many ways, artificial light combines aspects of the various types of light we've studied so far. To explore artificial light, we'll draw an interior with a single light source on the ceiling. We'll locate the shadow vanishing point directly below the light source, on the ground plane. In this situation, the shadows of objects in front of the shadow vanishing point will project forward in space. Objects behind the shadow vanishing point will project back, behind the objects. And objects straddling the shadow vanishing point will project horizontally away from it. In this exercise, we'll project the cast shadows of a block, a cone, a cylinder, and a sphere.

**Light and Irregular Forms**

Of course, many things we draw, such as still-life objects, trees, and people, are irregular. For many of these objects, using a bounding rectangle helps you project shadows in oblique and artificial light.

**Summing Up Cast Shadows**

In the last two lectures, we've looked at five cases of cast shadow projection. In each case, we built the shadows using vertical heights associated with an object. To construct the shadows, we determined the direction or angle of the shadow and its length. The shadow's direction or angle originated from the base of the vertical. The length of the shadow was determined by a light ray glancing the top of the vertical. The point where the shadow's angle and light ray intersected defined the length of the vertical's shadow.

In the first case we looked at, left sidelight, the direction of the light and shadow was horizontal to the right. In right sidelight, the direction of the light and shadow was horizontal to the left. In both cases, the shadow's length was defined by the angle of a light ray intersecting the shadow's direction.

The third case was oblique light from in front of an object. Here, shadows of verticals receded behind the object to a shadow vanishing point on the horizon. The lengths of the shadows were determined by the intersection of a light ray with the shadow directional line. All the rays converged to a shadow trace point located on a vertical trace directly below the shadow vanishing point.

The fourth case was oblique light from behind an object. Here, shadows projected forward in space from a shadow vanishing point on the horizon. The lengths of the shadows were determined by the intersection of a light ray with the shadow directional line. All the rays converged to a shadow trace point located on a vertical trace directly above the shadow vanishing point. In this case, the point can be conceived of as being the light source itself.

The fifth case was an artificial light in a room. Here, the light rays radiated outward from the light source. They glanced the tops of verticals and continued to the ground plane to intersect the shadows' angle or direction. These angles originated in a shadow vanishing point located on the ground plane directly below the light source. The resultant shadows splay out from the center.

For the light to be consistent in both oblique and artificial light, all the shadows of vertical elements must recede to the same shadow vanishing point. The lengths of all the shadows must be defined by a light ray intersecting the shadows' directional lines. All light rays from a given light source converge at a shadow trace point located directly above or below the shadow vanishing point.

## Multiple Light Sources

Our goal has been to understand how to draw convincing three-dimensional form from the imagination using value to imitate the effects of light. Using a single light source is the clearest way to make form feel three-dimensional. But you could certainly experiment with using multiple light sources. For example, you could draw a single object and project all five light situations we've discussed.

With light coming from every side, the planes become evenly lit. One potential effect of this is to make form feel less solid or three-dimensional; many artists are interested in exploring such forms. Multiple light sources might also be of interest when the focus of the drawing is not really the object but the choreography of patterns of light and shadow. You might also be interested in looking at contrasting light sources, such as outdoor light from a window combined with interior light from an incandescent bulb. This situation can be especially interesting if you're working in color.

## Continuing Projects

You now know quite a bit about value, light, and shade and about constructing shadow. With this knowledge, consider trying these drawing projects:

- Draw into the cast-shadow drawings you've done in this and the previous lecture. Add value to all the planes and to the objects. As you think about using light and shade to create volume, also think about overall mood and value palette. And remember to consider hierarchies of contrast—how you use value compositionally.

- Play with projecting shadows onto different kinds of surfaces. Make sure the cast shadow reflects the angle or curve of the plane on which it falls.

- Draw geometric solids from your imagination, starting with a sphere. Practice working with the nine steps of light we discussed in an earlier lecture. Then try a block, a cone, and a cylinder. Finally, put a group of solids together in a still life.

- Invent a room, imagine a window as your light source, and construct a still life consisting of geometric solids in the room. Include a pattern on the floor based on a grid.

## Suggested Reading

Loomis, *Successful Drawing*, "Light on the Basic Forms," pp. 79–88.

Montague, *Basic Perspective Drawing*, chapter 8, "Shadows and Reflections," pp. 145–154.

# Value: Oblique Light and Cast Shadow
## Lecture 25—Transcript

In this lecture, we'll complete our discussion of cast shadows. We'll cover oblique light coming from both the front and the rear of objects. We'll also discuss artificial light.

Before we do, let's return to sidelight and a single post in the desert. A ray of light glances the post's top and continues to the ground. To draw the shadow, we extend a horizontal at a 90-degree angle from the post's base to intersect the ray at ground level. The shadow has two components: angle or direction, and length. The line coming from the base of the vertical post determines the direction or angle of the shadow, here 90 degrees. The light ray determines length. Oblique light gets a little more complicated, but these two principles apply. Remembering this can stave off confusion.

Let's start with oblique light from the front. This means the cast shadows will recede into space. Draw along here. Once again, try to put things approximately where I do, that way you'll have room for everything we'll draw.

Start with a single pole out in the desert with a mid-ish horizon. We'll imagine light coming from the left behind us, so the shadow will recede at an angle from the post's base to the right. This establishes the light and shadow's direction. If you extend the line of the shadow to the horizon, you get a new kind of vanishing point: a shadow vanishing point.

Add a light ray. This establishes the angle the light travels from its source. The point at which the light ray traverses the shadow defines the shadow's length—same idea as sidelight. As the angle of the ray rotates toward the vertical, the shadow gets shorter; as it moves toward the horizontal, longer. There's a second new kind of point we'll use here, a shadow trace point. That's where the light ray would intersect a 90-degree vertical passing through the shadow vanishing point. We're actually going to draw a block in two-point perspective with its shadow, but we'll do this one post at a time.

Let's add a second post, same size as the first but farther back in space. To do this, we'll need a right vanishing point for the posts. Place it to the left of the shadow vanishing point, then vanish the top and bottom of the existing post back toward the right vanishing point. Then add a new post behind the first and erase the two construction lines receding to the right vanishing point. Then draw the second post's shadow using the shadow vanishing point and trace point. Draw a line from the base of the new post toward the shadow vanishing point to establish its angle, then a line from the top of the new post toward the shadow trace point—this establishes the shadow's length. Erase the two new construction lines.

Next, we'll add another post, the back corner of the block. We'll need a left vanishing point. Then vanish the right post back toward that point and add the post. Erase the construction lines. From the base of the new post, draw its receding shadow toward the shadow vanishing point. Then draw a ray from the top of the post toward the shadow trace point. You've defined the angle and length of this post's shadow.

All the shadow directions converge toward the same point, the shadow vanishing point. All the shadow lengths are defined by rays of light converging toward the shadow trace point.

We need one more post. We'll use the existing posts on the left in combination with the right and left vanishing points to locate this. Erase the construction lines. We won't need the shadow of the post on the left; it'll fall in the interior of the block and our goal is a solid block with its shadow. If we were constructing something like a table, we'd add this.

Now, connect the posts to get a transparent block. To get the shadow of the block, we need to draw the shadow of the long edge receding to the right. We get this by connecting the first two post's shadows. Then connect the third post's shadow to draw the top right rear edge's shadow. Erase the internal shadow construction line, then the portion of the shadow we won't see if the block's opaque. And erase the internal construction lines.

You could add value to all the planes. Good idea to lighten all the lines first—erase them back so that they're just visible. The planes will feel more volumetric if they're not bound by line. If the light's coming from the left, depending on its elevation, the left-facing plane or the top plane will get the most light. I'll go with the left plane, top next, right plane least.

We also want to think hierarchically. If I want people to pay attention to the block, I locate the highest contrast in the block and in its relationship to the ground. I also make sure that the contrast in the two ground shapes is minimal in comparison. We generally don't want lots of contrast between the two ground shapes, and minimal contrast between the block and the ground, and within the block too. Do this and the edge where the ground shapes meet will pop, and the block becomes an afterthought.

We can accomplish this compositional goal using different palettes. This will inflect the quality of light and will correlate with mood and emotional quality. And remember, value's relative. It's not the value per se but the role it plays in the given value palette. What reads as a mid-light in one context could read mid-dark in another.

Let's rewind what we just did, but instead of starting with a post, we'll start by constructing a block using right and left vanishing points.

From the base of one vertical edge, draw an angle or direction for the cast shadow. This is an artistic choice, a compositional choice. Then, extend this diagonal to the horizon to establish a shadow vanishing point. The shadow length is another artistic choice. It could be short, medium, or long—up to you. To establish that length, we need a shadow trace point.

Draw a vertical line through the shadow vanishing point. Establish the length of the first shadow, then project a line from the top of the vertical through the shadow's end to intersect the vertical trace. The point of intersection will be the shadow trace point. Then, relate the shadows of all vertical edges to these two points. Erase the construction lines and define the cast shadow's shape. Next, establish a value structure for the drawing, and you want to think about mood and compositional value and hierarchy.

It's worth noting that as we move laterally from the shadow vanishing and trace points, the cast shadows get longer and the angle of the shadow to the vertical edge becomes more obtuse. As we move closer, the shadows get shorter and the angle more acute. I'd suggest reinforcing what you've just learned by playing around with it. Try light from the right, it will work the same way. You could also modify the object. Try a table, then a block on another block. And try cones and cylinders, too.

Let's look at oblique light coming from behind the object. This means the cast shadow will project forward in space. Start with a block, like the one we drew earlier. Erase the construction lines. From the central vertical's base, draw a line to represent the cast shadow's direction and length. Extend this back to the horizon to locate the shadow vanishing point. Draw a vertical trace through this point.

From the tip of the cast shadow, extend a line through the top of the central vertical and continue along this diagonal to intersect the vertical trace. The point of intersection is the shadow trace point. Line up the shadow vanishing point with the base of the far left vertical edge. Project a line forward in space from the vertical's base along this diagonal. This defines the shadow's angle. Then, line up the shadow trace point with the top of the vertical edge and project forward to intersect the first line. This defines the shadow's length. Erase your construction lines. Follow the same procedures on the right edge. Add the lines representing the shadows of the top left and right front edges of the block, and erase the internal construction line to complete the shadow.

Here, as we move laterally from the shadow vanishing and trace points, the cast shadows get longer, but in contrast to light from the front, here the angle of the shadow to the vertical edge becomes more acute with distance. As we move closer, the shadows get shorter, the angles more obtuse. Play around with this, too, like you did with light from the front, and play with the system itself. You could imagine a large light source behind the objects, with rays projecting both right and left from a central trace point.

Our last type of light is artificial light. In many ways, this combines aspects of the various types of light we've studied so far. We'll draw an interior, a room, with a light source, like a light bulb, suspended from the ceiling. We'll locate the shadow vanishing point directly below the light source, on the ground plane.

In this situation, the shadows of objects in front of the shadow vanishing point will project forward in space in front of the object. Objects behind the shadow vanishing point will project back, behind the object. And objects straddling the shadow vanishing point will project horizontally away from the shadow vanishing point.

I'd like you to use a sheet of 22 × 30-inch paper. Put it on your drawing board in the landscape position and lightly draw an 18 × 24-inch rectangle centered in the page. The drawing will be 18 × 24. The extra space will allow us to position right and left vanishing points outside the format shape. This will help us avoid distortion.

First, draw a horizon line across the page at about two-thirds of the way up. If you're measuring, make it 13 inches off the bottom of the page, or 11 from the bottom of the format. Add a central vanishing point.

Start with a wide-ish back wall—mine's 4½ by 10. It's vertically centered on the page and straddles the horizon so that two and one-half inches fall below and two and one-half inches above the horizon. Use the central vanishing point to draw the walls, floor, and ceiling. Locate the light source in the ceiling. Mine's positioned about two and one-quarter inches from the top of the page. All we need is a point, like a vanishing point. Draw a vertical line through this point. The light source functions as a shadow trace point, the vertical line as a shadow trace.

To find the shadow vanishing point we have to project this point onto the ground plane. From the light source, draw a horizontal along the ceiling to the right wall, then vertically down the right wall to the floor, then horizontally across the floor to the vertical trace. The point of intersection is the shadow vanishing point. Once you've got this point you can erase the projection lines.

Now we need some objects. Let's start with a transparent two-point block in the lower right. As you'll remember from our discussion of two-point perspective, to limit distortion we space the vanishing points far apart. I'll put mine on the horizon at the edges of the page. Now, construct a transparent two-point block like this one. Once you've got your block, erase the construction lines.

To draw this block's shadow, we need to project a light ray glancing the top of each vertical. Next, we'll project the shadow's direction from the shadow vanishing point through the vertical's base to intersect the ray. Then we can draw the vertical's shadow—should all sound familiar.

Let's start with the vertical closest to us in space. Project a line from the light source through the top. Then, from the shadow vanishing point, through the base. Do the same with the left vertical, then the right, and then the rear. Now erase your rays. Starting on the left, outline the shadow, then erase everything that wouldn't be visible if the block were opaque. Last, you could add some value to the cast shadow.

It's worth noting how many lines we made to construct the shadow's shape. I count 35 including the horizon. That's a lot of lines. The good news is that for many purposes eyeballing works just fine. If something feels off, then pull out a straight edge.

Let's add some curvilinear solids here. I've added a cone, a cylinder, and a sphere. Let's try doing this freehand, approximating the angles so you begin to get a feel for this.

We'll start with the cone. First, we'll draw a perspectival tile around the elliptical base. Then project a diagonal through the center from the shadow vanishing point and intersect this with a light ray. Then we'll draw a line from each side of the cone's elliptical base aimed at the shadow's intersection with the light ray and stop at the wall. From the point where the center line meets the wall, we'll draw a vertical to intersect the ray and connect the two sides. You can erase your construction lines and add some value.

Let's project the cylinder's shadow. Start out the same way. Draw a tile. Find the perspectival center. Project a line from the shadow vanishing point through the base's center point and out along the ground plane. Where this line traverses the ellipse's edge on the left, draw a vertical up to the top ellipse. From the light source, project a line through this point to intersect the line from the shadow vanishing point. From the shadow vanishing point, project another line along the left edge of the cylinder's base and continue forward a bit. Where this line touches the base, draw a vertical up to the top ellipse. From this point, project a line from the light source to the ground plane to intersect the line from the shadow vanishing point. Repeat this on the right side. Once you have these three lines connect them along a curve. Then erase what you don't need.

Now for the sphere. Start with a circle. Then draw a square tile in perspective around the circle. Verticals first, then top and bottom diagonals converging to the horizon, though this will be well off the page. Now we'll draw the cast shadow of the tile, then the tile's simple armature, then the cast shadow of the armature.

So let's see how we can apply what we've just learned to things we'd draw in a landscape, interior, or still life.

I've drawn a tree, like an Italian cypress, a door with a glass pane, and a pitcher. We have an artificial light source above—could be an interior light or a streetlight on a dark night—and a shadow vanishing point below.

Start with the tree. We'll draw a perspectival rectangle encompassing the cypress. Add an armature. Then project the rectangle and armature onto the ground plane and draw the tree's shadow. The door's already rectilinear. We can project it directly onto the ground plane. Then draw verticals down from the glass plane to the door's base and project them along the ground plane. Now, project light rays through the window's four corners and draw light passing through the window on the ground plane.

Let's do the pitcher. Draw a rectangle around the pitcher. Project it. Draw verticals from the top of the body of the pitcher to the bottom of the rectangle. Project these lines forward and draw the body's shadow. Project a light ray from the low point where the spout attaches to the body of the pitcher to the body's shadow. Draw the spout. Project a similar point for the handle, and draw the handle.

Using the bounding rectangle works for all kinds of irregular forms in an artificial or oblique light: cars, dogs, people, anything. The essential point here is that we can apply these concepts in a range of ways, from slow and precise to fast and gestural.

In these last two lectures, we've looked at five cases of cast shadow projection. In each case, we built the shadows using vertical heights associated with the object. To construct the shadows, we determined the direction or angle of the shadow as well as its length. The shadow's direction or angle originated from the base of the vertical. The length of the shadow was determined by a light ray glancing the top of the vertical. The point where the shadow's angle and light ray intersected defined the vertical's shadow.

In the first case we looked at, left sidelight, the direction of the light and of the shadow was horizontal to the right. In right sidelight, the direction of the light and shadow was horizontal to the left. In both cases, the shadow's length was defined by the angle of a light ray intercepting the cast shadow's direction.

The third case was oblique light from in front of the object. Here, shadows of verticals receded behind the object to a shadow vanishing point on the horizon. The length of shadows were determined by the angle of the light rays. All the rays converged to a shadow trace point located on a vertical trace directly below the shadow vanishing point.

The fourth case was oblique light from behind the object. Here, shadows projected forward in space, in front of the object, from a shadow vanishing point on the horizon. The length of the shadows were determined by the angle of the light rays. All the rays converged to a shadow trace point located on a vertical trace directly above the shadow vanishing point. In this case, the point can be conceived of as being the light source itself.

The fifth case was an artificial light in a room. Here the light rays radiated outward from the light source. They glanced the tops of verticals and continued to the ground plane to intersect the shadow's angles. These angles originated in a shadow vanishing point located on the ground plane directly below the light source. The resultant shadows splay out from the center.

For the light to be consistent in both oblique and artificial light, all the shadows of vertical elements must recede to the same shadow vanishing point. The lengths of all the shadows must be defined by a light source or shadow trace point located directly above or below the shadow vanishing point.

In this section, we've covered single light sources. Our goal has been to understand how to draw convincing three-dimensional form from the imagination. When most people work from their imagination this is, more or less, the norm. It's the clearest way to make form feel three-dimensional. That's not to say that multiple light sources are out of the question—you could take the ones we've covered and combine them. Draw a single object and project all five different light sources. With light coming from every side, the planes can become evenly lit. One potential effect is to make form feel less solid, less 3D, and this could be made visually interesting. There are many artists who've been interested in less than solid form.

There are other occasions when multiple light sources might be of interest. One could be when the focus of the drawing is not really the object, but instead, the choreography of patterns of light and shadow. Another would be when a contrast of light source is involved. You've likely seen someone sitting by a window. The plane of their head turned into the room is lit by a warm, orange-ish incandescent bulb. The plane facing the window goes blue, lit by cool exterior daylight. Especially if one's working in color, these kinds of situations can be very interesting to pursue. But, in the latter case, it would likely be preferable to use direct observation as a starting point rather than perspectival constructive methods.

You now know quite a bit about light, shade, and constructing shadow. There are quite a number of interesting projects that you could take on at this point. First, draw into the cast shadow drawings you've done with this and the prior lecture. You could add more objects, but certainly add value to all the planes. Of course, think about how you're using light and shade to create volume but also think about overall mood and value palette. And remember to consider the hierarchies of contrast, how you're using value compositionally.

Play with projecting shadows onto different kinds of surfaces. We did a bit of this but there are many engaging possibilities here. Make small gestural drawings. Remember, once you understand the concept, you don't have to rule things out precisely. Imagine a series of objects in a row. Here, the small cone casts its shadow on the ground plane and then climbs up the larger cone. This, in turn, casts its shadow on the ground plane and climbs up and across the block. The key is to make the shadow reflect the angle or curve of the plane it falls on.

One of the projects described in an earlier lecture on value involved drawing geometric solids—a sphere and a block—from observation. Now draw them from your imagination. Start with a sphere. Draw a format shape and make a horizontal division in the format. You've just drawn a tabletop with a wall behind it. Draw a circle. That'll be your sphere. Now, use value to create mood, hierarchy, and three-dimensional form.

Remember the steps of light on a sphere we discussed in the first lecture on value. Use those nine steps: highlight, light, half-tone, penumbra, umbra, reflected light, reflected shadow, cast shadow, and light from the object reflected into the shadow. Do the same thing with a block and a cone. A cylinder would be good too. Then try a still life of several of these put together, all from your imagination. Try lining them up along a horizontal. Imagine light from the side so that each object casts a shadow on the next.

In terms of compositional value, you'll generally want the least contrast among the large ground shapes and the greatest contrasts in your objects and their relationship to the ground. Procedurally, it's a good idea to attend to the value of the ground shapes first, the objects and cast shadows second.

Just like in life, you can't put a table on the floor unless you have a floor; you can't put a bowl on the table unless you have the table; you can't put fruit in the bowl unless you have a bowl. While there're no rules, it's generally much easier to assign values to the tabletop and walls first, then the objects and their shadows: work large to small, general to specific. Also, consider doing some of these, or any of these other projects I'll describe here, as reductive drawings. I described this approach in an earlier lecture on value. It's often a good way to quickly get value asserted in the whole drawing.

After doing these kinds of exercises, I ask my students at the University of Washington to draw a still life in a complex interior from their imagination. I ask them to invent a room, at least two walls meeting in a corner. But the room could also be more elaborate with a back wall, two side walls, a floor, and a ceiling. I ask them to imagine a window, which is the light source. In the room, there's also a table. On the table is a still life consisting of geometric solids. I also ask them to include a pattern on the floor based on a grid. I ask them to use value so that everything feels three-dimensional, but I also ask them to use value compositionally so that the objects on the table read as the focal point.

Note here how the still life is dominant in scale, elaborate in shape, contains zigzagging diagonals, hinges on the center of the format, and has relatively high contrast. This enables it to dominate the very intricate floor pattern. Also, note how the walls and cityscape are handled—all close value.

Here we get a very clear mood, an old library in moonlight, wonderful stage setting, all those books, and other items on the shelves. Each book has a size, shape, specific binding, and spatial orientation. Some are vertical, some horizontal, some sloping diagonally. There's a whole world there and yet it's all shrouded in mid-grays. That allows the still life table and window events to remain the area of focus.

And here's a final example. So many rhyming rectilinear structures: books, tables, and blocks, and gridded pattern, all in contrasting scales. The value of the gridded floor pattern's beautifully controlled. If the contrasts had been too high, it would have been way to attention-getting, but it sits there and plays its role because it exists in close value. Another thing I really like about this drawing is how each book has a real shape and size. Some are vertical, others lean at various angles.

For this project, use a good quality paper. Consider its surface, value, and chroma. Making good choices here can really benefit the drawing.

A next project is to invent a still life from your imagination using your knowledge of basic solids and light and shade to construct the drawing. The space, here two walls and a tabletop, are easily constructed using linear perspective. The five objects are simple combinations or permutations of cones, spheroids, and cylinders. That's not to exclude observation in any of the projects I've just described. If you're drawing the geometric solids and run into a problem, set something up that's similar, analyze what you're seeing, then go back to your drawing and apply what you've observed.

With the two other projects, you might want to research a type of room, furniture, window, or a floor pattern. Use online resources, compile your own photographs of things, and collect the kinds of objects you'll need. When using photographs you want to make sure you're doing just that, using the photograph, not copying it.

I'll give you an example. I want a particular type of window for my drawing. I find a picture of what I want online, but the picture has the window in a wall parallel to the picture plane—I want the window in a side wall. So I take the data about the window type, molding, thickness, et cetera, and adapt it to my drawing.

Some of my students draw still lives of invented objects. Once you understand form and light, you can draw as if you were playing with clay. In this regard, I'd note that William Bailey doesn't generally set up a still life and make a drawing. Instead, he uses his knowledge of line, shape, volume, and the illusion of space to construct these drawings from his imagination. Similarly, to make this pastel drawing, Norman Lundin didn't set up this table in this room. Instead, he calls on a breadth of knowledge to construct the drawing.

That's not to say artists who work this way won't look at a specific cup or a pitcher for reference, or the play of light on a wall. But many drawings people assume are made by direct observation are instead synthesized in the mind of the artist and are worked out on the surface of the page.

To conclude, we can wed what we studied earlier about geometric solids and perspective to our knowledge concerning light and shadow to create believable space and volume drawn from our imagination. There's a whole world to explore here.

# Texture: Mark Making and Optical Value
## Lecture 26

In common speech, *texture* refers to the look and feel of a surface or material. In drawing, the word *texture* is used in three distinct but related ways. First, there's the actual three-dimensional texture of the drawing itself. This encompasses both look and feel and includes the physical texture of the drawing surface and materials. Next, there's visual texture, which relates to look only. A crazy scribble and a set of carefully ruled parallel lines are the same to the touch, although visually, they have a different feel. This kind of visual texture is connected to artistic approach. The third type of texture is related to the texture of the subject: Think hair versus skin or wood versus marble. Some artists take great pains to simulate these kinds of textures in their drawings and paintings, while others are more interested in the weave of the drawing itself. In this lecture, we'll begin to explore texture and mark making.

**Actual Texture**

Today, actual texture plays a much greater role in painting than in drawing, but it has a significant place in drawing's history. Before papyrus and paper, people scratched their drawings into rock. Such drawings are called *petroglyphs* ("rock carvings"). One example is the Anasazi Newspaper Rock in Utah.

© alex grichenko/iStock/Thinkstock.

Drawing with incised lines has also been commonplace in ceramics. And many types of printmaking, such as woodcuts and engravings, depend on incised mark and line; these can be felt on the blocks used to make the prints, though not on the prints themselves.

A number of 20th-century artists also used incised line as a drawing tool, but the most common way we experience actual texture in drawing is in the paper. As noted in an earlier lecture, paper can be very smooth, very rough, and any texture in between, and the choice of surface in a drawing is significant. For example, pencil on smooth paper allows for fine detail. In contrast, to achieve the kind of optical mixing of value he wanted in his drawings, Georges Seurat chose a paper with tooth. If you'd like to see how this works, drag charcoal lightly over a rough paper; you'll note that the dark material catches on the high ground, while the recessed part of the paper's texture remains white. Nevertheless, at a distance, our eyes mix the black and white, and we see gray. The lighter the pressure you use, the lighter the gray that will result, but if you push the charcoal into the paper's crevices, you'll get robust darks.

**Visual Texture: Hatching**
The second type of texture we encounter is purely visual. So far, in the drawing projects we've undertaken we've generally applied value in a smooth and continuous way, but we can also use a wide variety of lines and marks to create optical value with a range of textures.

For example, one type of mark used to generate tonal value is *hatching*. This is made of nothing more than lines. If the lines are drawn close together, the result is a dark gray. If they're spaced out, the result is a lighter gray. Discontinuous line, the number of hatch directions, staggered hatching, line thickness, and even the speed of execution (deliberate versus gestural) also affect the kind of value created with hatching.

Another important factor in hatching is the hatch's direction. One common approach is to have the hatch follow the form of the subject like a cross-contour. Value changes that capture the play of light on planes already create the illusion of three dimensions. Applying the value following the axis or axes of the form compounds this illusion. Hatching may also imitate the direction of the light source.

Use a nib pen, brush and ink, and graphite to try some hatching. Make some swatches at first, varying the spacing, the number of directions, and the line continuity. Then draw some geometric solids using hatching.

Here's a review of ways in which hatching can be controlled:

- Through spacing: Closer spacing equals darker values.

- Through continuity or discontinuity of line: More continuous lines equal darker values.

- By varying the lengths of the lines moving into the light: Staggering line lengths can create the sensation of a graduated value.

- By varying the thickness of the line: Thicker lines result in darker values.

- By changing the tonal value of the material: With ink, for lighter values, dry the brush or add water to the ink; with pencil or charcoal, use a range from hard to soft and vary the pressure as you draw.

- By increasing the number of hatch directions: More directions result in an increase in darkness and density of the hatch.

When working with hatching or other mark-making systems, remember to think compositionally. Organize the value with the drawing's focal hierarchy in mind.

### Other Forms of Mark Making

Hatching and cross-hatching are important modes of mark making, but the catalog of human mark making is vast. Among the first tools our ancient ancestors used were their own hands, as can be seen in the Cueva de las Manos in Argentina.

© Sohadiszno/iStock/Thinkstock.

Of course, using the hand as a mark-making device is still with us today. The contemporary American artist Chuck Close, for example, used his thumbprint as a mark-making device to create a series of portraits. The central idea here is that we can use any type of mark to create optical value if we apply the principles we used in hatching: Wide-spaced, discontinuous, light marks will read as light value; dense, overlapping, and dark marks will yield a darker value.

As an experiment in mark making, lightly outline a dozen or more one-inch squares on a piece of paper. Fill each with a different kind of mark or optical value. Vary the density, continuity, and pressure to create different tones. If you get stuck, think adjectively. Try to make textures that are delicate, sharp, scratchy, blunt, bushy, coarse, choppy, fuzzy, jagged, and fluffy. You might even keep a sketchbook of different kinds of marks—single hatches, cross-hatches, curving marks, wavy marks, stippled marks, scribbles, and so on. In each case, the marks might be thin or thick, light or dark, short or long, slow or fast, and rigid or flowing. You can also craft your own mark-making tools with sticks, tongue depressors, and other common items. As a follow-up project, apply these textures to form.

## Suggested Reading

Guptill, *Rendering in Pencil*, chapter 4, "Interpreting Nature's Tones and Textures," pp. 31–40.

————, *Rendering in Pen and Ink*, chapter 4, "Practice in Tone Building," pp. 25–28, and chapter 5, "Elementary Steps in Value Study," pp. 29–31.

# Texture: Mark Making and Optical Value
## Lecture 26—Transcript

Our next topic's texture and mark making. The word texture comes from the Latin *textura*, meaning weaving. And many textures like this, or this, have a woven quality. The first is a close-up of the Dürer woodcut we've seen before, the second from an 1888 Van Gogh portrait of the postman Joseph Roulin. In common parlance, texture refers to the look and feel of a surface of material. In drawing, we use the word texture in three distinct but related ways.

First, there's the actual 3D texture of the drawing itself—that's both look and feel. The surface we draw on can be rough or smooth—that's physical texture. And some drawing materials, like oil pastels, leave texture on the page that you could detect blindfolded.

Next, there's visual texture. This is look only. A crazy scribble and a set of carefully ruled parallel lines are the same to the touch, though visually they have a different feel. This kind of visual texture is connected to artistic approach and, at times, what we might call the artist's handwriting. Much of what we've studied so far has had to do with the nouns and verbs of drawing. It's a sphere, or a block, or a figure in a room. But physical and visual texture are adjectival—they qualify the nominal content. Texture can make it a fuzzy sphere, or a gleaming block on a table or an anxious person in a room, and all this has a lot to do with the feel of a drawing.

The third type of texture is related to the texture of the subject. Think hair versus skin or wood versus marble, and some artists take great pains to simulate these kinds of textures in drawings and paintings while others are more interested in the weave of the drawing itself. Let's look more closely at each of these types of texture.

Today, actual texture plays a much greater role in painting than in drawing but it has a significant place in drawing's history nonetheless. That very first drawing we looked at from the Blombos Cave is a case in point. This is real 3D texture—you could close your eyes and feel the drawing with your fingertips. But it's also visual. The etched grooves consist of distinct planes;

those facing the light appear light, the others dark. The light lines make the dark ones feel darker and vice versa: simultaneous contrast. So our eyes are drawn to these high contrast events.

Before papyrus and paper, people scratched their drawings into rock. They're called petroglyphs, literally rock carvings like the Anasazi Newspaper Rock in Utah. Drawing with incised lines has also been commonplace in ceramics, and with functional ceramics, the drawn elements are experienced through both sight and touch. Many types of printmaking, like woodcuts and engravings, depend on incised mark and line, though, as in the Dürer, we don't see 3D texture in the print, and we would in the block used to make it.

A number of 20th-century artists used incised line as a drawing tool. Jean Dubuffet, for instance, drew with incised line in cement. But the most common way we experience actual texture in drawing is in the paper. As noted in an earlier lecture, paper can be very smooth, very rough, and anyplace in between.

This pencil drawing by Lopez Garcia is on a relatively smooth paper. Pencil on smooth paper allows for fine detail. Note the pristine handling of the edges and the very gentle gradations of value in the walls and ceilings. This wouldn't be possible on the paper Seurat uses here; it has too much tooth. You've probably seen some of Seurat's paintings like this one, *The Lighthouse at Honfleur*. The method he developed, along with Paul Signac, is referred to as pointillism. You place small dabs of color one next to the other—say, a red next to a blue. At a distance, they'll appear to combine to make a violet: optical mixing.

Color printers work the same way using four inks—blue, yellow, red and black—along with the white of the paper. The wide range of colors we see, often in very smooth transition, is an illusion. The reality is thousands of tiny little dots arranged in varying proportions. Now, Seurat wanted this same kind of optical mixing in his drawings. By choosing a paper with tooth, he could do this without having to make thousands of little dots. In effect, the paper did it for him.

Drag the charcoal lightly over the surface and the dark material catches on the high ground. The recessed part of the paper's texture remains white. Our eyes mix the black and white and we see gray. The lighter the pressure, the lighter the gray; more pressure, darker gray. Push that charcoal into the paper's crevices and you get robust darks. As we begin to consider texture, surface choice will play a compelling role.

The second type of texture is purely visual texture. So far, we've applied value in a smooth and continuous way, and many artists, like Antonio Lopez Garcia or Norman Lundin, often use value just this way. These drawings are both physically and visually smooth. But we can use a wide variety of lines and marks to create optical value with a range of textures.

The type of mark used to generate tonal value in the Dürer is called hatching. It's made of nothing more than line. Put the lines closer together for a dark gray, space them out for a lighter gray. Like Seurat's black and white dots, it's a type of optical value. If we look at a section of the back wall and compare it to the side plane of the gridded picture plane, we see that the marks themselves are similarly black, but by changing the spacing, Dürer makes the wall appear a dark gray and the side plane of the gridded picture plane a light gray. Same thing in the woman's hair: away from the light, tighter spacing, darker value; in the light, wider spacing, lighter value. Looking higher up in the back wall, we note another technique: the use of discontinuous line to produce lighter value.

Another factor affecting value is the number of hatch directions. On the thigh, we have a single hatch, tighter spaced away from the light, wider spaced toward the light. In contrast, look at the calf. Here we have two directions in the hatch, crosshatches, and this produces a darker optical gray. And he uses another trick. On the thigh, not all the hatches are of equal length—some end before others. Staggered hatching, the part closest to the light has less density of line, so it looks lighter.

Another important factor in hatching is the hatch's direction. One common approach is to have the hatch follow the form like a cross contour. On the table leg, we get horizontals and verticals, the two axes of the table leg itself; on the artist's arm, two curvilinear directions following the axes of the drape.

Value changes that capture the play of light on planes already create the illusion of three dimensions on a two-dimensional surface. Applying the value following the axis or axes of the form compounds the illusion. Now, this isn't a rule, and in fact, Dürer doesn't do this everywhere. For instance, some of the cross hatches in the walls, windows, and in the table's edge, are diagonals.

Let's take a look at the woman's head. Her forehead's lit; her eye sockets in shadow. The front plane of her head's lit, the underside of her jaw and neck are in shadow. The top planes of her breasts are lit, the undersides in shadow. All of this tells us that the light's coming from above left. Looking at the crosshatching diagonals in the wall above her head, we see that they imitate the direction of the light, and this is another common practice in hatching and crosshatching.

Jacob de Gheyn II, a 17th-century Dutch artist, was a great practitioner of hatching and he employs many of the same principles as Dürer. We see discontinuous and continuous hatches, single hatches, crosshatches, hatches following the axis or axes of the form, and hatches following the direction of the light. But there are a couple new things here, too.

Most obviously, the range of value and color of the ink—we have both a light cool gray and a darker brown. In the figure on the left, there are different concentrations of inks. Parts of the drapery behind the right leg are like a whisper while there's a much fuller concentration under the left arm. Now, my guess is that he started out very faint. As he became surer of the proportions, he darkened the ink, especially in the shadow areas. Similarly, there are both dark and light tones of the brown ink. Note the central figure in relation to the one behind her.

A second factor he introduces is line thickness. Let's look at the drape on the thigh of the woman on the right. The hatches on the shadow side are thicker and taper as they move into the light.

A third factor is the way speed of execution affects the quality of the hatch. If we look at the hatches in the central woman's abdomen and pelvis, they're similar to Dürer's—very deliberate. But the legs of the woman on the right, or the arm of the small figure in the rear, are more gestural. This is a more scribbled approach to hatching. As we saw earlier with line, speed can be a very expressive attribute.

Here's that Van Gogh portrait. Though the feel is different than the Dürer or the de Gheyn, a lot of the underlying grammar is identical. We have single hatches and crosshatches. We have different kinds of spacing, a variety of line thicknesses, a variety of solutions of ink, and we often have the hatch following the axis or axes of the plane concerned. Look at the wall: horizontals and vertical, the two axes of a wall. Or the top of the cap. Here, a single hatch pulls around the surface, following the cross contour.

Hatching's extremely versatile. This drawing's by one of my recent graduate students. Many of the hatches are angled or curved following the planar form of the petals. Others are scribbled and subsume an area in shadow.

This much more aggressive use of hatching is by another recent grad student. You can see how certain areas are treated with relatively light pressure, like the wall behind the students drawing, while other areas, like the students themselves, are really leaned into. This adds up to compositional value. What's the subject? Students drawing in a classroom. What gets the highest contrast? The students in relation to their drawings. What do you look at first? The students drawing. Good value organization. The drawing makes use of single hatches, crosshatches, and in some places, several other layers of mark, but often they're not associated with the axis or axes of the subject.

This use of hatching became common in the late 19th and early 20th century. Many artists wanted to depict space in a flatter way than artists like Dürer and de Gheyn. In some of Giorgio Morandi's etchings, for instance, you'll see multiple directions of hatching, including directions that have nothing to do with the axes of the objects. This can create a great deal of density, like a scrim across the picture plane uniting the surface and also creating a degree of spatial ambiguity. The value changes in the objects suggest 3D volume, while the hatching directions have a flattening effect.

We find something similar in this portrait by Ann Gale. The central scribbled hatching floats like a scrim in front of the sitter's head, while other hatches attach to the 3D form of the head, neck, and shirt, and others yet attach to the space behind the figure. You'll also note she's drawing, hatching, with her eraser.

So let's try some hatching. I'll use a nib pen. Let's start with a single hatch, just verticals. Make a small swatch. Now another, but tighten the spacing a bit. And another with tighter spacing yet.

Let's add horizontals in these swatches to create crosshatches. We'll echo the vertical spacing in the horizontals; the tighter the spacing, the darker, the greater the effect of optical value. In other words, the tighter the spacing the more convincing the sensation of tonal value.

To get a lighter sense of tonal value with a tightly spaced line let's try a discontinuous hatch. Then a discontinuous crosshatch. Now, let's make a swatch that's lighter at the top and darker at the base—a staggered hatching. We'll use a pattern of gradually shorter lengths. Then compound this with horizontals tighter spaced at the base and opening up and becoming discontinuous as we move into the light.

And now thick to thin and we can compound this with across, tighter to wider spaced. Now let's add some speed, verticals, and horizontals zigzagging. And let's try that with a brush. We could also try thick to thin and then across. To get a lighter hatch we could add water to the ink, but for now let's make a lighter value by drying the brush to deplete the ink. Then turn the hatch into a crosshatch.

Let's apply all this to draw a one-point block. We'll start with a dry brush and discontinuous line. You'll remember, when using value, we generally don't want visible outlines, much less strong ones. Outlines tend to kill the illusion of three dimensions.

Next, the block's cast shadow. We'll imagine light coming the left side. The front face will be the lightest, top plane next, side plane darkest. Cast shadow a bit lighter than the side. I'll do the hatching with the nib pen.

Let's start with the dark plane with a tightly spaced vertical hatch, then cross it with diagonals receding toward the vanishing point, the two axes of the plane. Make the cast shadow a bit lighter, a bit wider spaced—horizontal one way, back toward the vanishing point crossing it.

On the top plane, we'll use a wider-spaced horizontal and diagonals receding toward the vanishing point. As these move into the light, they'll get discontinuous. Let's apply a vertical staggered hatching in the front face and cross this with a horizontal that becomes discontinuous.

Now, let's try hatching with graphite. We'll draw a cone sitting on a table in front of a wall. Start with a light pencil. Make a rectangle, a format shape. Add a horizontal division—a table and wall.

Here, let's try a faster, more scribbled hatching. Ground plane, still with light pencil, horizontals, and then diagonals receding toward the vanishing point. Draw across the format shape so value extends across the rectangle.

Let's go a bit darker for the wall. You could use a bit more pressure or tighter spacing or a somewhat softer pencil. Scribbled horizontals and verticals for the wall, then erase to restore the format shape.

We'll imagine light coming from the right and draw with the eraser to create the light plane of the cone. Now, with a softer pencil, we'll begin to hatch in the shadow side of the cone. Two directions: up toward the apex, and around the horizontal axis in curves. Project the cast shadow and add hatching here, too. Where you want more dark, add more hatching; where you want things lighter, draw in with the eraser.

Let's review the ways we can control hatching. First, through spacing. Closer spacing equals darker; wider, lighter. Next, through the level of continuity or discontinuity of the lines. More continuous, darker; more discontinuous, lighter. Then by varying the lengths of the lines moving into the light. Longer, darker; shorter, lighter. And by varying the thickness of the line itself. Thicker, darker; thinner, lighter. We can also change the tonal value of the material. To get lighter values, we can dry the brush or add water to the ink. With other materials like pencil or charcoal pencil, we can use a range from hard to soft. With all the materials, we can change the pressure as we draw. Lastly, we can increase the darkness and density of the hatch by increasing the number of directions.

Another factor to remember is speed. We can hatch slow and controlled or rapidly, gesturally, or even in a scribbled manner. To enhance the sensation of three-dimensional form, we can follow the axis or axes of the form in the hatch. Another strategy is to let the hatching follow the direction of the light. Many of these strategies were employed in this student's drawing.

We also want the hatching to work compositionally. That means the values need to be organized to reflect the drawing's hierarchy. Here, the organization of value contrast makes the figure function as the general focus. The head is the focal point; all the complexity in the mirror and ground are treated in lower contrasting values. If you wanted to compress or flatten the form, multiple directions disassociated from the axis or axes of the objects can be useful.

One other note here: Many hatched drawings, woodcuts, and etchings are modest in size. The Dürer, for example, is about 3 × 9 inches, the de Gheyn about 10 × 13, the Van Gogh 12½ by 9½, the Morandi 4¾ by 6. In contrast, the smooth drawing by Lopez Garcia is 32¼ by 26¾.

When looking at examples it's a good idea to pay attention to the dimensions. If you're trying to incorporate something you've seen into your own drawing, working at a corresponding scale can be helpful in understanding the new method or technique. Of course, that shouldn't preclude experimentation at different scales once a method or technique's been understood.

To get more practice with hatching try drawing other geometric forms. Then invent still lives from your imagination and use hatching to create the light and value structure. Then try it from observation. Use the subjects we've tried to date: still life, an interior, landscape, a self-portrait, and another figure if you have someone to pose for you.

Hatching and crosshatching are important modes of mark making, but the catalog of human mark making is vast. Among the first tools our ancestors used were their own hands. There are many examples, from The Cueva de las Manos in Argentina to the Gua Ham cave in Indonesia, to these from the Elands Bay Cave in South Africa. And using the hand as a mark-making device is with us today. Chuck Close used his thumbprint in a series of portraits, including this one of the composer, Philip Glass. Much larger than the hatched drawings, this is five feet tall and over three feet wide. To get a sense of the scale even in reproduction, well, we know how large a thumb is.

The central idea is that we can use any type of mark to create optical value if we apply the same principles we used in hatching. Wide-spaced, discontinuous light marks will read as light value; dense and overlapping dark marks will yield a darker one. If you apply sophisticated visual thinking, finger painting will produce sophisticated results.

Try this now. Lightly outline a dozen or more one-inch squares; fill each with a different kind of mark or optical value; vary the density, continuity, and pressure to create different tones. If you get stuck, think adjectively: make something smooth then rough, hard then soft, loud then quiet. Give yourself a list of adjectives. Make textures that are delicate, sharp, scratchy, blunt, bushy, coarse, choppy, fuzzy, jagged, and fluffy. Then apply them to form, just like we did earlier with hatching—first with blocks and cones, and then other objects and subjects. Here's a spoiler alert: I'm going to show some examples of swatches of marks, so see what you can invent before looking at these.

Arthur Guptill was an artist and illustrator who wrote a number of books on drawing in the early- to mid-20th century. In some of his books, he made extensive tables of marks. Here are just a couple. You'll find a full range of what he did in his books *Rendering in Pencil* and also in *Rendering in Pen and Ink*. He played with a variety of hatches and crosshatches and made other tones of closely spaced lines, dashes, and dots, as well as other, less regular groupings of marks, and he worked through many of these in a host of gradations from light to dark. It's a great idea to keep a sketchbook of different kinds of marks. Start your own catalog; see how many you can invent.

When using pencils, try a wide range from hard to soft, and remember to vary the sharpening, this'll allow for a greater variety of mark. You could have single hatches, crosshatches, curving marks, wavy marks, stippled, scribbled, and irregular marks. In each case, the marks could be thin or thick, light or dark, short or long, slow or fast, and more rigid or flowing. As we've seen, marks needn't be dark on a light ground. You can use your erasers to draw light marks on a marked or shaded ground. And try drawing with several pencils at once.

If you're stippling, a handful of pencils can create a ground of small dots pretty rapidly. I'm using all 22, but if you want it light just use the Hs; for dark, the Bs. You can do similar things with ink using a bunch of sharpened chopsticks. And you can make your own mark making tools. This is a tongue depressor cut to a zigzag. It can hatch, stipple, and make a range of other marks.

As you invent new textures, marks, and optical values, apply them in your drawings. It can be an interesting project to do the same drawing multiple times but using different systems of mark and texture each time.

In an earlier lecture, I recounted the story of Degas meeting his friend, the poet Mallarme. Degas, who was trying his hand at poetry at the time remarked, "Your métier, your field, is hellishly difficult. I'm never able to really get at what I'm going for and yet I'm so full of ideas." Mallarme is reported to have responded, "My dear Degas, one doesn't make poetry out of ideas. You make poems out of words." And this applies here. At one level, drawings are nothing more than a collection of dots, dashes, stipples, smudges, ticks, blots, splatters, and scribbles.

I'd like to return to some of the drawings we've looked at before, as well as a couple new ones, and pay special attention to how these artists use texture and mark. Grab a sketchbook or some paper and some pencils, pen and ink, and a couple brushes of varying size. That way you'll be able to try some of the things you see. Not a matter of drawing the objects, just the squiggles, blots, and ticks.

Rembrandt's regarded as one of the most inventive artists in this regard, the categoric opposite of fussy and rendered. This drawing's about six and one-half inches tall by about four and three-quarters wide. My guess is he started with line—wild, rapid, darting lines made with a small pointed brush. These marks set up the figure and window, serpentines in the skirt contrasting with the more staccato marks in the sleeves and hands.

Now, look at the scale of the large blot of ink moving from the right wall over Saskia's shoulder and spilling over her head and torso. He has a good linear structure and doesn't think anything of making a crazy blot right through the center, but it works great. Light's coming in through the window; her hand and arm get the light and throw shadow back across her head and torso, which in turn casts a shadow back onto the wall. I'd also guess that the mid-gray blot of wash was first, followed by the darker iteration that cascades down her arm and hip revealing light glancing the shoulder and arm. Probably a couple minutes work.

Here's another, it's about $7 \times 10$ inches. We have both a linear structure and areas of wash through both the architecture and the figures followed by some instances of rapid scribbled diagonal hatching. The lines, marks, and blots are wild, but we do get a very clear sense of space, of where things are: What's in front and what's behind. And while things are somewhat generalized, take a look at the standing turbaned figure on the far right. No rendering of drapery, no real anatomy—his hand looks like a mitten—but the looping calligraphy in the hood draping down the back roughly follows the cross contour over the shoulder, yielding volume, and overall the stance and costume feel specific.

While the mark making in the last drawing was overwhelmingly linear, here Rembrandt deploys the brush to create value shapes. This drawing's about five and three-eighths by seven and one-quarter inches. There's little rendering to speak of. Instead, brush shapes are posed one against another to suggest water, trees, and sky. The tree just left of center is a wonderful invention of rapid, looping, gestural brush strokes. There's an equally masterful command of a range of values from light whispers to much more aggressive darks. You'll learn an enormous amount about using brush and ink by taking this apart and making each shape and value you see in this drawing.

Speaking of brush and ink, let's take another look at Zhào Mèngfǔ's hand scroll, it's about 11 × 42 inches. Like the Rembrandt, it's a treasure trove of mark making. In the first lecture, I noted that Chinese has its roots in a picture-based writing system. In the colophon of another one of his paintings titled *Elegant Rocks and Sparse Trees*, Zhào Mèngfǔ relates writing to painting. He advises using flying white cursive script for rocks.

Now, flying white refers to a somewhat dry brush quickly drawn across the surface so that the white of the page mixes with the mark: optical value. Flying white cursive's deployed here by Mǐ Fú, an 11th-century Song dynasty poet and calligrapher. Do you see how flying white's applied to both? But that's not the only visual connection between the calligraphy and the rock. Both demonstrate dramatic moves from thick to thin, from flowing to staccato, and contrasts of angular to curvilinear.

This dramatic character is zhàn, meaning to fight, war, or battle. This is what the generic character looks like—pretty amazing improvisation. The noted art historian and former Princeton Professor, Wen Fong, described Mǐ Fú's character this way, "He painted the character by giving free reign to his brushwork, allowing the stroke to twist and turn sculpturally in space." It's not hard to see how the character and rock both share calligraphic and sculptural form.

For the trees, Zhào Mèngfǔ advises using seal script. Here's an example of seal script by Zhào Mèngfǔ himself, totally different from the cursive. Both the seal script and the trees are much more uniform in value and thickness, much less contrast in the marks. And in both, short arms protrude from longer spines. He goes on to counsel clerical script for bamboo. Here's an example of clerical script, it's a rubbing from a stele from the Eastern Han dynasty. That's 25–220 C.E. In contrast to the uniform stroke quality of seal script, here you'll note the many dart-like tapering strokes.

There's no bamboo in *Twin Pines, Level Distance*, but Dèng Yǔ, a contemporary who followed Zhào Mengfu's teaching on the subject, shows how you can apply these pointy, dagger-like marks to suggest similarly shaped bamboo leaves.

Zhào Mèngfŭ ends the colophon, declaring, "People who comprehend this must know calligraphy and painting are originally the same." And that makes sense when you have a pictographic language and a long tradition of valuing the pictorial quality of writing. Thinking this way allows Zhào Mèngfŭ to relate mark to texture on a conscious level.

In the next lecture, we're going to conclude our discussion on the ways artists use texture, mark, and optical value. We'll also discuss projects that will get you using these ideas and techniques.

# Texture: How Artists Use Texture
## Lecture 27

In this lecture, we'll learn more about how artists use texture, mark, and optical value. We'll begin by studying drawings by five artists. As we'll see, each drawing has a pronounced textural personality and mood that are related to formal and material choices. We'll then go into detail about the primary factors that affect texture in a drawing, including paper or drawing surface, modifications made to the surface, choice of drawing tool, and more. We'll close with a look at creating simulated or trompe l'oeil textures.

**Texture and Materials**

Seven primary factors affect texture:

- Paper or drawing surface

- Modifications made to the paper or surface

- Choice of drawing tool

- Preparation or modification of the tool

- Application method (e.g., drawing directly on the surface versus transferring material via a brush)

- Physical technique (e.g., hand motion, pressure applied)

- Modification of the mark (e.g., compounding, blending, smearing, smudging, and erasing).

In combining these seven factors, the number of textural possibilities is nearly infinite.

## Paper or Drawing Surface

As we've noted, papers span a wide variety of surface patterns, both regular and irregular, with textures from very smooth to very rough. Using a smooth paper for a still life of shiny, reflective objects could be a reasonable choice because the paper itself is shiny and reflective. With a smooth paper, the light bounces off an even surface, as opposed to a textured paper, in which many different planes reflect light in different directions, reducing shininess. In contrast, using a rough paper could be a reasonable choice for a landscape featuring a craggy cliff on a stormy night. The point here is that a given paper can have qualities that relate to the subject of the drawing.

Surface texture also affects the ease with which you can draw different kinds of edges. With less tooth to the paper, it's much easier to draw clear, crisp edges and develop small details. This might be desirable for a detailed study of a branch and some leaves. But to draw the same branch on a tree in a forested area in the distance, a more textured surface could help to create the sense of a mass of foliage.

As we've already noted, it's also the tooth that pulls the material off the drawing implement and holds it on the surface, which can affect how dark the material looks. With the same material and the same pressure applied, a toothier paper can create a darker value than a smoother one.

## Modifications to the Paper or Surface

A portion of a paper's surface can be modified to make it smoother or rougher. For example, to make paper smoother, burnish it with the back of a spoon, the side of a butter knife, or even a dense eraser. To make it rougher, use a piece of 220-grit sandpaper.

## Choice of Drawing Tool

Like paper, drawing materials have their own textural characteristics. For example, graphite is shiny and reflective, while the family of carbon and charcoals is comparatively matte. Again, with a still life of shiny objects, it would be reasonable to use graphite on a smooth paper. Both the graphite and the paper are relatively reflective. With a stormy landscape, charcoal on a rougher paper could be a reasonable choice. That's not to say that it would be wrong to draw each of these subjects with different materials. It's just that they'll feel different—more reflective or more matte, smoother or more jagged, crisper or more atmospheric—depending on the tools used. Such characteristics are at the heart of how a drawing feels.

## Preparation or Modification of Drawing Tools

An additional factor in creating texture is preparation or modification of your drawing tools. For example, earlier, we learned a number of ways to shape a pencil's tip: pointed, flattened, or turned into a wedge. Each of these shapes creates different textures.

In using wet media, you can dilute the ink or partially dry the brush before applying it to the surface. And you can use different brush shapes and types of bristle.

## Application Method

As we've seen, the method of application also affects texture. Materials can be applied directly or indirectly to a surface. For example, graphite or charcoal can be rubbed with a tortillon, a blending stub, a brush, or a chamois, then transferred to the surface. Powdered graphite or charcoal could be applied similarly. Artists also use many other tools as applicators, including felt, facial tissue, paper towels, cotton swabs, and make-up sponges.

With wet media, the range of application tools is extremely varied, including brushes of all sizes and shapes, countless types of nibs, and sponges. Blotter paper or other absorbent materials can be used to modify wet media on the drawing surface.

## Physical Technique

The way in which marks are physically made is influenced by a number of factors, including the position of the surface in relation to the body (on an easel versus on a desk), the joint of motion (shoulder, elbow, wrist, or fingers), the position of the hand, and the amount of pressure exerted.

## Modification of the Mark

Once you have some mark on the surface, you can modify it in many ways. Indeed, the number of textural possibilities skyrockets as you begin to layer, combine, blend, smudge, smear, and erase. Exploring the possibilities of mark modification could fill hundreds of sketchbooks over many years.

When you combine materials, you need to be aware of their native characteristics. Pay attention to how the order of application affects the way materials appear on a given surface. For example, graphite is slick, and many materials won't adhere to it well. It's easier to put graphite on top of charcoal or ink than vice versa—but there's no harm in trying unlikely combinations.

## Simulated or Trompe l'Oeil Texture

Students often ask how to draw the texture of metal, rock, or water, but there is no single drawing "recipe" that will work. Metal, for example, can be shiny stainless steel, rusted iron, or bent aluminum. Rock can be a jagged cliff or polished marble. And water might be in a pitcher at lunch or in the ocean at night. Further, the way each material looks is affected by a host of factors, such as spatial location and light. A distant tree reveals much less of its bark's surface texture than one up close. And we'll see more or less texture depending on the position, distance, and strength of the light source. For all these reasons, providing specific instructions for drawing these elements is of limited use.

That said, there are ways to study specific textures. The key is to determine the distinguishing visual characteristics of a subject at a given distance and in a given light source, then relate that information to specific drawing materials and procedures.

In drawing simulated textures, start simply. Do a study of just one interesting texture, not a full-blown drawing. For example, find a piece of wood with an interesting grain pattern.

First, analyze the material to determine its underlying visual characteristics. With certain textures, a black-and-white photo of the object can help you see the underlying characteristics more clearly. Or try making a rubbing or a photocopy. A photo, rubbing, or photocopy will each have much less visual data than the objects themselves, which can work to your advantage in trying to distill a principle. In looking at this example of wood grain, a black-and-white photo reveals that you could lay down a fairly consistent ground of value, then use a darker, nearly vertical mark to draw the echoing grain shapes.

© srrupi/iStock/Thinkstock.

You might also make a study of a reflective surface, such as an empty paint can from the hardware store. Before you start drawing, think about what material and paper you want to use. On a test sheet, experiment with blending tools and erasers to approximate the quality of the edges you see in the reflections on the can. Above all, study the can carefully to understand exactly what in the room is being reflected on its surface, rather than just copying a random pattern of lights and darks.

You can apply these same methods of analysis to rock, fur, water in a glass, or anything else that piques your interest.

## Suggested Reading

Sale and Betti, *Drawing*, chapter 6, pp. 193–222.

Smagula, *Creative Drawing*, chapter 6, "Texture," pp. 132–149.

# Texture: How Artists Use Texture
## Lecture 27—Transcript

In this lecture, we'll learn more about how artists use texture, mark, and optical value, and we'll discuss some projects that will get you experimenting with all this.

Let's start with five drawings: the first, the Bailey still life; the second, the Monet, *View of Rouen Across the Seine*; third, this Van Gogh landscape; fourth, this Picasso from the *Human Comedy* series; and fifth, a Käthe Kollwitz self-portrait. Each has a pronounced textural personality and mood and this is related to formal and material choices.

It would be good to have a sketchbook or some paper on hand. If you've started a sketchbook for mark and texture, use that. It's actually a good idea to have two sketchbooks for the purpose: one smooth, the other with a rougher paper. This lets you see how a given drawing tool and technique interacts with surface characteristics. Again, don't worry about drawing objects, just the marks.

While all five drawings use value, the Bailey's the only one that features much of what we might call shading, and although we sense volume and directional light, it's the softest and most reserved. Quiet. No drama. This drawing measures 39½ by 42 3/8—almost square, the least dramatic of shapes. The directions in the drawing? Mostly horizontals and verticals with a few gentle diagonals. The paper's softly toned, closing down the value range on the light end. As we saw in an earlier lecture, the drawing exists between about a one and a-half and four on our value scale.

Some of the distinctions we perceive at edges are not always differences of value, some are differences of color; the paper versus a similar value of graphite. And the mark and texture follow suit: soft, even, without incident. All the choices, from the choice of materials, to their handling, to compositional decisions, all work together toward the same end, a feeling of quiet repose and stability. So, make some soft, light, continuous tones with your graphite now.

The Picasso's the polar opposite, a horizontal rectangle, $9\frac{3}{8} \times 12\frac{1}{2}$ inches, with a seeming endless array of popping and stabbing white, dark gray, and black shapes. While there are some horizontals and verticals, diagonals rule, and the marks, most in high-value contrast, cover the page in an active, high-volume pattern. So, with brush and ink, make some of these Picasso marks. You could spend some real time with this drawing cataloging the wealth of brush strokes, from those that create the plant's leaves to those creating the patterns on the wall and floor.

The Monet's someplace in between the first two: not as quiet as the Bailey, not so much horizontality and verticality; not as tight a value palette but not as high-volume as the Picasso, none of the diagonal fireworks, and not a single black-white contrast. The sheet of paper, $13 \times 19\frac{3}{4}$, is white, lightly tinted blue. It has a slight vertical tooth that serves as an architectural support for the many vertical stresses in the drawing.

The drawing was executed with black chalk in a very free, scribbled hand, but because many of the marks sit into tonal grounds of mark of similar value, they don't feel highly contrasted. They give the sense of a gentle breeze in the air. Even the dark boats are partially subsumed in their shadows and reflections and in the dark banks behind them. The more contrasting scribbled lines of the boats' reflections convey the gentle wavelike surface of the water. With some charcoal or black chalk if you have it, try marks like these—scribbles and scribbles on top of other scribbles.

The Van Gogh also occupies a place between the extremes of the Bailey and the Picasso, but it's extreme in its own way in the invention and deployment of mark. The page is about $19 \times 24$. The drawing was done with brown ink in various dilutions over black chalk. Overall, the value and scale of mark relate to linear and atmospheric perspective. In a letter to his brother Theo, he wrote: "The two views of La Crau are the best things I've done in pen and ink." And, indeed, they're both beautiful drawings. The one we're looking at is in The British Museum's collection. The other's in Amsterdam's Van Gogh Museum.

Get yourself a good reproduction or download a high-res file of one or both. Give yourself some time to go through them. Make every different mark you can find and try varying the dilution of ink as you see it. Even in a small section like this, there's plenty to unravel.

The Kollwitz is similar in size to the Van Gogh. It's 18¾ by 25, drawn with charcoal on a brown laid Ingres paper. Squint—you'll see that the head, arm, and hand all condense into one close value shape. This tells us the value range in the figure's tight as all similar value in the mid and dark range. The major value contrast occurs between that big value shape and the paper itself.

While there's some modeling, it occurs among very proximate values. The top of the cheekbone is just slightly lighter than the side plane; the whites of the eyes, all but indistinguishable from the lids, save for the bit of line separating them. What really distinguishes the arm from the head and hand is not value but mark making: visual texture. It creates contrast, telling us that two things are different. The eye and head reveal relatively slow mark— that conveys focus and thought; the mark in the arm, action and movement. The hand slowed again, though like a hand poised to launch a dart: potential energy.

The drawing's structure expresses an idea about drawing, that it requires a focused intellect and a steady hand, but also an ability to spring into action. Also note this single linear stroke describing the page or drawing board— that's a poetic choice. You can see how much she's done with the broad side of the charcoal. In fact, look at the stub she holds between her fingers; same width as the zigzag in her arm. Try some of this mark making now.

We just reviewed five drawings. Expand on this by looking at drawings you love. Get the best resolution reproductions you can. Look at what the drawings are made of—not the people, or flowers, or buildings, but the marks. Then use similar materials and surfaces at a similar scale and draw the marks, lines, and gradations of value. Then apply what you've learned in your own drawings.

Studying materials and surfaces will really help you learn about texture. There are seven primary factors: The paper or drawing surface. Then any modifications made to the paper or drawing surface. The choice of drawing tool. Next, the preparation or modification of the tool. Fifth factor, the application method. For example, we could draw directly with compressed charcoal or we could rub a brush against it and transfer the material to a surface. Next, there's the physical factor, how the mark's physically drawn. That includes the physical position of our bodies and the drawing, hand position, hand motion, and hand pressure. Last, number seven, is modification. This can mean compounding, blending, smearing, smudging, and erasing marks. In combining these seven factors, the number of textural possibilities is just about infinite.

The paper or other drawing surface is our first factor and there are three main sub-factors here: texture, value, and color. As we've noted, papers span a wide variety of surface patterns, both regular and irregular, with textures from very smooth to very rough. As we saw with Seurat, the paper can do a lot of work. Now, Seurat's concern was with the visual texture of the drawing, not with simulating the texture of materials like skin or cloth.

But let's say I want to simulate the textures of objects. This is our third way of thinking about texture, often referred to as trompe l'oeil, French for fool the eye. We'll go into more detail about this later. For now, imagine I'm drawing a still life of shiny, reflective objects. A very smooth paper will help. Not only is the smooth paper, well, smooth, but smooth papers are also shinier—they're more reflective. That's because the light's bouncing off an even surface. The surface of a textured paper is made of many different planes reflecting in different directions. This reduces shininess. On the other hand, if I were drawing a landscape, a stormy night sky over a craggy cliff descending into a turbulent sea, a rougher paper might bring out these physical qualities.

Surface texture will also affect edges: less tooth, much easier to control edges and small details; lots of tooth, harder to get precise details, but easier to get fuzzier edges. Let's say I'm doing a detailed study of a branch and some leaves. Smooth paper will readily allow me to be as precise as I want. But if I were drawing the same branch on a tree in a forested area in the distance, a more textured surface could well help me create the sense of a mass of foliage.

As we've already noted, it's the tooth that pulls the material off the drawing implement and holds it on the surface, and this can affect how dark the material will look. With the same material and the same pressure applied, a toothier paper can create a darker value than a smooth one.

This is willow charcoal on Strathmore 500 Series Bristol Plate, a very smooth paper. This is the same charcoal on a Strathmore 500 Bristol Vellum, a much rougher paper. And here's some graphite on the smooth plate. And on the rougher vellum. The difference in value is apparent.

You can modify a portion of a paper's surface to make it smoother or rougher. To make it smoother, burnish. You can use the back of a spoon, the side of a butter knife, or even a dense eraser. This is something called a bone folder. It's used to fold paper in bookmaking and origami; works for burnishing too. Whatever you use, test it first to make sure it won't leave any marks.

This is the rougher paper, the Strathmore 500 Bristol Vellum. Do a little burnishing and you see the effect. You can also roughen a surface. I'm using a piece of 220-grit sandpaper. Note the difference in the look of the graphite on the roughened area.

Along with paper, the textures we get will have everything to do with the drawing material we use. Each creates unique textures and each material is complex. With a set of pencils spanning 10B–10H you have 22 different drawing tools right there. Like paper, drawing materials have their own textural characteristics. Graphite's shiny, it reflects light. The family of carbon and charcoals is comparatively matte.

So back to that still life of shiny, reflective objects, or a drawing that I want to have an overall shiny or reflective texture. Drawing with graphite on a smooth paper would be reasonable. The materials have that built in. On the other hand, if I were drawing the stormy night sky over a craggy cliff descending into a turbulent sea, charcoal on a rougher paper would be a reasonable choice. Now, that's not to say that it would wrong to draw each of these subjects with the other set of materials, it's just that they'll feel different—more reflective or more matte; smoother or more jagged; crisper or more atmospheric. And these characteristics are at the heart of how a drawing feels, so in choosing materials consider the feel of what you're going for.

A further factor is drawing tool preparation or modification. We learned a number of ways to shape a pencil's tip—pointed, flattened, or turned into a wedge. Each of these creates different textures. On the wet media side, we can dilute the ink or partially dry the brush before applying it to the surface, and we can use different brush shapes and types of bristle.

Then there's the method of application. We can apply material directly or we can also apply many materials indirectly. We've already seen that we can rub the graphite or charcoal with a tortillon, a blending stub, a brush, or a chamois, and then apply it to the surface.

Artists use many other tools as applicators, like felt, facial tissue, paper towel, cotton swabs, and make-up sponges. Many other things you have around the house can be used too; each will create a somewhat different texture. A variation's to apply the material to an intermediary surface, then rub some felt or similar tool on the intermediary surface and transfer it to the drawing.

As you've seen, you can also create a powder from some materials and transfer that to the surface. With wet media, the range of application tools is extremely varied. There are brushes of all sizes, shapes, and textures, from soft small pointed rounds, to short hard bristled ones, to medium-sized wedge shapes, to much larger brushes. And there are countless types of nibs and even a chopstick, or any stick for that matter, can be used to apply wet media.

That same stick brushed against an old toothbrush can be used to create splattering marks. You may want to mask areas when doing this. And no reason not to draw directly with the toothbrush. Many tools can be used to flick wet media across the page. Sponges of all kinds will make many other types of textures possible. And blotter or other absorbent materials can be used to modify wet media on the surface. Not to forget the Eland Cave and Chuck Close's portraits, hands and fingers can be put to great use, too.

You've likely seen the next technique in a 1940s detective film. The bad guy receives a call, he writes down a phone number on a pad, tears off the top sheet, and runs out the door. The detective jimmies the lock, rubs a pencil over the blank sheet, and the incised telephone number emerges, white against black.

So let's say you want a thin white edge in an otherwise dark ground, maybe the highlight on a piece of molding. Put a sheet of tracing paper over the drawing. With a sharpened pencil or stick, incise a line in the tracing paper's surface with enough pressure to create a groove in the underlying sheet. Apply value and the white line emerges. Best to know where you want that line, but if you want to get rid of it, try filling in. Whatever the surrounding dark is, get a well-sharpened version and work it into the groove, then blend with a pointed tortillon or stump. You can create all kinds of white on black patterns this way: hatchings, scribbles, really anything you can draw with line.

The next factor involves the way the mark is made physically. First off is the position of the surface in relation to the body. The page could be flat on a desk or other surface, or the page could be in a vertical position on an easel. The page's position is related to the joint of motion. We can move from the shoulder, from the elbow, from the wrist, from the fingers. At the desk, people tend to draw at a smaller scale using elbow, wrist, and fingers. Standing at an easel, shoulder, elbow, and wrist is more common.

Then there's hand position. With the paper on a horizontal surface, we can hold the hand the way we write or palm the implement for a different range of movement. With the drawing surface in a vertical position, we can hold it something like a scalpel or underhand. There are many possibilities. Each will give us a different range of motion and suggest different kinds of mark and texture. Note how particularly Käthe Kollwitz holds her charcoal. Of course, one could hold the implement in one's mouth or between one's toes, and people have done both. More commonly, people draw with their non-dominant hand, this often in an effort to arrive at freer-looking, more random marks and textures, all worth trying.

Our last two physical factors are hand motion and hand pressure. I can create an area of mark vertically, horizontally, or diagonally. I can use a circular motion or a figure eight. I can move my hand in small increments or large increments. I can apply a continuous pressure for an even tone or a discontinuous pressure for an uneven one.

Once we have some marks on the surface, we can modify it in many ways, and the number of textural possibilities really skyrockets as we begin to layer, combine, blend, smudge, smear, and erase. Exploring this could fill hundreds of sketchbooks over many years.

The simplest way to modify a mark is with some kind of compound texture using the same tool. For instance, I can create a tonal swatch with charcoal, then, using the same charcoal, mark into it in a contrasting way. Or I could create a tonal swatch with charcoal, then mark into it with a carbon pencil, or graphite, or ink, or any of these, and any others, in any combinations. And I could mark on top of these with an eraser. First a pencil type, then the kneaded. It's endless.

When we combine materials, we want to be aware of their native characteristics. Pay attention to how the order of application affects the way they appear on a given surface. Graphite's slick—many materials won't adhere to it well. Easier to put graphite on top of charcoal or ink than vice versa, but no harm in trying unlikely combinations. Make swatches; label them so you know what you've done.

Then there's a whole world to be discovered in blending, smearing, and smudging. We've talked about nine tools we can use for the purpose: the tortillon, the blending stub, brushes, a chamois, a piece of felt, facial tissue, paper towel, cotton swabs, and make-up sponges. So, start with nine swatches of a given material. Here, I've used vine charcoal. First blend, then smear, then apply. Now, do the same with each of the remaining tools. You could also experiment by repeating this same test on a contrasting paper and you could try using multiple tools on the same swatch.

There's an unlimited amount to discover here. Each week choose a material, say an 8B pencil or an 8H; run it through its paces. Over time, you'll develop a very intimate sense of what each of your materials does alone, in combination, and subjected to various modifications.

So, let's talk about our third type of texture, simulated or trompe l'oeil texture. Over the years, I've had students ask, how do you do metal? Or rocks? Or water? Reasonable enough; they all have different textures. But for most purposes it's of limited practicality to learn a recipe for each—there's too much variety. Metal could be shining stainless steel, rusted iron, or bent aluminum. Rock could be a sheer cliff or polished marble. And water could be in a pitcher at lunch or in the ocean at night.

The way each material looks is affected by a host of factors, like spatial location and light. A distant tree reveals much less of its bark's surface texture than one up close, and we'll see more or less texture depending on the position, distance, and strength of the light source. And we have to relate the way we draw anything to the overall compositional hierarchy and mood of the drawing. So it's of limited use to say, for tree bark use a 2B pencil on its side on a rough paper. That said, there are ways we can study specific textures, and we'll look at wood grain and reflective metal.

I've mentioned that many artists and professors say that learning to draw is all about learning to see, and that's certainly the case here. We need to determine the distinguishing visual characteristics of a subject at a given distance in a given light source. If we can relate that to specific drawing materials and procedures, we'll be in good shape to proceed.

In drawing simulated textures, start simply. Do a study, not a full-blown drawing. Don't try to create an entire still life, just one texture that you're interested in learning about. We'll look at wood grain first. If you were doing this on your own, you'd want to get a piece of wood with an interesting pattern of grain.

The first step's analysis—the goal's to determine the underlying visual characteristics of the subject. With certain textures, a black and white photo of the object can help you see the underlying characteristics more clearly or making a rubbing or a photocopy. All three have a lot less visual data than the objects themselves and this can work to your advantage in trying to distill a principle.

Here, the black and white shows you how you could lay down a pretty consistent ground of value. Then using a darker, more or less, vertical mark, draw the echoing grain shapes, all the while paying attention to the spacing and proportion. And that's pretty much the way Magritte draws his wood grain in this celebration of texture and mark, though the values are lighter, more high key. So, give it a try. Try graphite on a fairly smooth paper and then on a more textured one, and then try different grains.

Let's take a look at a very different kind of texture, a reflective surface. You'll need an empty paint can from the hardware store or something similar. Highly polished reflective surfaces like mirrors produce reflections with sharp edges. The less polished the metal, the fuzzier the edges. The can you find may be more or less polished. This one is by no means the dullest metal, but it's much less polished than a mirror—the edges are gauzier. Whatever the case, when looking at reflective surfaces, it's helpful to understand what's being reflected instead of just trying to copy a random pattern of lights and darks, so let's sort this out.

To control the reflection, I'll place the can in a cardboard box. Let's start on the left. The yellowish vertical band is the reflection of the left flap folded into the box's interior. The band's lighter toward the interior of the can, that's the reflection of the close edge of the flap. It gets gradually and slightly darker toward the left edge of the can, representing the flap receding into the box. Then we get a thin dark stripe, the reflection of the much darker back plane of the box. We see something similar on the right side though the reflected flap's darker. That's because I've lit the can from the right side and the right flap's in shadow.

You'll also note that light from the can gets reflected back onto the right flap. The bright vertical stripe to the left of the flap's reflection is a reflection of the light shining from the right. Let's look at the curving edge, yellowish to whitish, near the base of the can in the center. That's the reflection of the front edge of the box reflected into the curving can. It disappears into the light's reflection. The curving edge above it, lightish to darkish, is the reflection of the table's edge meeting the much darker room. The blur behind would be me, my camera, and tripod.

The next couple pieces are a little harder to see because the contrast is low, so I put some white foam core inside the box to heighten this. The receding diagonal of the bottom of the flap reflects as a curve; same thing on the other side. And the cast shadow of the flap onto the box's floor plane reflects too. Knowing what's going on, I think you'll be able to make out these relationships in the original version. It really all boils down to seeing the shapes and value of what's being reflected.

Several years ago, I had a grad student who got interested in reflective surfaces and did a group of drawings and paintings of a paint can—this, a very iconic example. Before starting your own drawing, think about what material and paper you want to use and do some tests. Experiment with your blending tools and erasers to approximate the quality of the edges in the reflection, then do a couple of compositional sketches to figure out placement and format shape, then analyze what you're seeing and draw. It's a great situation to play with and create variations. Other kinds of objects positioned to reflect in the can be interesting. Try an egg, or a lemon, or a bottle.

Then move the can out of the box onto your still life table so it reflects the room. Dissect what's happening. The box is like a simple room, so you have some preparation for the complexity of an actual room. Or put the can on a wood grain tabletop, or on something reflective, like a mirror or metal baking sheet. You could make all the surfaces in your setup reflective. Or use a piece of patterned material—stripes are interesting. You could apply the same methods of analysis we used in looking at wood grain or reflective surfaces to rock, fur, water in a glass, or anything that piques your interest.

Varying materials is another way to explore texture. It's a great project to draw the same thing, same size, composition, lighting, but change the paper and drawing material. For instance, try graphite on a smooth paper, then on a rough paper. I think you get the idea.

A little foreshadowing here; my grad student who did the paint cans actually did many of these in color, our next topic, and this will be a great project to remember and reprise after we've covered some color basics.

Returning to texture, remember, it's all about the feel and look, and even the smell of the piece. Van Gogh was very aware of all of this. He wrote to his brother Theo in April of 1885 about the painting he was working on, *The Potato Eaters*. He wrote this:

> I've tried to bring out the idea that these people eating potatoes by the light of their lamp have dug the earth with the self-same hands they are now putting into the dish, and it thus suggests manual labor and—a meal honestly earned.

He goes on to talk about the texture of the painting in terms of weaving. I'd love to know if he was aware of the etymological connection. He writes:

> I've held the threads of this fabric in my hands all winter long and searched for the definitive pattern—and although it is now a fabric of rough and coarse appearance, the threads have now been chosen with care and according to certain rules. ... It would be wrong to give a painting of peasant life a conventional polish. If a peasant painting smells of bacon, smoke, potato steam, fine. ... A painting of peasant life should not be perfumed.

# Color: Color Theory and Color and Light
## Lecture 28

The next three lectures focus on color. First, we'll look at some definitions and notions surrounding color theory. Then, we'll explore how color functions in nature. Finally, we'll analyze a number of artists' paintings and drawings to see how they actually use color. And you'll have the opportunity to apply what you learn in a range of exercises and drawing projects.

### Pastels

For the drawing projects in our lectures on color, use chalk pastels. These are made from pigments ground into a powder and held together with a water-based binder. They're relatively easy to use, especially if you've worked with charcoal.

Pastels run from soft and powdery to hard and brittle. The soft pastels spread and blend more easily, while the hard pastels can be sharpened to a point with a knife or razor blade for more precise work. Some manufacturers make pastel pencils that can also be used for more detailed work.

Pastels can be purchased both individually and in sets. If you purchase them individually, try these 14 colors to get started: green, blue, blue-violet, red-violet, red, orange, yellow, yellow ochre, raw sienna, burnt sienna, Van Dyke brown, white, black, and gray. If you purchase a set, look for a similar range of colors.

Many manufacturers make light-to-dark gradations of their colors and number these. The darkest version usually gets the lowest number; the purest grade gets a middle number; and the lightest gets the highest number. A good way to expand on a basic set is to get three of each color. For example, choose a green and get the darkest, purest, and lightest versions. Another way to build on a set is to get three versions of the same color with different qualities. For example, purchase an iconic blue, another blue toward green, and another toward violet. You might also expand your collection by buying both soft and hard pastels in similar colors.

As with most of the materials we've discussed, there is no standardization among manufacturers. Two "ultramarine blues" made by two manufacturers may well be different. And there are a wide variety of color names, some particular to a single manufacturer.

Pastels, like graphite and charcoal, can be hatched, blended, layered, and manipulated in myriad ways. Pastel papers tend to have a fair amount of tooth, which serves to abrade the chalk and hold it to the surface.

## Color and Light

As you may remember from high school physics, Isaac Newton passed white light through a prism and observed that it split apart into bands of color. He described the spectrum he saw as consisting of seven colors: red, orange, yellow, green, blue, indigo, and violet. The number of colors derived from Newton's belief that the color spectrum had an underlying connection with the seven-note musical scale and the number of days in the week, among other things. Newton arranged the colors in a circle—the first color wheel.

Physics tells us that color is determined by the distance between waves (wavelength) of a given wave of light. This is referred to as *wave quality*. Red has the widest wavelength; as we progress around Newton's circle, wavelengths get narrower.

An object or substance appears to be a certain color because it reflects waves of that length and absorbs all others. All else being equal, the lightness or darkness of an object or substance is determined by the quantity of light waves it reflects or absorbs. White objects, such as white drawing paper, reflect most light waves. Black substances, such as ink, absorb most light waves.

## The Color Wheel

Newton also showed that he could pass his bands of colored light back through a prism and get white light, but pigments behave differently. If you mix seven pastels to match Newton's seven colors, you won't get white but a darkish mud.

For artists, the most basic group of colors consists of a triad: red, yellow, and blue. These are referred to as *primary colors* because they can't be produced by mixing other pigments. The next three colors are known as *secondary colors* and are made by mixing the primaries. As most of us know, yellow and blue produce green, blue and red produce violet, and red and yellow produce orange. If we mix intermediary steps between any of the six primaries and secondaries, we get six new colors, referred to as *tertiaries*. These are yellow-green, green-blue, blue-violet, violet-red, red-orange, and orange-yellow. And we could mix each of these 12 colors with its neighbor to create another 12 hues. As more transitional colors are added, the visual path around the color wheel becomes smoother.

On the wheel of primaries and secondaries, the colors that are next to one another are called *adjacent* or *analogous colors*. Here, each color shares something with its neighbor. Orange and yellow both share yellow; orange and red both share red. These represent smoother transitions than yellow to red. A general principle in applying color in a given drawing is to use colors that share common elements where you want smoother transitions.

Colors are also thought of as having temperature. Yellow, orange, and red are the warm colors, while green, blue, and violet are cool. Like the warm and cool groups, there are other, more subtle, groups. For example, the three colors that share yellow—yellow, orange, and green—form a group. Note, however, that not all adjacent colors are equally similar. The temperature divide is significant. A pure yellow feels more similar to a pure orange than to a pure green. Although yellow and green share yellow, green contains blue, a contrasting cool color. Yellow and orange share yellow, and neither contains anything cool; thus, they share warmth, as well.

Other significant groupings include those that contain two primaries and their secondary, or two parents and their offspring, such as yellow, blue, and green; blue, red, and violet; and red, yellow, and orange.

The opposite of analogous colors are *complementary colors*. These pairs of colors sit opposite each other on the color wheel, putting each one as far away as possible from its opposite. The three complementary pairs are yellow and violet, orange and blue, and red and green. While analogous colors share a component color, complements have nothing in common. For example, there's no yellow in violet and no violet (or red or blue) in yellow.

We could say that analogous colors are like two grays. They have contrast—we can tell them apart—but they share some elements. Each has some amount of black and some amount of white. But complementary colors are extreme. They're like black and white, with none of one in the other.

The three pairs of complements have different personalities. The yellow-violet pair has the greatest value contrast of the three, followed by orange and blue. Red and green are the most similar in value.

## Properties of Color: Hue, Value, and Saturation

In an earlier lecture, we noted that each color has three attributes: hue, value, and saturation. *Hue* coincides with the color's name; it's the yellow, green, or blue character of the color. *Value* refers to the color's lightness or darkness. (Any color can be made lighter by adding white, known as a *tint*, or darker by adding black, known as a *shade*.) *Saturation* refers to the color's level of purity. We can create versions of any color, stretching from very gray at the achromatic end of the scale to the most intensely saturated at the other. When you change the value of a color by adding white, black, or some other neutralizing color, you also lower the saturation.

## Color and Contrast

If drawing with value is like playing checkers, drawing with color is like playing three-dimensional checkers. With value, an area can be either lighter or darker. Thus, tonal value in and of itself offers one kind of contrast. With color, we can have contrasts happening along three scales simultaneously: hue, value, and saturation. If all three are the same, the color will be identical, and we won't see any distinction between two shapes. But if we vary one factor even a bit—say, keep the hue and saturation about the same but lighten the value—we get contrast and differentiation. Varying all three attributes results in high contrast.

As we've seen, warm to cool represents one type of contrast. Another is contrast of amount. All else being equal, the greater the amount of a given color, the more dominant that color will feel.

## Simultaneous Contrast of Hue, Value, Saturation, and Temperature

In the first lecture on value, we learned that value is relative. White surrounded by black will appear brighter, and black surrounded by white will appear darker. We experience color similarly. Red appears brighter if surrounded by black and dimmer if surrounded by white. Colors also appear more saturated as the ground's hue moves from similar to complementary.

In terms of drawing, this means that it's smart to block in overall color first. Because the way color reads is contextual, finishing one object before going on to the next can result in real problems. The color that looked right at first could look all wrong when an abutting color is added.

## Color and Content

It's important to note that color has symbolic meaning. Some such meanings are local and culturally specific, while others associations are more widespread. Not surprisingly, the warm colors—red, orange, and yellow—are often associated with heat, warmth, fire, sun, and energy. Red is particularly associated with heart, passion, and love, but it can also signify blood, violence, and danger. Green has associations with growth, life, and freshness, and blue is often construed as calm or sad. In the West, white is associated with day, reason, calm, and purity. Black has associations with night, terror, and death but also with elegance and romance. Of course, many of these associations are matters of local culture. Among the Chinese, white is associated with death, and red is the color of prosperity.

## Light and Color in Nature

Most of what we've discussed so far would come under the heading of color theory. But in order to use color in drawing, it helps to understand how we actually see color. We talk about the nominal color of an object as its *local color*. But when we look at most things, we actually see many more colors than the local color, and the colors we see are influenced by environmental factors, including the color of the light source, the direction of light, and the reflectivity of the object's surface and the surrounding objects and surfaces.

These same factors hold true indoors and outdoors, but outdoors, other factors come into play, as well. For example, the atmosphere lends its color to what we see. As hills and trees recede into space, they take on more and more of the color of the atmosphere itself. That's because, with distance, there's more atmosphere between you and what you're seeing. A sun-filled sky can tinge everything with golden tones. Other skies might suffuse a landscape with blue, brown, or gray.

## Steps of Light in Color

In the lectures on value, we saw that we could create the illusion of light and volume using anywhere from two to nine values. With color, the number of possibilities for modulating form increases exponentially. For example, volume can be created by modulating a single color from light to dark, from warm to cool, or from light to dark and warm to cool simultaneously. In the next lecture, we'll learn more about how we can use and create form in just about any kind of color palette.

### Suggested Reading

Albers, *Interaction of Color*.

Mendelowitz, Faber, and Wakeman, *A Guide to Drawing*, "Color," pp. 114–121.

Pumphrey, *The Elements of Art*, "Value and Color," pp. 147–187.

# Color: Color Theory and Color and Light
## Lecture 28—Transcript

The next three lectures focus on color, a fascinating subject. First, we'll look at some definitions and notions surrounding color theory, then at how color functions in nature, and we'll analyze a number of artists' paintings and drawings to see how they actually use color. And you'll have the opportunity to apply what you learn in a range of exercises and drawing projects.

I'd suggest using pastels—the chalky kind, not the oily ones; they're more versatile. Chalk pastels are made from pigments ground into a powder and held together with a water-based binder. They're relatively easy to use, especially if you've worked with charcoal. Pastels run from soft and powdery to hard and brittle. Rembrandt, Art Spectrums, Schminke, and Sennelier are on the soft side; Prismacolor Nupastel, Cretacolor, Holbein, and Richeson on the hard side. Some people prefer one type to the other; many artists use both. The soft pastels spread and blend more easily. The hard pastels can be sharpened to a point with a knife or razor blade for more precise work. Some manufacturers make pastel pencils that can also be used for more detailed work.

You can purchase pastels both individually and in sets. If you purchase pastels individually, I'd suggest 14 to get started: a green, a blue, a blue-violet, a red-violet, a red, an orange, and a yellow. And four earth colors: a yellow earth, like a yellow ochre; an orange earth, like a raw sienna; and a red earth, like a burnt sienna. I'd also suggest getting a darker, less saturated brown, like a Van Dyke brown or a burnt umber; and a white; black; and gray.

Many manufacturers make light to dark gradations of their colors. They number them. The darkest version usually gets the lowest number, the purest grade gets a middle number, and the lightest gets the highest number.

A good way to expand on the basic group is to get three of each color when available. For example, choose a green and get three versions: the darkest, the purest, and the lightest. A further way to build on a set is to get three different greens, or blues, or reds, ones that have different qualities, like a center iconic blue, another more toward the green, and another more toward the violet. And you could also expand by buying both softs and hards of similar colors. Now, you can also purchase a set. If you go this route, look at the range of colors to see what bases are covered in light of what I just suggested regarding individual sticks.

As with most of the materials we've discussed, there's no standardization between manufacturers. Two ultramarine blues made by two different manufacturers may well be different, and there are a wide variety of names, some particular to a single manufacturer, so it's a good idea to look at the sticks and not just depend on the names until you know the brand.

Pastel, like graphite and charcoal, can be hatched, blended, layered, and manipulated in myriad ways. Pastel papers tend to have a fair amount of tooth, and that serves to abrade the chalk and hold it on the surface.

As you may remember from high school physics, Isaac Newton passed white light through a prism and observed it split apart into bands of color. This is an illustration from his 1704 book, *Opticks*. He described the spectrum he saw as consisting of seven colors: red, orange, yellow, green, blue, indigo, and violet. The number of colors—seven—derived from his belief that the color spectrum had an underlying connection with the seven note musical scale and the number of the days in the week, among other things. He arranged the colors in a circle—the first color wheel. The letters at the ends of the spokes along the circle's circumference show the musical note in scale order he associated with a given color.

Physics tells us that color is determined by the distance between waves, or wavelengths, of a given wave of light. This is referred to as wave quality. Red has the widest wavelength and, as we progress around Newton's circle, wavelengths get narrower. An object or substance appears to be a certain color because it's reflecting those waves and absorbing all the others. The green block looks green because it absorbs all other wave qualities and reflects the green ones back to us. Similarly, the yellow reflects the yellow, and the red the red. All else being equal, the lightness or darkness of an object or substance is determined by the quantity of light waves it reflects or absorbs.

White objects, like the white paper we draw on, reflect most of the light waves coming at them. Black substances, like the ink we use, absorb most of the light waves coming at them. That's related to what we experience with a white or silver car being cooler than a black one in summer heat, and this was actually tested at the Lawrence Berkeley National Laboratory in 2011. They found the cabin air temperature of a white or silver car to be 9 to 11 degrees lower, on average, than an identical black one. In any case, here the yellow block reflects more light than green or red, so the yellow appears lighter.

Newton also showed that he could take his bands of colored light, pass them back through a prism, and get white light. Pigments behave differently. Take seven different pastels, same as his colors, mix them together, you get a darkish mud. That said, the color wheel is still very much with us today, though we've adapted it to our own purposes. And this has to do with how pigments, as opposed to light, are mixed and how colors relate.

For artists, the most basic group of colors consists of a triad: red, yellow, and blue, referred to as primary colors. They're primaries because you can't make them by mixing other pigments. The next three colors, the secondaries, are made by mixing the primaries: Yellow and blue produce green; blue and red, violet; red and yellow, orange. Taken together, this yields a color wheel of three primaries and three secondaries. To get familiar with all this, I'd suggest drawing along with what we'll be discussing. Here, you could lay your primaries and mix secondaries or make a primary/secondary color wheel.

If we mix intermediary steps between any of the six primaries and secondaries we get six new colors referred to as tertiaries. These include yellow-green, green-blue, blue-violet, violet-red, red-orange, and orange-yellow. You could mix these, too. And we could mix each of these 12 colors with its neighbor to create another 12 hues.

One of the things you'll note is that, as we add more transitional colors, the visual path around the wheel is smoother: more legato, less staccato. For our purposes, a six-color wheel will do fine to help us understand the basic relationships among the colors, but these same relationships would apply to a 12 hue, 24 hue, or 48-hue wheel.

We think of colors as having temperature. You'll likely note that yellow, orange, and red form a group—these are the warm colors. Green, blue, and violet are the cools. With yellow at the 12 o'clock position, the color wheel reveals the warm colors dividing from the cool, from the top right to lower left, along a diagonal. One side feels like day, the other like night; one like sunshine and warmth, the other like a cool stream in a dark forest. They represent different temperatures and different moods.

With yellow at the 12 o'clock position, our color wheels reveal the hues organized from top to bottom, light to dark. As we noted, with fewer transitional colors, the visual path's choppier; more transitional colors, smoother. That's because transitional colors share elements of the hues on either side. Red and orange both contain red, so they feel similar. Same with blue and violet; they share blue. And both are smoother transitions than, say, yellow to red, or yellow to blue. These feel like big jumps because these colors have nothing in common. In the six-color wheel, we glide through orange to get to red, glide through green to get to blue—smoother.

So when we want smooth transitions, we use colors that share common elements, and colors that share common elements or qualities will appear to hang together and form a shape. When we want abrupt transitions and when we want an area to feel like an independent shape, we'll do the opposite. On the wheel of primaries and secondaries, the colors that are next to one another are called adjacent or analogous colors. Each color shares something with its neighbor. Like the warm and cool groups, there are other more subtle groups. The three colors that share yellow form a group: yellow, orange, and green.

Though, it's worth pointing out that not all adjacent colors are equally similar. The temperature divide's a significant one. A pure yellow will feel more similar to a pure orange than to a pure green. While yellow and green share yellow, green contains blue, a contrasting cool color. Yellow and orange share yellow and neither contains anything cool, so they share warmth as well; same thing with red, orange, and violet. Other significant groupings include the ones that contain two primaries and their secondary, two parents and their offspring: yellow, blue, and green; blue, red, and violet; and red, yellow, and orange, already mentioned as the warm group.

The opposite of analogous color is complementary color, also referred to as opposite color. That's because these pairs sit opposite one another on the wheel. That puts each one as far away as possible from its opposite. Our three complementary pairs are yellow and violet, orange and blue, and red and green. While analogous colors share a component color, complements have nothing in common. There's no yellow in violet and no violet, or red, or blue in yellow. There's no orange, or red, or yellow in blue and no blue in orange. There's no red in green and no green, or yellow, or blue in red: nothing in common.

We could say that analogous colors are like two grays—they have contrast, we can tell them apart, but they share elements. Each has some amount of black and some amount of white. There's something different, but something shared. We get some contrast—how much depends on how much is different and how much shared. On our value scale, a number seven gray and a number eight gray share a lot. Not a lot of contrast. Not unlike blue and violet. On the other hand, a number two gray and a number six gray share much less, more contrast. Not unlike yellow and green. But complementary colors are extreme. They're like black and white: no white in black, no black in white; no yellow in violet, no violet in yellow. Nothing in common; highest contrast.

That said, the three pairs of complements have different personalities. The wheel's organized top to bottom, light to dark, so the yellow-violet pair has the greatest value contrast of the three pairs. Orange and blue follow—most people find these more mellow—and red and green the most similar in value.

In an earlier lecture, I noted that we think of each color as having three attributes: hue, value, and saturation. Hue coincides with the color's name—it's the yellow, or green, or blue character of the color. Value refers to the colors' lightness or darkness. Any color can be made lighter or darker. A color made lighter by adding white's called a tint. One made darker by adding black, a shade. Some color wheels plot tints and shades radiating from each hue. White, black, and gray are referred to as neutrals; they're considered colorless. When added to other colors, they don't change the hue of that color, they change its value, making it lighter or darker.

That's the theory. It doesn't always work that way. Mix black with yellow, you'll get a green, not a dark yellow. Even in the example here, the dark yellow has a greenish cast. There are also a number of ways of making things lighter or darker that don't depend on adding white or black. For instance, you can apply a color transparently, on a light ground it'll appear lighter; more opaquely to make it darker, or apply it to a darker ground. The ground could be the paper or a color that's been spray fixed. And the decision to blend or not will also affect the color's apparent value.

The third attribute of color is saturation. This refers to the color's level of purity. We can create versions of all our colors stretching from very gray, at the achromatic end, to the most intensely saturated at the other. Often, when we change the value of a color by adding white, black, or some other neutralizing color, we're also lowering the saturation. When analyzing a color, we want to understand it in relation to these three scales: hue, value, and saturation.

Again, in theory, you can create all possible colors, all secondaries, tertiaries, of every value and saturation, using the three primaries and black and white, but it doesn't work that way with pigments. We'll come back to this later. The essential point here is to begin to be able to read hue in something that's somewhat neutral. Look at the more neutral versions of the color in these wheels. Can you still feel the underlying color?

You may have heard it said that you get neutral gray by mixing complements. That's not quite true. The actual color you get will depend on several factors. There's the material: pastel behaves one way, oil paint another. Then there's how you actually mix the colors, and there's the specific pigment—not all blues are the same. Let's take a look at how this works.

Here are three pairs of complements. Overlay yellow on violet, then violet on yellow—two different colors. So order matters, but neither's a gray, though both are more neutral than yellow or violet alone. Same thing with blue and orange, or red and green. So far, I've mixed directly, but if I blend, I get a different color, and if I apply the color on the swab, it's more neutral. The colors have been more thoroughly mixed. The neutrality will be more pronounced if I use neutral versions of my compliments to start with. Here, a more neutral blue and orange.

We're entering into the world of chromatic grays, colorful grays, neutral versions of their parent colors, and I can make each one a little warmer or a little cooler. Adding white, a neutral, will not only lighten, it will increase its neutrality, as will adding a neutral gray. This kind of color is extraordinarily useful because so many of the things around us are not saturated namable color and we often need to make subtle distinctions between things.

If drawing with value is like playing checkers, drawing with color is like playing three-dimensional checkers. With value, an area can be either lighter or darker. So tonal value, in and of itself, offers us one kind of contrast. With color, we can have contrasts happening along three scales simultaneously: hue, value, and saturation. If all three are the same, the color will be identical—we won't see any distinction between two shades.

But if I vary one factor even a little bit, let's say keep the hue and saturation about the same, but lighten the value, I get contrast and differentiation. Or instead, I could keep the hue and value about the same and change the saturation. Or I could keep the value and saturation and change the hue. Or I could vary all three: hue, value, and saturation. That means a lot of contrast.

With two shades and three variables, there are eight possible scenarios. Hue, value, and saturation could all be the same or all be different, or any two could be the same and one different, or any two could be different and one the same. But there are more than eight possibilities because of the amount we could vary any of these factors could be anywhere from a little to a lot along a sliding scale. So the actual number of specific contrasts you could create with only two shades is nearly infinite, more than you could move through in a lifetime.

There're a couple other types of contrast we need to consider. One we've already mentioned is warm to cool; another's contrast of amount. All else being equal, the greater the amount of a given color, the more that color will feel dominant.

In the first lecture on value, we learned that value is relative. White surrounded by black will appear brighter; black surrounded by white, darker. We experience color similarly. A red surrounded by black appears brighter; surrounded by white, dimmer.

Here, we have an identical red in three different red grounds. Each time the central red appears to be a somewhat different color. In the brightest ground, it's the most muted; in the darkest, the brightest. As the ground gets darker and less saturated, the internal square appears to get lighter, more saturated, more orange. Not surprisingly, the red square's more saturated in a neutral ground.

Here we have four different saturated ground colors. The first, a red variant; the next a violet, a color containing red; then a blue; and finally red's complement, green. The red appears more saturated as the ground's hue moves from similar to complementary. The same blue-green appears greener in a blue and bluer in a green. The same violet appears redder in a blue and bluer in a red-violet. And a color that's pretty gray in a bluish ground's bluer in an orange one. You could make some color studies of your own along these lines.

Many of these and related principles were outlined by Johannes Itten and his student and later colleague, Josef Albers. Both were professors of art in Germany at the Bauhaus. Albers would go on to teach at Yale. In 1963, he published one of the seminal 20th-century works on color, aptly titled *The Interaction of Color*. Of course, artists have been aware of color's relative nature for some time.

In 1885, Van Gogh wrote to his brother about his painting *The Potato Eaters*. He explained that it really needed to be hung on a golden colored wall. He wrote, "…it simply mustn't be seen without being set off in this way. It will not appear to full advantage against a dark background and especially not against a dull background." Van Gogh understood that a painting on the wall is very similar to a rectangle of color inside another rectangle of color.

In terms of drawing, this means it's smart to block in general color overall first because the way color reads is contextual. Drawing one object, finishing it, and then going on to the next can result in real problems. The color that, at first, looked right, could look all wrong as abutting color is added—the same situation as with value but more so.

We should note that color has had symbolic meaning. Some of this is local and culturally specific; some associations are more widespread. Unsurprisingly, the warm colors—red, orange, and yellow—have been associated with heat, warmth, fire, and energy. Red particularly, with heart, passion, and love but also with blood, violence, and danger. Think stop sign.

Green has associations with growth, life, and freshness, and in the U.S., money. Blue is often construed as calm or embodying the coolness of water, and as in the blues, sadness. White, at least in the west, has been associated with day, the Apollonian, reason and calm, and also associated with purity, like brides in white. Black has associations with night, terror, and deaths but also with elegance and romance—think limo, tuxedo, and black party dress. Of course, a fair amount of this is a matter of local cultural. Among the Chinese, white's associated with death and red's the color of prosperity.

Most of what we've just discussed would come under the heading color theory, but in order to use color in drawing it helps to understand how we actually see color. When talking about objects, like these blocks, we refer to their greenness, yellowness, or redness as their local color. When we look at most things, we're seeing many more colors than their local colors. In fact, here are 16 colors that are present in the image of the blocks. The four in the center are obvious—a red, a yellow, and two greens—but some of the others might seem more curious and a number of these don't really have names. The reason why we have so many colors here is that local color is influenced by environmental factors.

The first factor's light. The green block is receiving most light from above right, and we see three main colors associated with this. The top ridge of the block receives the most light and is the lightest. The side plane gets the next largest amount of light and it's a bit darker. The front plane receives the least light, it's darkest. But the color isn't only getting darker, it's also moving from the yellow to the blue. The light to dark shift is accompanied by a warm-cool shift. Why? Because the light itself is yellow. As Leonardo observed, "Il colore dello alluminato participa del colore dello alluminante." "The color of the object receiving light is affected by the color of the light source."

We see similar progressions across the yellow and the red blocks' planes, though the right face of the yellow block's in the shadow of the red block, so it receives more light from above left. As you may have already noticed, there's a second factor affecting the color here, and that's reflectivity.

Leonardo comments on this, too. "Li colori delli obbietti illuminati s'imprimono nelle superfite l'u del altro." "The colors of objects receiving light reflect on the surfaces, one to the other." For example, look at the bottom right edge of the green block. It goes an orange-ochre or orange-green kind of color. That's because the reflection of the red block is mixing with the green local color on its surface. If we look at the shadow side of the yellow block we see the same thing. The red block is reflecting onto the yellow surface to create a succession of earth tones that contain both yellow and red. As we move across the yellow plane, the color gets progressively darker and redder.

Now, you might ask, why isn't the yellow reflecting into the red? Well, it is, just not that much. To reflect color, a surface has to receive a sufficient amount of light. The right plane of the yellow is pretty much in shadow, so it reflects less. The blocks aren't only reflecting one onto the other, they're also reflecting down onto the white surface. The reflections of the lighter planes are lighter, the reflection of the shadow planes are darker. All the reflections are pretty neutral but can you seeing color in the neutrals? Do you see how the reflection of the yellow cube is more yellow, the red more red? When thinking about reflective color, the other major factor is the surface concerned. A more highly reflective surface will, by definition, produce a more defined reflection. That means greater saturation and higher value contrast.

There are a couple of other things worth pointing out here. Generally, the light tone or halftone will have greater saturation than the highlight or shadow side. The very lightness of the highlight subtracts from its saturation, and unless there's some very strong reflection into the shadow side, it'll appear less saturated.

So while we name colors for convenience that's green, or red, or yellow, what we actually see is the name color affected by the direction of the light, the amount of light a given surface receives, the color of the light, and any reflected color from other objects in the environment.

Indoors, under incandescent light, illuminated planes go warmer and shadows generally cooler. Under fluorescent light, illuminated planes go cooler and the shadows can appear warmer. Had the blocks been lit with blue daylight through a window, the illuminated planes would go cooler.

Moonlight through a window would be different again. At night, we'll often get strong contrasts of light and shadow and strong saturation in an artificially illuminated area. That's because dark is the default and light, like a street lamp or a car's headlight, will illuminate some portion of the scene. And imagine those blocks at night sitting on a shelf in a half-dark closet. Well, without strong light the saturations all diminish and the contrast of light and shadow are reduced. We may not even be able to tell the blocks' colors at all.

In this example, the blocks were posed in a photographer's studio, indoors. But these same factors hold true when we move outdoors, and there are a couple others that come into play as well. In an earlier lecture, I discussed color and atmospheric or aerial perspective. We noticed that distance affects the way we perceive color. When things are closer, their colors appear to have greater value contrast and greater saturation. As they recede, less.

One way of thinking about this is that the atmosphere, like the yellow bulb on the blocks, lends its color to what we see, and as things like hills and trees recede into space they take on more and more of the color of the atmosphere itself. That's because, with distance, there's more and more atmosphere between us and what we're seeing. Here, we get an admixture of light blue.

Leonardo explains this:

There is another kind of perspective which I call Aerial Perspective… In an atmosphere… the remotest objects seen through it, as mountains, in consequence of the great quantity of atmosphere between your eye and them—appear blue and almost of the same hue as the atmosphere itself.

And when the sky is cool, the shadows of objects in the landscape tend to reflect that coolness. On the other hand, a sun-filled sky can tinge everything with golden tones. Other skies will suffuse a landscape in brown. A cloudy dusk can go indigo-blue, an overcast day to violet-grays, and winter cold to icy ones. Like the blocks, many surfaces in nature reflect color. Water, of course, would be an obvious example. But color's reflecting in nature more subtly all the time, just like in the colored blocks.

In the lectures on value, we saw how we could create the illusion of light and volume with as few as two values—a light and a dark to stand for everything from highlight to form shadow to cast shadow. Or we could use three: a light, a half tone, and a dark. Or nine, one each for the highlight, light, and halftone, then two steps for the form shadow, then a reflected light, a reflected shadow, a cast shadow, and light from the object reflected into the shadow.

What's clear is that there's no right way, but different approaches will yield different results. The more or less on-and-off value of the Daumier has one feel, the more modulated approach in the Lundin another. With color, the number of possibilities for modulating form increases exponentially. In the next lecture, we'll take an in-depth look at how artists use color. For now, I'd like to look at some of the ways artists modulate form.

In the woman's flesh, Vermeer modulates light to dark and, simultaneously, warm to cool, all in a fairly neutral complementary orange-blue range. Cézanne's values are much closer and his saturation much greater, but he also modulates warm to cool—here, analogous yellow to green. Van Gogh also modulates warm-cool in the head, like Vermeer orange-blue, though much more saturated. And Wayne Thiebaud pumps the saturation and compounds this with high-value contrasts. While Monet moves light to dark in the man's head, he stays within the warm, though the form shadow is more neutral.

But, in the woman's dress, the lights are cool and the form shadow goes warmer. And let's look at the woman's back in this William Merritt Chase pastel. The highlights are cool, the surrounding light warm. As we move into the form shadow, we go cooler; into the umbra, warmer.

In the next lecture, we'll learn more about how we can use and create form in just about any kind of palette.

# Color: How Artists Use Color
## Lecture 29

In the last lecture, we looked at both landscape photos and artworks and saw how color creates a quality of light and mood. And mood is an important consideration in making a drawing; it leads us to select a specific palette. Within the confines of a given palette, we can create a visual hierarchy, using color and value to structure focal areas and focal points. We also saw that we can attend to the illusion of space, volume, and light with color. In this lecture, we'll look at the work of a number of artists to learn how they use specific color palettes.

### Working with Color

As you begin to work with color, try to pay attention to your everyday feelings about it. Many people viscerally feel the difference between a blue sky and a cloudy one or the difference between a field of flowers in the afternoon sun and a dingy bus station at night. Why do some places feel uplifting, romantic, scary, or depressing? Analyze what's going on around you in terms of color and use what you learn in your drawings.

You actually know a lot more about certain aspects of color than you might think. For example, you coordinate the colors of the clothes you wear every day, and you know that business attire projects a serious mood through its fairly neutral palette. With casual clothes or sports clothes, the palette is more saturated, and the mood is lighter. Similarly, you've likely thought about mood and palette in decorating your home or office. You may have a brown study or a yellow bedroom. Each of these palettes projects a different mood.

We're also constantly barraged with the work of professional designers and illustrators who put color to work to create mood and evoke an emotional response in order to sell us things. Examples of this can be found everywhere—even the cereal aisle of your local supermarket. The sweet children's cereals are packaged with bright, saturated colors, while the healthy, whole-grain options have much more neutral packaging. Try to become more aware of how color is used around you by professional designers and note your reactions.

## Palette and Mood

In the last lecture, we saw how a sense of light, mood, and emotion can be affected through palette choice. The essential character of a palette is defined through limitation. Artists have used certain common color limitations, or palettes, for centuries. These palettes include the following:

- Monochromatic. Working with a monochromatic palette is really a form of working with value, though hue plays a part. A blue painting will feel different—cooler and icier—than a warm gray or an orange painting.

- Expanded monochrome. This type of palette admits a bit of color outside the monochrome.

- Dominant hue. Related to both the monochrome and expanded monochrome palettes is the dominant hue palette. Here, the artist chooses a range of colors and mixes a sufficient quantity of one other hue to each one to ensure that the one hue will be dominant.

- Analogous. A next step in palette complexity is the analogous palette. This type of palette uses colors that are next to one another on the wheel. Examples include red-orange-yellow, orange-yellow-green, and green-blue-violet.

- Complementary. Another common palette is one based on complements. These include: yellow-violet, orange-blue, and red-green.

- Split complementary. Related to the complementary palette is the split complementary. Examples include yellow with red-violet and blue-violet, red with yellow-green and blue-green, and blue with yellow-orange and red-orange.

- Double complementary. This palette is based on two sets of complementary colors, for example, red-green and orange-blue. The Eakins watercolor we've looked at throughout the course uses this palette.

- Earth tone. The neutral earth-tone palette is also common. This type of palette was used quite a bit by Picasso, Georges Braque, Juan Gris, and others during the heyday of Cubism.

## Color Application: Flat Color, Open Color, and Gradations

Another set of factors to be aware of in working with color has to do with the relationship of color to shape. Here, *flat color* refers to broad areas of unmodulated color enclosed in a shape. This is the way many of us colored in pictures as children: Draw the shape of the apple and color it in red. One of the hallmarks of this use of color is that the colors of individual things don't partake of the color of a light source, nor does color reflect from one object to another. Color remains in its bounded shape.

With *open color*, we see marks and multiple small areas of color within shapes, and the edges of the shapes themselves are much less strictly defined. This approach is common when areas or surfaces are built out of mark and the sensation of color depends on optical mixing.

Another way in which shapes are treated with color is through *gradation*, moving from, say, light to mid-dark to dark. This approach is most common in naturalistic work, where the goal is to create a convincing illusion of three-dimensional form in space.

## Summing Up Color Principles

Here are some important principles we've learned about color:

- When using color, a first and defining choice is palette selection, which inflects light, mood, and emotion—the overall flavor of the work.

- Once you've made that decision, the next step is to think hierarchically and compositionally. Think about relative contrasts; in other words, consider relative hue, value, and saturation contextually to move the viewer through your drawing. Remember, areas of higher saturation and value contrast will become focal zones.

- Pay attention to the effects of atmospheric perspective. With distance, objects take on the color of the atmosphere. When things are closer to us, their colors appear to have greater value contrast and greater saturation. As they recede, they have less value contrast and saturation.

- All else being equal, warm colors will tend to advance and cools to recede, but saturation will generally trump this principle. In other words, a saturated blue bowl—a cool—will easily advance against a backdrop that is a neutral, warm tan.

## Suggested Reading

Guptill, *Watercolor Painting Step-by-Step*, chapters 7–10, pp. 65–98.

Loomis, *Creative Illustration*, "Color," pp. 145–179.

# Color: How Artists Use Color
## Lecture 29—Transcript

In the last lecture, in both the landscape photos and the artworks, we saw how color creates a quality of light and mood. And mood is an important consideration in making a drawing. It will lead us to select a specific palette. Each of the images we looked at have this, a specific palette that creates a mood. Within the confines of the palette, we can create a visual hierarchy. We use color, and value that's part of color, to create focal areas and focal points and attend to the illusion of space, volume, and light like we did with a value palette.

As you begin to work with color, it's a good idea to pay attention to your everyday feelings surrounding color palettes and mood. Many people viscerally feel different between a blue sky and a cloudy one, or the difference between a field of flowers in the afternoon sun and a dingy bus station at night illuminated by weak fluorescents. Why do some places feel uplifting, romantic, scary, or depressing? Analyze what's going on in terms of color and you'll have excellent material at your disposal.

You actually know a lot more about certain aspects of color than you might think. You coordinate the colors of the clothes you wear on a daily basis, shirt and pants, suit and tie, dress, handbag, and shoes. These are all examples of coordinating color and projecting mood or setting a tone, based on palette.

Business attire projects a mood through palette: serious, sober. The palette's fairly neutral, achromatic. Casual business attire projects a different mood. The color sends a different signal, as does an evening gown, and golf clothes another, palette's more saturated. Kids' clothes are often even more so. And clowns are like a whole kid's closet, all mashed-up, kind of anarchic.

Similarly, you've likely thought about mood and palette in decorating your home or office. You've coordinated the color of your walls, and flooring, and furnishings. A brown study, a pink bedroom, and a sleek neutral living room all have different palettes. They project different moods.

We're also constantly barraged with the works of professional designers and illustrators who are putting color to work to create mood and evoke an emotional response in order to sell us things. Many good examples can be found in the cereal aisle of the supermarket. The sweet kids' cereals are packaged with bright, saturated colors. The mood's upbeat and fun, like a lot of kids' clothes, toys, and cartoons. Healthy, whole grain, high fiber cereals targeted at adults are packaged in much more neutral boxes. Here, serious brown ochres dominate, the colors earth and grain, nothing sweet, nothing artificial.

Same is true of greeting cards. Next opportunity, compare the kids' birthday cards with condolence cards. The former have a lot in common with kids' cereal boxes. The latter are generally much less saturated, often soft pastels. So take a look around your home or office. Analyze the palettes in individual objects, in clothing, or in entire rooms. Then make swatches of colors to represent the palette of what you've analyzed.

In the last lecture, we saw how a sense of light, mood, and emotion can be affected through palette choice. The essential character of a palette is defined through limitation. Limitation is key. If we throw every color at a drawing or painting, they tend to cancel each other out. If we copy colors indiscriminately, we lose control of mood and hierarchy. There are certain common types of palettes that artists have used for centuries. It would be a good idea as we go through these to make swatches of color to represent the palette of each work.

Perhaps the most simple color limitation is to use one chroma. We refer to this as a monochromatic palette. This well-known example is by Ingres. Picasso's *Guernica* is another famous monochromatic work. The contemporary American artist, Mark Tansey, works just about solely, in monochromes, from blues to greens to oranges and reds. This is really a form of working with value though hue plays its part. A blue painting will feel different, cooler, more icy, and less humid, than a warm gray, much less an orange painting.

An expanded monochrome palette admits a bit of color outside the monochrome. Whistler was supremely conscious of color. His painting known colloquially as *Whistler's Mother* was actually titled, *Arrangement in Grey and Black No. 1*. He titled many of his paintings to reference specific palette limitations. While in London, he did a group of color studies of the Thames at night and in early morning like this one titled *Nocturne in Blue and Silver*. It represents a subtle variation on a dark cool monochrome to incorporate small traces of warm lights.

Degas uses an expanded monochrome on the warm side of the spectrum here. Looking at these two works, you can really appreciate Leonardo's notebook entries on the subject. Colors of individual things partake of the color of the light and color reflects from one object to another. The more you look for this, the more you'll see well beyond the local color of individual objects. You'll see how environmental factors of light and reflection permeate the scene before you.

Related to both the monochrome and expanded monochrome palette is the dominant hue palette. Let's say I want a palette where yellow is dominant. I could take a group of colors, like the range of primaries and secondaries, and add a sufficient quantity of yellow to each so that when they're put into action yellow will be the dominant hue, or green, or red violet. And you can do this to varying degrees and vary value and saturation as well. This portrait by Whistler exemplifies the approach. While there are yellows, earth tones, and darks, which have admixtures of cools, the predominant hue is red.

A next step in palette complexity is the analogous palette. Here Monet uses a blue-violet-red palette for this 1904 painting of the Houses of Parliament. Though there are some blues, the painting has a strong violet-red presence. You'll also note that the values of the color are all pretty close in the mid- and mid-dark range. As with a number of Monet's paintings, there are multiple versions of this scene. I've counted at least 19. Each uses a different set of palette limitations to create the sense of mood, season, time of day, and atmospheric conditions.

Moving clockwise around the wheel, from violet-red, Cézanne uses analogous orange-yellow-green, here the value is mostly in the mid-range. Delacroix, in a more neutral range, takes us the next step around the circle in this watercolor, analogous yellow, green, and into blue. And Monet completes the circle with his view of Waterloo Bridge, London, at dusk, green-blue-violet. Though much more saturated than the Delacroix it feels like a whisper because the value range's so close, mostly in the light- to mid-range.

I hope you're beginning to get a feel for the personalities of these palettes. Each has a specific and different flavor.

Another very common palette is one based on compliments. This Degas uses a yellow-violet complimentary system. Try to imagine it without the figures. Pretty much a yellow painting though most of the yellows are fairly neutral, listing to tan or ochre, earth tones.

Our earth tones, themselves, are very important. We can mix them with primary, secondary, and tertiary colors to make them more neutral. Yellow with yellow ochre or Van Dyke Brown will give us a neutral yellow. The figures, most dressed nominally in white, list to the violet, light and fairly neutral. Also note that the door on the left, the central decorative framing of the doors, and the molding at the top of the walls has admixtures of yellow, violet, and the yellow earth, pretty neutral. This Turner is also a yellow-violet painting, but the violet is warmer, more toward the red and just about everything is very neutral. In contrast, this yellow-violet Wayne Thiebaud is pumped. Actually, the ground is modest, a light violet. The high saturations are saved for the malts, excellent hierarchical use of saturation and value contrast to create a focal area.

The essential point here is that a yellow-violet palette, or any palette for that matter, is not one thing. It can be pulled in many different directions, each one with a different mood or flavor. And I hope you see how environmental light and mood are tied to palette, whether indoors or outdoors. It's all about defining a range of value and saturation within a palette limitation. There are endless permutations within any given palette, whether it's monochromatic, analogous, or complimentary.

Traveling around the globe to the Netherlands, we get Vermeer employing an orange-blue limitation. The woman's jacket is a somewhat neutral blue and the sliver of abdomen we see is orange. But look at the back edge of the table. It's a neutral orange against a neutral blue-gray wall. Her skirt's treated in neutral oranges with shadows that have admixtures of the cooler blue. The painting, *A Last Judgment*, behind her is similarly rendered in neutral oranges and blues, as is the tiled floor under the table.

We get a different blue-orange palette in this 18th-century pastel by Rosalba Carriera. The ground's a neutral, more towards the blue, but with hints of warm. Why don't the compliments in the ground create a lot of contrast? Because they're similar in neutrality and in value, they've been made to share qualities. All the high-value contrasts and vivid saturation go to the figure's head.

Whistler shifts the orange and blues farther into the neutrals. He calls this *Mother of Pearl and Silver*.

You'll notice that Vermeer, Carriera, and Whistler all follow the same solid strategy. Greater saturation and value contrast in the objects, less in the ground.

These photos that we looked at earlier—also orange-blue—embrace the same organizational principle. The Canaletto, that we've looked at repeatedly, also operates in neutral orange-blue. The sky and the domes of Saint Mark's Cathedral are mostly cool. The whole bottom section and tower neutral warm. I'd call this orange-blue though the piazza's pavement extends a bit into the red. Odilon Redon takes the same palette but pumps the saturation.

And let's look at our last complementary pair, red and green, here decidedly neutral in Robert Nanteuil's pastel. The ground, neutral green, the flesh toward the red, but the flesh in the shadows goes toward the green. Here's, another portrait by Gilbert Stuart, the 18th-century American famous for his portraits of George Washington. Here the range is much more saturated. A lot of it clearly announces itself as red or green. But pay attention to the "white dress." It's primarily rendered in species of green.

Eakins also opts for red-green here. Imagine it without the objects and kid. The upper ground shape, green, and the bottom red, both toward the neutral—and squint, both similar in value. Result? Not too much contrast.

Give the kid and the objects higher value contrasts and some pumped saturation. That's color working compositionally. And we'll revisit Monet here in Venice. His green-red takes the reds toward the violet. And another permutation, a drawing by Turner, a pinkish ground, all very light, with our major event, the boat and related sky, receiving the saturation and the value contrast.

The examples we've looked at so far are all Western, but these palette ideas are much more widespread. This is a section of a Ming Dynasty late 16th-century hand scroll. It employs a red-green complimentary system, neutral red-browns in the tree trunk and side planes of the exposed earth, in the ground, greater saturation in the seated Lohan's robe.

A related color palette is the split-complementary palette. A yellow with both red-violet and a blue-violet is an example, or a red with a yellow-green and a blue-green, or a blue with a yellow-orange and a red-orange. You could make some swatches of those palettes.

David's *Oath of the Horatii* is based in both red-green and orange-blue. Some of the color's obvious, but a lot of the color here's subtle, neutral. At first, you might not recognize the hue. Look at the center female figure's skirt. That's a neutral orange, the upper part of her garment a neutral blue. Or look at the herringbone pattern on the floor, basically, a neutral red, the columns a dark neutral blue, the arches above, neutral reds.

Eakins is also straddling red-green, orange-blue. The sky's blue with traces of orange, the thin landscape a neutral orange-green, the water, blue, green, and orange. The skulls are orange and red earths. The flesh is modulated white and red-orange to neutrals tinged with blue.

This early 15th-century Chinese scroll, *Eighteen Songs of a Nomad Flute: The Story of Lady Wenji* uses a similar set of palette restrictions, red-green, orange-blue. The ground shifts from neutral orange to neutral green in a consistently light value range. The tents, figures, and other important elements get the higher saturations and greater value contrast to the ground.

This late 16th-century Indian example from the court of Akbar the Great employs a similar red-green, orange-blue palette, again, more neutral in the ground and more saturated in the figures. Van Gogh's The Night Café uses a similar palette, but here the color's much more saturated and the greens are extending into the yellow, giving it a somewhat acidic feel.

Modigliani dwells mostly in the hot colors goes with the subject, reds in the drape to oranges in the flesh. He introduces a single blue event, mid-dark, in the pillow, a complement to the light flesh's orange. This sets off the model's head and chest, the focal area. He uses the deep dark values in the head and around the neck and chest to further this emphasis.

Another palette variation is the neutral earth-tone palette. Here's Picasso's 1910 portrait of the art dealer Ambroise Vollard. You'll note that the head is mostly warm, everything else much more neutral and cool. We could also conceive of this as a species of an orange-blue or red-green complementary system. This type of palette was used quite a bit by Picasso, Georges Braque, and Juan Gris, and others during the heyday of cubism. In some examples, you don't get much of the warms at all. In others, the warm earths dominate.

In an earlier lecture, we saw how we could mix complements to produce colors that were more neutral. We also learned how we could use more neutral versions of the primaries and secondaries to get further neutrality. We can extend on this using earth colors. Each of the warms has a sister earth color. You can think about these as less saturated versions of the primary and secondary colors themselves.

For yellow, we have colors like yellow ochre. For orange, those like raw sienna. For red, those like burnt sienna. Mix your violet, blue, and green with their complementary earth and you'll get an earth variant of the true complement. A variant on this is to mix a second earth, a darker neutral earth with the cool and warm earth. Or with the cool alone. And you can also use whites and grays to further neutralize these colors.

There are another set of factors we want to be aware of in considering color. This has to do with the relationship of color to shape. We can have flat color. Broad areas of unmodulated color enclosed in shape, or to put it another way, defining the edges of a shape. In Van Gogh's *The Night Café*, much of the color functions this way. The red fills the shape of the wall, the light blue the tabletops, the mustard green, the side plane of the pool table. This is the way many of us colored in a picture when we were kids. Draw the shape of the apple and color it in red.

In contrast to flat color, we have open color, like in this Monet. Here, within the shapes—the sky, the water, the planes of the bridge—we see a range of colors—greens, blues, and violets. Here there are marks and multiple small areas of color within the shapes, and the edges of the shapes themselves are much less strictly defined. The approach is very common when areas or surfaces are built out of mark and the sensation of color depends on optical mixing. Meaning our eye perceives blue-green where there are lots of individual blue and green marks or smudges in an area, or orange when there's red and yellow, the same idea as in Seurat's use of colored dots.

Another way in which shapes are treated with color is through gradation. Take a look at the upper section of the back wall in this Vermeer between the orange curtain and the painting. First, there's a gradation from light to a mid-dark, that's the shadow of the curtain. Then from that neutral-cool mid-dark to a lighter warm, that's the reflection of the curtain, then cooler and more neutral, getting lighter as we move toward the painting's frame. We're likely experiencing the effects of simultaneous contrast here. The dark frame is making the wall seem lighter. The wall is making the frame appear darker. We feel similar gradations in the woman's skin and garments and many of the other surfaces.

This approach is most common in naturalistic work, like in Vermeer and Eakins where the goal's to create a convincing illusion of three-dimensional form in space.

To recap, in a given shape or area we can have flat color, multiple colors or gradations, some artists and traditions use one approach, others combine them. Take Van Gogh, for instance, flat color in the walls but marks of different color in the floor and something in-between on the pool table's surface. Modigliani mixes-it-up, too. We get some real gradation in the woman's torso suggesting three-dimensional volume but that's about the only place. The rest is pretty flat. While we get some mark making in the bed, the red is pretty-much flat color within a shape, as is the dark pillow, and the woman's hair and eyes.

Certain artists and traditions embrace flat color palettes. Let's return to Ugolino's *Last Supper*. If we removed the figures and all the stuff on the table, we'd have a more-or-less orange-yellow/blue-violet complementary palette. The back wall and floor are blue-violet neutrals. The right side wall, the tablecloth, and the bench are orange-yellow. While the figures' robes are modulated, they act a lot like flat color, red, blue, green, orange, and a dark cool. That's because they're modulated tonally. They get lighter or darker but within a garment's shape, there's no color change. The colors themselves are repeated rhythmically across the surface. The eye tends to connect the similar colors and moves us around the table.

*Court Ladies Preparing Silk* functions in a similar way. Here, too, the ground is fairly neutral and mid-tone. The ladies' hair and heads pop light and dark against the mid-tone ground and the colors of their robes—blues, reds, pinks, and greens—are much more saturated than the ground. They repeat rhythmically and move us back and forth through the painting.

One of the hallmarks of this use of color is that it's non-Leonardian. The colors of individual things don't partake of the color of a light source. Nor, does color reflect from one object to another. Color remains in its bounded shape.

While there's much more gradation in Raphael's *School of Athens*, the color is set-up in a similar way. Take the figures away it's all neutral. The figures' drapes carry all the saturation and the colors repeat rhythmically across the surface. For instance, take a look at the light blue drapes and how they choreograph your movement through the painting.

Breughel was one of the great practitioners of this use of color. Here, in *Children's Games*, the ground is mostly earth tones, pretty neutral. The figures get most of the saturation, yellows, reds, blues, greens, and other colors move us around the surface. And Mondrian uses color in a similar way.

Let's sum-up a couple principles here. When using color, a first and defining choice is palette selection or color limitation, because, that gives us light, mood, and emotion, the overall flavor of the work. It could be cool, acidic, or any number of other things. Once we've made that decision the next step is to think hierarchically and compositionally, thinking about relative contrasts, meaning we're considering relative hue, value, and saturation contextually.

And this is something you already know something about. You experience it every day. Why are stop signs red and white? Because there's very little red in nature, so it will have a lot of contrast to its likely color environment in the country. And similarly, there's not a lot of saturated red in most cities so it'll get our attention. Why the white? Because it's really different than red, it's very light and totally unsaturated so lots of contrast, you can't not notice the word stop.

The same principle's used in advertising all the time. This photo's highly organized. Why do we go to the lips first? Highest saturation. They're also in the center. Then the sunglasses; lots of light-dark contrast, diminishing amounts of saturation and value contrast as we move to the head. And least saturation and contrast in the ground. It's all neutral. Most people will dependably move through the photo in that order.

Let's take a closer look at how artists use color hierarchically and in relation to broader compositional considerations. In this Cézanne, the pears are the focus. They're the objects. They're in the center and they overlap the table, partially obscuring it so they win out over the table. And the use of color is making a contribution, too. The pears are yellow and green, the table orange and green. Now, at first, you might think orange and green should have greater contrast because yellow and green are analogous and there's red in orange and green and red are complements. So what's going on? Well, for one thing the yellow and green in the pears is more highly saturated than the orange and green in the tabletop. Why? Because, the green has a bit of orange in it and the orange has some green. And the green and orange are also very similar in value. While the yellow and green of the pears has a higher value contrast. And the value contrast of the pears to the ground is accentuated by these thin slivers of dark green related to the pears' edges. On the underside of the pears, these act as cast shadow. Higher saturation and value contrast add up to focal zone.

Let's take a look at the Vermeer in this regard. Squint at it, it helps to suppress details. Notice that the highest contrast is one of light to dark. The light shape is composed of the woman's headscarf, head, and neck, down to the white fur front of her jacket. The light shape is framed by the similar darks of the painting behind her, the shadow side of her headscarf and dark jacket. There's not a single contrast in the painting that can top this. It makes sense. The painting's all about her. She's the focal point. And she's made so through this juxtaposition. But it's not just her head and upper torso. Vermeer wants to bring attention to what she's doing, using a balance. How does he do this? Put the hand in the center, on a diagonal, and reward it with high contrast. Again, here, value contrast. The light fingers of the chiaroscuro hand are set-off by the dark picture frame. Note the other hand, much lower contrast situation. So overall, we go first to her, her upper torso, and her right hand.

It's a narrative painting, telling a story. Though the specifics are debated, it falls into the category of the Christian Vanitas, works that, in one way or another, convey the message that life and its pleasures are transient, that the more important reality is eternal life. So she's weighing things. She's poised between the Last Judgment behind her, the riches on the table before her, the mirror reflecting youth and beauty, and the window's light that literally illuminates her. And these are precisely the things that reveal themselves next, again, through their relative contrast.

You'll note that all the detail in the side plane of the table and the patterned floor beneath it are all brought into more neutral and close-value range, less contrast, and everything's tied to the geometry of the format. He's using the color with the organization based on the armature of the rectangle. We get stresses on both the vertical and horizontal halves and as we've noted, the hand's center stage. We even get a stress along the diagonal following her gaze down through the scales to the dark blue drape in the lower left corner.

The David is also highly organized. The men form a rectangular, aggregate grouping, hinged on the center and full of active diagonals. They get the highest saturations and the highest value contrasts. And this is set up in relation to the ground. The light arms and swords are framed by the dark behind. Not surprisingly, this defines the focal zone.

Put the light thing in a dark environment and we'll look. Same idea as the white stop on the red stop sign. Or in the Vermeer, the large light shape in the woman's upper torso set against the dark ground. The women in the David form a sleepier, more horizontal, group. While the men thrust up, the women slump down. Their saturation and value contrast follow suit. Move to the architecture and saturation and value contrasts are reduced even more.

We could sum this up as a principle regarding color and composition. If you want the viewer to pay more attention to the objects than the ground, make sure the ground has less contrast of hue, value, and saturation, than the objects. That's what David is doing, and Breughel, and Eakins, and Cézanne, and even Mondrian. We've seen that, with any palette, no matter the limitations, we can create a visual hierarchy with focal areas and focal points. Equally, within any palette, and in any range of hue, value, or saturation demanded by the hierarchy, we can create the illusion of light, space, and volume.

Earlier, we noted that distance affects the way we perceive color. With distance, objects take on the color of the atmosphere. And when things are closer to us, their colors appear to have greater value contrast and greater saturation. As they recede, less.

A second principal goes like this. All else being equal, warm colors will tend to advance and cools to recede. But saturation will generally trump the effect of warm advancing and cool receding. In other words, a saturated blue bowl, a cool, will easily advance against a neutral warm—say a neutral orange wall and table. And high-value contrast can often override high saturation. We see a lot of this play out in the Eakins. The warms are predominantly in the foreground. Looking at the water, in particular, the foreground's more saturated and has greater value contrast. As we recede, it gets cooler and more neutral, more like the atmosphere. Especially the way it appears at the horizon, because, at the horizon the sky is more neutral. As we move higher in the page and forward in space the saturation of the blue increases.

We see a similar application in the David, though as we recede here, we move into the dark. Forget the figures for a moment, look at the floor. More saturation and contrast close to the picture plane. More neutral and less value contrast as we recede. Moving back to the columns and the space behind, we get even less saturation and value contrast. At an abstract level, the same thing is happening in the Mondrian. The saturated primary colors advance in front of the neutral white ground.

In the next lecture, we'll talk about creating volume and put all this knowledge into practice in some complex drawing projects.

# Color: Color Drawing Projects
## Lecture 30

We concluded the last lecture with a discussion of atmospheric perspective and saw that we can create the illusion of spatial depth using color. We'll continue in this lecture with a discussion of how we make objects appear three-dimensional. Then, we'll move into a number of drawing projects that use color.

### Color and Volume

If we draw a block with all planes identical in color, we get relative flatness. But if we make a differentiation in color, we can get dimension.

We can create volume in any palette and in any range of values. We can also increase the contrast, lighten or darken the value range, or shift into another hue. And we can accompany a change in value with a change in saturation, making the color more saturated in the light and less so away from the light. We can also modulate the hue in this progression across the planes of an object. We could start with a warm, say an orange, on the plane closest to the light, and move to a cool, say a blue, on the plane farthest from the light.

Artists use specific palettes to create a mood and quality of light, and they use relative contrasts of hue, value, and saturation to create a visual hierarchy of focal points. Within the given palette and hierarchy, artists create the illusion of space, volume, and light. Thus, it's reasonable to start a drawing by asking: What's the intended mood or flavor? Make a determination about mood and palette first, and let all else follow.

If you're working from observation, use the same principles. That means carefully considering the color and value of all the elements in a still life as you set it up, including the wall, table, and lighting. When working from a landscape, it means organizing the color you see and interpreting it in a way that serves the mood of the drawing.

## Pastels and Palettes

In these lectures on color, we've outlined different palettes, including analogous, complementary, and so on. Working with a palette means making a selection of pastels to use for a given drawing. The goal here is to limit the number of colors while maintaining a range from light to dark and saturated to neutral. This yields both cohesion and the opportunity for contrast. For instance, for an orange-blue complementary drawing, you might select a cool blue; a warm blue; a saturated orange; an earth orange; a dark, neutral brown; a gray; and a white. Note that this selection includes a warm and a cool version of your cool color, a saturated and an earth version of your warm color, a dark, and two neutrals, giving you the opportunity to mix a great range of colors. For analogous palettes, follow the same model. For instance, for a yellow-green palette, you could select a saturated yellow; an earth yellow; a cool green; a warm green; a dark, neutral brown; a gray; and a white.

It's a good idea to create test sheets to play with the relationships of the pastels you plan to use in a given palette before making a drawing. This will give you options when you approach the drawing.

## Palette Exploration: Drawing Geometric Solids

As an exercise for this lecture, we'll do a series of drawings to explore color palettes; control hierarchy; and create space, volume, and light. Keep the compositions here simple. First, divide a rectangle along a horizontal to yield a tabletop and wall. Then, imagine a block, sphere, cylinder, cone, or other solid lit by a single light source. Next, think about mood and palette. Use value and color hierarchically so that the object is the focal point, and use color within the given palette to create the illusion of volume, space, and light. Think in four to nine steps of light as you move across the large planes of the table and wall and the object itself.

For this exercise, use colored paper, which immediately asserts mood and provides an underlying unifying hue for the drawing. This shared hue allows you to create smooth transitions where you want them. Where you don't want smooth transitions, work opaquely so that the paper is less visible. Try a number of variations of palettes and papers.

Monet loved these kinds of experiments. He often repeated the same painting or drawing over and over again but varied the light, mood, and palette. Look online to find his series of *Haystacks*, *Waterloo Bridge*, *The Houses of Parliament*, and *Rouen Cathedral*. You'll find multiple versions of each that explore color and light.

### Color Projects

Once you've made some color studies of geometric objects, try creating a still life from your imagination. The utility of working from your imagination is that you can't copy details. You have to think abstractly about the large color relationships. Start by making small, monochromatic, gestural sketches in pen or pencil to find a composition. Then, look at your single-object color studies to get ideas about possible palettes to apply to the still life and do a small color study. This can consist of just smudges of color that relate to the shapes in the composition. Line up your color studies and take a couple steps back to judge the overall flavor and mood. To make the drawing, use the same principles you used to draw the geometric solids. The goals of this exercise are to:

- Select a range or palette of color and value to create a mood.

- Use that palette to create a hierarchical structure that features focal areas and focal points.

- Create the illusion of volume, space, and light within the hierarchical structure.

As you work, keep in mind these key points from earlier lectures:

- First, make sure you're thinking compositionally. Be attentive to the format shape and its large divisions and to positive and negative shapes. Build your objects using shapes and geometric solids.

- Be aware of the eye height or horizon, which will indicate how much of any plane you will see.

- Work from the large decisions to the small, adding detail last.

Also make sure that your paper's color relates to the color system with which you're working. You might start with fairly neutral colors, which will allow you to attend to proportion and placement first. Once these issues have been resolved, add analogous or complementary colors, working up from lower to higher saturations.

Follow this exercise with a still life drawn from observation, but take the same care with the palette. Be prepared to drape a wall or table and be choosy with your objects and the type and direction of light. Think about how everything relates in terms of mood, hierarchy, space, and volume.

**Unnamable Color**
A common problem people have when starting out with color is that they conceive of it in terms of namable color—primaries, secondaries, and the like. These are all useful, but a command of all the grays—and the ability to see the grays as color—is all but essential.

Similarly, many beginners see a white bowl or a black hat and immediately grab the white or the black pastel to fill in that section of a drawing. But the white bowl is rarely white, and the black hat is rarely black. When we look at something that's nominally white or black, we're actually seeing a whole range of color.

Just as with value, light is the reason we see any color at all. The color that anything appears to be is directly related to the color and strength of the light source. It's also tied up with the way in which surfaces share color through reflection. When we look at any given area, we're often seeing the accumulation of multiple factors creating the instance of color. In many cases, the differences are small. For example, a gray may be just slightly warmer, cooler, darker, or lighter or more to the yellow and away from the red. The more you look analytically, the more you'll learn to see these small differences in color.

A good exercise that can help you analyze unnamable color is to draw a still life of white objects on a white table in front of a white wall. As you work, you'll find that almost nothing is truly white. Instead, there is a great deal of color, color reflection, and interaction.

Often, students believe that they're not getting as wide a range of color as they'd like in a drawing. In response, they may wind up using every pigment in their kit, resulting in a depletion of mood and hierarchy. In many cases, a better approach is to try to find more color within the palette's restrictions. Remember, color is relative. By changing an abutting color, you can make an existing color feel lighter or darker, more neutral or saturated, or warmer or cooler.

Many times, you don't need a new namable color. For example, if you're working in a red-green complementary system and you feel that your red is not projecting enough, you can modify the ground rather than adding a new color to accentuate the central red object. There's no rule here, but because most people err on the side of too many random colors, it's useful to look for some less obvious solutions.

**Additional Projects**

Make a portrait or self-portrait that brings to bear all the thinking you used in setting up your still life. Keep in mind that the environment, lighting, point of view, costume, and palette all combine to create mood and meaning. And remember, every surface can be affected by reflected color, including flesh.

Next, take a cue from Monet and go outside. Draw at different times of day under different weather conditions. A sunny day or a gloomy, overcast day each presents a palette—a defined range of color with a specific emotional thrust. After drawing several landscapes from observation, bring your drawings inside. Use these drawings, as well as your knowledge about composition, space, and color, to construct a second landscape from your imagination.

Finally, as we've noted, environmental factors influence color. Using two different color and light environments in the same drawing can be an interesting project. One classic way to approach this problem is to use an interior with a view out a window. Less common, though no less interesting, is to look from the outside into an indoor space.

## Suggested Reading

Eagle, *Pastel Painting Atelier*.

Enstice and Peters, *Drawing*, chapter 10, "Using Color in Drawing," pp. 216–229.

# Color: Color Drawing Projects
## Lecture 30—Transcript

We concluded the last lecture with a discussion of atmospheric perspective and spoke about how, using color, we can create the illusion of spatial depth. We'll continue here with a discussion of how we make objects appear three-dimensional.

If we draw a block with all planes identical in color, we get relative flatness. But make a differentiation in color, here in value, and we'll get dimension. We can create volume in any palette and in any range of values. We could increase the contrast, lighten the range, or darken it and we could shift into any hue, green, yellow, or red. Or we could move more neutral, to the warm, or neutral to the cool. Each time we've used one color and changed its value.

But we could accompany the change in value with a change in saturation, more saturated in the light, less as we move away. We could do this in the cool range and in the warm. And we could also modulate hue in this progression. Here, using complements orange and blue, progressively cooler as we move away from the light. Or we could use adjacent color, here, yellow, green, and blue, and here accompanied by diminishing saturation.

Cézanne modulates his pears from yellow through green and into a darker, less saturated green. And the ground's less saturated with less internal value contrast that the pears. In Biglin's skin, we move from a light warm to a darker, less-saturated warm, to darks that are, in places, much cooler. Like the Cézanne, the two ground shapes, have much less contrast than the figure.

The Vermeer, like the Eakins, is naturalistic. The modulation of the woman's skin is similar to Biglin's, light and warm, to darker and a bit cooler, to darker and cooler still, and the ground contains much less contrast than the figure. Each artist uses a specific palette to create a mood and quality of light. Each uses relative contrasts of hue, value, and saturation to create a visual hierarchy with focal points. And within the given palette and hierarchy each artist creates the illusion of space, volume, and light. So a reasonable procedure to follow is to ask, what's the intended mood or flavor?

Remember the photos we looked at in the last lecture. Grass isn't always green, nor is the sky blue. Make a determination about mood and palette first. Let everything else follow. If you're working from observation, use the same principles. That means carefully considering the color and value of all the elements in a still life as you set up, down to the wall, table, and lighting. When working from a landscape, it means organizing the color you see and interpreting it in a way that serves the mood of the drawing. And there are good reasons for leaning on reality even when you want a naturalistic result. Artists do this all the time. It should be clear that even very representational artists don't copy what's before them.

In our discussion of value, we noted that focusing on an object rewards it with high-value contrast and clear definition of edge. With color, we'll perceive greater saturation in the object or area receiving the eyes' focus. And this is the visual principle Vermeer uses in his treatment of the woman's head in relation to the painting behind her. He paints the painting as if he's seeing it peripherally.

Our consideration of color started with what would be termed color theory. We spoke about color abstractly. We talked about blue and red and said that mixing the two makes violet. But when we use pigments, like pastel, we have many blues and reds to choose from, each a different color. And not all blues and reds make violet. So I'd suggest making tests to see how your pigments actually behave.

Here's one way. Make swatches of your colors running in horizontal rows across your page. I've made four rows of 14 colors with space below the second, third, and fourth row. I've used a yellow, a center green, a center blue, a blue-violet, a red-violet, a center red, a center orange, a yellow earth, an orange earth, a red earth, a dark brown, a black, a gray, and a white.

Select one pastel—I'll use yellow—and mix it with all the colors in all four rows. After each one, wipe the pastel to keep it clean. The first row I'll leave as is. The second, I'll blend with a cotton swab. Then use the material on the swab to create a new swatch in the space. In the next row, I'll add yellow's complement, violet. And, again, mix and sample with the swab. In the final row, I'll add a neutral gray. And once again, mix and sample to create new swatches. Having done this, you'll likely think of variations of this test. For instance, you could try applying a color, spraying it with workable fixative, and then applying another color on top, semi-transparently. It's pretty endless. There's an amazing amount you'll learn by putting each stick through its paces.

In these color lectures, I've outlined different palettes, analogous, complementary, etc. Working with a palette means making a selection of pastels to use for a given drawing. The goal is to limit the number of colors while maintaining a range from light to dark and saturated to neutral. This yields both cohesion and the opportunity for abundant contrast.

For instance, for an orange/blue complementary drawing I might select a cool blue, a warm blue, a saturated orange, an earth orange—like a raw sienna—a dark neutral brown, a gray, and a white. For a red/green system, I could select a cool green, a warm green, a saturated red, an earth red—like a burnt sienna—and the dark brown, gray, and white. And for a yellow/violet: a blue-violet, a red-violet, a saturated yellow, an earth yellow—like a yellow ochre—and the brown, gray and white.

In each case, you have a warm and cool version of your cool, a saturated and earth version of your warm, a dark, and two neutrals. This gives you the opportunity to mix a great range of color. Some might add a light and dark version of each color for greater value contrast.

For analogous palettes, you could follow the same model. For instance, for a yellow/green palette I could select a saturated yellow, an earth yellow—like a yellow ochre—a cool green, a warm green, and the brown, gray, and white.

As a variant, I could leave out the cool green and the resulting drawing would feel warmer. It's a great idea to create test sheets to play through the relationships of the sticks you'd use in a given palette before making a drawing. This will give you options when you approach the drawing.

Now I'd like you to do a series of drawings to explore color palettes, control hierarchy, and create space, volume, and light. So you can really concentrate on this, and it's plenty, I'd like you to compose very simply. Take a rectangle and divide it along a horizontal yielding a tabletop and wall. Then imagine a block, sphere, cylinder, cone, or other solid lit by a single light source.

Then, think mood and palette. Employ value and color hierarchically so that the object is the focal point. And use color within the given palette to create the illusion of volume, space, and light. Think in four to nine steps of light as you move across the large planes of the table and wall and the object itself. I'd suggest using colored paper. The great thing about colored paper is that it immediately asserts color and mood. It also provides an underlying unifying hue for the drawing. You can use this to help create smooth transitions where you want them because you have a shared underlying color. Where you don't, work opaquely so that the paper is less visible.

A pack of mixed sheets of colored construction paper or a pad of colored pastel paper will work well. It's difficult to handle the pastel at a small scale so I'd recommend paper that's at least medium size. Common measures are 11 × 14 inches, 12 × 16 inches, and 12 × 18 inches. Canson Mi Teintes makes a selection of papers in larger 19 × 25-inch sheets.

I'll outline 10 palettes to start with and illustrate this with student examples. A lighter warm paper with analogous color. Here, yellow. To begin a drawing like this, it makes sense to start linearly with a light yellow. A lighter warm paper with complimentary color. That could be yellow-violet, orange-blue, or red-green. A lighter cool paper with analogous color. Here, blue to violet to violet-pink.

For the complementary and analogous drawings use the palettes I just outlined to help you choose your pastels. A light cool paper with complimentary color. Here, orange-blue. Note how the pastel is used transparently in the tabletop and walls so we get optical mixing. The oranges in the wall become much more neutral than in the saturated front plane where it's applied opaquely. A darker warm paper with analogous color. Here, red to orange and yellow. A darker warm paper with complimentary color. Here a red-green on a neutral red earth tone paper. For a red-green compliment, you could use a central red, burnt sienna, two greens, a dark brown, and white. A darker cool paper with analogous color. Here, blue to green. A darker cool paper with complimentary color like orange on a dark blue ground. This uses one orange, one blue, and white, and the blue of the paper itself. A neutral earth paper with analogous color. A neutral earth paper with complimentary color. Here, yellow-violet, starting on a neutral yellow earth ground. It's actually a piece of cardboard.

Over time, work your way through all the primaries and secondaries in both their analogous and complimentary palettes. Once you've covered the bases, extend out, and make further experiments. Start with a yellow monochromatic palette and extend it to a darker red, like a burnt sienna, a small change but a very different feel from the straight-up yellow monochrome. Or take an orange-blue and extend into yellow for the lightest tones, combining the idea of an analogous palette with a complimentary one. Or straddling certain terrain, here, we're starting with an earth-tone ground. It has both an orange and a red character. Overall, the palette has aspects of an analogous red-violet-blue but also feels a bit like an orange-blue compliment.

There are endless variations to be played with here. Monet loved these kinds of experiments. He repeated the same painting or drawing over and over again but varied the light, mood, and palette. Look up his *Haystacks*, the *Waterloo Bridge*, and the *Houses of Parliament*. There are multiple versions of each that explore color and light.

And, of course, there's the *Rouen Cathedral*. Here, pretty much a split-complement, yellow to blue-violet-red. The façade and sky are pretty cool and shady, here in full sunshine with a more-or-less orange-blue complement.

We can take any palette—monochrome, analogous, complementary, or earth tone—and make it light, mid-tone, or dark. Similarly, we can make any of these highly saturated, mid-saturation, or very neutral. So the number of potential palettes is nearly inexhaustible.

Once you've made these first color studies try creating a still life from your imagination. Start by making small monochromatic gestural sketches in pen or pencil to find a composition. Then take a look at the single-object color studies to get ideas about possible palettes to apply to the still life.

Then do a small color study. It needn't be highly articulated or detailed. It can consist of smudges of color that relate to the shapes in the composition—shouldn't take more than a couple of minutes—and you might want to try a couple variations. Then line up your color and take a couple steps back. You're trying to judge the overall color and mood. Choose the one that you think works best.

Depending on the complexity of the drawing, you may want to get larger, better-quality paper for this, and the following projects, like those 19 × 25-inch Canson Mi Teintes. To make the drawing use the same principles you used to draw the geometric solids. Here are some student examples: one, in an analogous palette, another, complimentary. You'll note how the darkness of the paper sets-up the mood of the drawing.

The utility of working from your imagination is that you can't copy details. You have to think abstractly about the large color relationships. The goal is to: Select a range or palette of color and value to create a mood; use that palette to create a hierarchical structure that creates focal areas and focal points; and within the hierarchical structure, create the illusion of volume, space, and light.

There are a number of key points from earlier lectures that you want to be sure to consider. First, make sure you're thinking compositionally. Be attentive to: the format shape and its large divisions; those positive and negative shapes; build your objects using shapes and geometric solids; be aware of the eye height and the horizon—this will indicate how much of any plane you'll be able to see; work from the large decisions to the small, detail come to last.

Make sure your paper's color relates to the color system you're working with. This is an excellent example. The neutral tone works as a base for the overall color mood of the drawing. It's useful to start fairly neutral and monochrome. This lets you attend to proportion and placement first. Once these issues have been attended to, add analogous or complimentary colors, working up from lower to higher saturations.

Follow this with a still life drawn from observation but take the same care with palette. Be prepared to drape a wall or table and be choosy with your objects, and type, and direction of light. Think how everything relates in terms of mood, hierarchy, space, and volume. If you don't have enough colored objects on hand, go to a local thrift store and pick-up an assortment of objects that can complete different color palettes.

Then try an interior. This is a pastel by Norman Lundin, very much in the neutral range, naturalistic, and at the same time, abstract: four large interlocking shapes. The floor and ceiling of a similar mid-dark value sandwich the light warmer walls in between. The highlighted edge of the central wall and its reflections in the ceiling and floor become the focal area, the very light highlight near the floor, the focal point.

The Lundin is, in one sense, typical of many naturalistic works in that it depends on very neutral color. It looks nothing like the primaries and secondaries in the color wheel. We begin to get neutral color like we find in the Lundin at the very inner and outer rings of a more complex wheel that gets into the tints and shades of a given hue. But even here, the color is more saturated than what we find in Lundin's interior. That's because most of the colors of things we routinely see have no common name.

We could say that, in the beginning, there was yellow, red, and blue, and they begat orange, green, and violet, and in the next generation they begat yellow-orange, orange-red, red-violet, etc. But the colors we're talking about now, these very neutral colors, though they're related to these early progenitors, they occur many generations later.

Van Gogh, quite aware of this fact, wrote in an 1885 letter:

How typical that saying is about the figures of Millet: "Son paysan semble peint avec la terre qu'il ensemence!" "His peasant looks like he was painted with the earth he's sowing." How exact and how true. And how important it is to know how to mix on the palette those colors which have no name, and yet are the real foundation of everything.

A common problem people have when starting out with color is that they conceive of it in terms of namable color, primaries, secondaries, and the like. They're all useful, but a command of all the grays, and seeing the grays as color, are all but essential.

Similarly, many beginners see a white bowl or a black hat and immediately grab the white or the black pastel and start filling-in that section of their drawing. But the white bowl's rarely white and the black hat's rarely black. When we look at a nominally white or off-white wall, we're actually seeing a whole range of color. The walls in this photo are all painted the same color, a warm off-white. But because of context, they appear as different hues and saturations. The primary light source's out of the frame. It's a window, below, on the left wall. So that wall is darker, partly silhouetted. The ceiling and right wall receive light directly from the window and are predictably lighter.

But the walls are affecting one another. Can you see how the dark of the left wall's reflected into the corner of the ceiling and right wall? As we move away from this dark reflection, we get lighter where the maximum light from the window reaches both surfaces. As we move farther to the right, the strength of the window's light diminishes and the two surfaces get progressively darker. We also see the effects of simultaneous contrast on the left wall, looks darker against the two light walls than in its interior. And the interior is receiving reflected light from both the lighter parts of the ceiling and right wall.

As to color, it's all very neutral. Here are six swatches sampled from the walls. The left column is from the left wall, the center column from the ceiling, the right column from the right wall. The top row samples are taken from the central corner where the three walls meet, the bottom row, from the lightest part of each surfaces' interior. The left column's darker than the center and right. That's expected. The left wall's in partial silhouette. And the top row's darker than the bottom. That's expected, too. That represents the corner versus the lightest part of each wall. So those are the value relationships. But can you see these as colors? As related to hues—to reds, oranges, blues, and violets? That's the goal. As Van Gogh says, "They're the real foundation of everything."

We'll look at the bottom row first. The ceiling and right wall are not only lighter but much cooler than the left wall. Their hues are neutrals more toward the blue-violet. The lightest part of the left wall lists warmer, more toward the orange. Why? Well, the ceiling and right wall receive daylight from the window, and daylight, if there's no direct sun, is cool in color. And the lightest part of the left wall is warmer than the lightest part of the ceiling or right wall but it looks cool compared to the left wall's corner. So all this is relative.

Let's look at the top row, overall, warmer than the bottom row. Why are the ceiling and right wall warmer in the corner? They're getting the reflection of the left wall. And why are they still cooler than the left wall? They're still getting more daylight than the left. Color is mixing on the surfaces. The color of the light's mixing with the reflected color of the warm wall.

Just as with value, light is the reason we see any color at all. The color that anything, or any part of a thing appears to be, is directly related to the color and strength of the light source and it's also tied up with the way in which surfaces share color through reflection. When we look at any given area, we're often seeing the accumulation of multiple factors creating the instance of color.

Often the distances are small. The gray is just slightly warmer, or cooler, or darker, or lighter, or more to the yellow, away from the red. You've already seen how we can use our compliments, earth tones, and neutrals to create these chromatic grays. And the more you look analytically, the more you'll learn to see small differences in walls and ceilings and in art, too.

This is just what we find in the Canaletto. The shifts of hue and value in the tall tower consist of taking a neutral a bit this way, then that. Same in the David. While many people are drawn to the drama of the figure, the subtle changes of value and chroma in the architecture create a compelling underlying drama if you know what to look for in the light tones, and in the mid-range, and in the darks.

There's a good exercise that can help you analyze unnamable color. The project involves drawing a still life of white objects on a white table in front of a white wall. A variant is to draw a white toilet on a white tile floor in front of a white wall. In both cases, you'll find that almost nothing's white, just like the white walls we looked at earlier there's a lot of color, color reflection, and interaction. This is a kind of drawing that can be done in several different palettes. If you do this with an incandescent light source, an orange/blue complementary system and related neutrals can be a good place to start.

Another common problem students experience is to feel that they're not getting as wide a range of color as they'd like in a drawing. So they wind up using every pigment in their kit. Often, a better approach is to try to find more color within the palette's restrictions. Remember, color's relative. By changing an abutting color, you can make an existing color feel lighter or darker, or more neutral or more saturated, or warmer or cooler—here greener or bluer. And it's often not a new namable color we need.

For example, you're in a red-green complementary system and you feel your red is not projecting enough. So you want to add a new stick. Maybe some violet or yellow to accentuate the central red object. But keep Van Gogh's words in mind. "How important it is to know how to mix those colors which have no name." So instead, you modify the ground. You pull it into a slightly greener neutral and the red projects in a much more dominant way. There's no rule here but since most people err on the side of too many random colors, this may help you discover some less obvious solutions and avoid some common pitfalls.

Another great project is a portrait or self-portrait. But bring all the thinking you used in setting up your still life to bear here. There's a passage in E. L. Doctorow's novel, *City of God*. He writes:

> After the set is lit, the camera is positioned, the actors have taken their place, costumed, their hair dressed to indicate economic class, education, age, social status, virtue or the lack of it, 95 percent of the meaning of a scene is established before anyone says a word.

It's actually very good advice to anyone using a model. The environment, the lighting, point of view, costume, and, of course, palette all combine to create mood and meaning.

Remember, every surface can be affected by reflected color, flesh included. In the Vermeer, note how the color of the jacket reflects up into the shadow side of the woman's arm and the orange skirt reflects up into the fur trim. So compose your set-up with all this in mind. And if you belong to a life-drawing group bring your pastels and apply specific palettes in your drawings.

Here we have an analogous orange, yellow, green on a neutral pink ground. High saturations are saved for the figure and we get high-value contrast between the figure and the dramatic cast shadow. The green of the wall is applied transparently and mixes optically with the neutral pink paper to create neutral green-grays.

Then take a cue from Monet and go outside. Draw at different times of day under different weather conditions. A sunny day or a gloomy overcast day, each present a palette, a defined range of color with a specific emotional thrust. After drawing several landscapes from observation, bring your drawings inside. Use these drawings, as well as your knowledge about composition, space, and color to construct a second landscape from your imagination.

We've noted environmental factors that influence color. Using two different color and light environments in the same drawing can be an interesting project. One classic way to approach this problem is to use an interior with a view out a window. Less common, though no less interesting is to look from the outside, in.

Another great exercise is to adopt a palette from a drawing, painting, film still, or other source that piques your interest. You can eyeball the color and make some swatches with your pastels. You could also use digital sampling to distil a palette.

Congratulations. This lecture concludes our study of the major formal elements of drawing. A good deal of the art in drawing has to do with how you balance all these pieces. Central to doing this well is having a sense about what you're trying to bring out. Like a composer orchestrating a piece of music or a director editing a movie scene.

A well-executed drawing, at an abstract level, controls the way the viewer moves through it. In this sense, all drawings are abstract. And it's through these relationships that meaning, broadly defined, emerges. I've chosen three drawings to review some major considerations in this regard. The first is the Degas, a quick scribble done on a sleepy night in a brothel. While quick and gestural, every mark and smudge is made in reference to the geometry of the format shape. The woman and the man ride one diagonal. As a counterbalance, the table straddles a diagonal the format central horizontal quarters creating two mirrored wedge shapes: top and bottom.

Though there's not a lot of shading, we get an impressive sensation of depth. There are three depths of space. The woman, table, and bottle occupy the foreground. They clearly overlap the man in the mid-ground. The background is signaled by the diagonal line behind the man. That indicates a visual event, perhaps furniture, or molding, seen peripherally on a wall, behind him. The use of diminishing value, line weights, and level of detail all work to create the illusion of a depth of space.

We also experience volume, primarily through cross contour. Many of the internal marks in the figures, while describing drapery or a part of the body, are really creating volume. Note the strap over the woman's shoulder, and the many marks tracing over her back, and the internal line on the man's shoulder. This line gives us two planes, top of shoulder and front of chest. The highest value contrast is associated with the woman's head: focal point. Her body's next. That's the greater focal area.

Here's, Xià Guī's *Mountain Market, Clear with Rising Mist*. The format's divided at the horizontal half, with stresses at the horizontal quarters. There are stresses at the vertical half and quarters, too. We get space and atmosphere through a deft manipulation of line, mark, and value. The closer marks are more pronounced, tightly spaced, and darker. As we recede in space, value and detail are subsumed by the atmosphere.

Last, the Eakins watercolor. Every piece is tied to the geometry of the format, to the horizontal half, vertical half, horizontal quarter, and the diagonals. The ground, without Biglin, his scull, and their reflection, is like a whisper. All the light-dark contrasts, the contrasts of saturation are reserved for the main subject in relationship to the ground. All the strong directions, the important diagonals, are similarly reserved for Biglin. He's the solid, weighty thing, against all the water and atmosphere. His head and torso are the focal point, with the scull the focal area.

As you work through the projects using color, ask yourself what you're trying to bring out and keep all these elements of formal language in mind. They'll help you get there.

# The Figure: A Canon of Proportions
## Lecture 31

The next four lectures focus on the figure. We'll start with constructive figure drawing. As the name implies, this involves building the figure using a set of principles. A great deal of drawing involves proportion and measure, and that applies here, too. We want to control the figure's proportions. Thus, we'll start with linear proportions for the figure—what's termed a *canon of proportions*. Then, we'll apply volumetric solids to make the figure dimensional. Next, we'll look at both the skeletal system and the major muscles in the body to see how we can use anatomical landmarks based on this knowledge. We'll also see how we can locate a figure in a believable spatial environment by relating what we've studied about the figure to linear perspective. In the final lecture in this section, we'll discuss a number of drawing projects involving the figure.

### Human Proportions

Students routinely ask what the correct proportions are for drawing a figure. Both the historical record and nature would indicate that there's no right answer to this question. Indeed, in his book *Master Class in Figure Drawing*, the teacher and artist Robert Beverly Hale wrote, "The forms of the body have no exact shape and never have had except in the mind of the individual artist. They have always varied according to the knowledge, the style, and the time of the artist. They have always been created by the artist to conform to his ultimate purpose. … Drawing is not a mere act of copying, but a highly creative act controlled by the artist's expressive intent."

If we think of almost any artist, we can see that each interprets or reinvents proportions of both male and female figures to suit his or her own purpose. As Leonardo put it, "We, by our arts, may be called the grandsons of God." In this field, you get to make any kind of figure you want to.

To some extent, the human proportions we see in art are related to the wide range of proportions we see in nature. Think, for a moment, about runway models, sumo wrestlers, ballerinas, NBA players, and jockeys; these categories evince widely different sets of proportions. Although you may notice fewer extremes, the same is true of any random group of people you see at the supermarket or on the subway.

In the early 1500s, Dürer became very interested in human proportions. He wrote, "I know of no one who has written about a system of human proportion, except a man, Jacobus [Jacopo de Barbari], a native of Venice. He showed me how to construct a man and a woman based on measurements. I was greatly fascinated by his skill and decided to master it." And master it he did. Dürer made hundreds of drawings of variations on human proportion while experimenting with different methods of figure construction. This work culminated in a lengthy study of the subject, published in 1528 and titled *Four Books on Human Proportion*. Like his other book on drawing, this work is all about measure.

Returning to the question about correct proportions, there is no one answer—not in art and not in the world in which we live. There are endless combinations. But following in Dürer's footsteps, we can start with one set of proportions, then play with variations.

## Constructing Human Figures

Before we begin drawing complex figures, it's useful to return to some of the procedures introduced in one of the first lectures. We found that we could draw complex still-life objects more easily by breaking them down into simple constituent shapes—rectangles, trapezoids, hemispheres, and so on. We'll follow that same idea as a first project in drawing the human figure.

For this project, we'll adopt the method Dürer used in his 1528 book, drawing three views of the same figure: a front, or anterior, view; a side, or lateral, view; and a rear, or posterior, view. After completing this drawing, you'll have a ready method for inflating, compressing, lengthening, or shortening any of the pieces you want, and with practice, you'll be able to create figures with the kinds of proportions you want to draw.

The general steps for this exercise are as follows:

- Because humans are basically bilaterally symmetrical, draw a vertical centerline.

- Establish height proportions. Divide the centerline into segments with horizontal lines to mark locations for anatomical events, such as the top of the shoulders, bottom of the chest, and so on.

- Establish width measurements, that is, distances to the right and left from the centerline that define the width of the shoulders, the width at the top of the pelvis, and so on.

- Draw 16 specific shapes to block in the figure's proportions, then introduce contrapposto to make the figure feel more natural.

- Introduce cross-contours and geometric volumes to create the illusion of three-dimensionality.

- Integrate the cross-contours with contours to create a more naturalistic figure.

As is common in figure drawing, we will use the head as our standard unit of measure.

**Variations in Male and Female Proportions**
There are clear differences between the male and female body. Of course, the obvious ones are breasts and sexual organs, but there are also differences of measure that affect overall shape. Chief among these is the shape of the pelvis. The male pelvis has a greater height-to-width ratio. In the female, the ratio is greater width to height. In addition, the opening in the male pelvis is more constricted, and the male pubic arch is more angular and acute. The female's is more curved and obtuse.

From the Renaissance to contemporary superhero comics, artists and illustrators have also adopted certain conventions for male and female figures. Common among them are the following:

- The male is drawn taller, and the female is shorter.

- Overall, the female is drawn more curved, and the male, more angular.

- The male's shoulder width is greater than that of the female

- The female's hips are wider.

- When we look at the relationship between shoulders and hips, the male has wide shoulders to narrower hips. The woman's shoulders and hips are more equal in measure.

- The female's torso and limbs are made slimmer in ratio to their height.

We see some of these same differences in the images below by Leonardo and Botticelli.

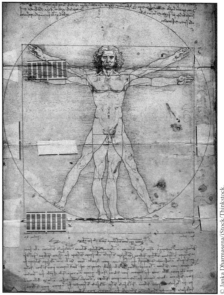

## Contrapposto

The figure we've been drawing is in a static position, facing straight forward, with everything lining up horizontally and vertically. But we don't generally stand like that. Instead, we tend to put more weight on one foot. This position is called *contrapposto*. The shoulders, hips, and knees line up on a diagonal. With a standing figure, the hip taking the weight goes up, while the other hip is low. The bottom of the pelvis and the knees follow suit. The shoulders move opposite to the hips and thighs.

Try to apply this idea in your drawing of the figure. You'll note that the angles of the shapes change rather than the shapes themselves. The whole assemblage rotates together.

In this lecture, we've seen how we can use a canon of proportions to draw a figure. We've also seen how small changes in proportion and position can influence the feel of the figure. We'll continue this drawing in the next lecture, adding two more views, posterior and lateral, and we'll learn how to make the figure feel more three-dimensional.

## Suggested Reading

Dürer, *Four Books on Human Proportions*.

Dürer and Strauss, *The Human Figure by Albrecht Dürer*.

Loomis, *Figure Drawing for All It's Worth*, "Ideal Proportion," pp. 26–29.

Reed, *The Figure*, pp. 9–19.

Winslow, *Classic Human Anatomy*, "The Proportions of the Whole Figure," pp. 249–261.

# The Figure: A Canon of Proportions
## Lecture 31—Transcript

The next four lectures focus on the figure. We'll start with constructive figure drawing. As the name implies, it involves building the figure using a set of principles. A lot of drawing involves proportion and measure, and that applies here, too. We want to control the figure's proportions so we'll start with linear proportions for the figure, what's termed a canon of proportions.

Then we'll apply volumetric solids to make the figure volumetric. Next, we'll look at both the skeletal system and the major muscles in the body and see how we can use anatomical landmarks based on this knowledge. Then we'll see how we can locate a figure in a believable spatial environment by relating what we've studied to linear perspective. In the final lecture in this section, we'll discuss a number of drawing projects involving the figure, both from the imagination and from observation.

Students routinely ask me what the correct proportions are for drawing a figure. Both the historical record and nature would indicate there's no right answer to that question. We've been drawing people for a very long time. In summer 2001, *ARTnews Magazine* ran an article on the oldest drawing of a person that had yet been discovered. It dated back about 32,000 years and was found in the Chauvet Cave in the south of France.

It was drawn in charcoal on the cave's rock surface. The article describes the drawing as depicting the hips, pubic area, and legs of a woman. Jean Clottes, a leading French scholar involved with Chauvet described it as "an exceptional image of the lower body of a woman... associated with a bison figure."

The drawing's not unlike some of the sculpted female figures, colloquially referred to as Venus figurines. These have been found across Europe and date from about 40,000 years ago to as recently as about 12,000 years ago. The Chauvet drawing's also, not unlike graffiti I've seen in several of the men's rooms at the university where I teach. A lot of the work surrounding the nude has, unsurprisingly, has had to do with sex, from Chauvet to Picasso to 1950s pin-up art and anime. The point is, artists, from the very beginning, have drawn the body with an expressive idea, or aesthetic, in mind. And that has, to a large degree, determined the kinds of proportions used.

As a teenager, I had the good fortune to study figure drawing with the artistic anatomy with Robert Beverly Hale at the Art Students League in New York. He was a knowledgeable teacher and artist and the first curator of American Painting and Sculpture at the Metropolitan Museum. In the book *Master Class in Figure Drawing*, which was based on his teaching, he wrote:

> The forms of the body have no exact shape and never have had except in the mind of the individual artist. They have always varied according to the knowledge, the style, and the time of the artist. They have always been created by the artist to conform to his ultimate purpose. … Drawing is not a mere act of copying, but a highly creative act controlled by the artist's expressive intent.

It echoes the sentiment expressed by Leonardo, that tracing nature, while useful, doesn't fulfill, in his words, the final aim of this science. He goes on to tell us what's important for artists, is being able to reason about nature with their minds. That echoes Hale's concept of ultimate purpose. Of course, we can't know the ultimate aim of the person who drew that first female figure in the Chauvet cave but the choices in the depiction, like those in the Venus figurines, are very specific.

A look back at two Renaissance versions of female figures bear out Hale's assertion about the forms of the body having no exact shape. Botticelli favors a tall, lithe, model-like woman. Michelangelo, who was 11 when Botticelli painted his *Birth of Venus*, quite another, Eve's been pumping iron. There are few women I've seen in my many decades at the gym who could match her pecs, lats, and triceps.

And if you think of Rubens, El Greco, Ingres, Modigliani, Soutine, Freud, well, each interprets or reinvents proportions, of both their female and male figures, to suit their own purpose. As Leonardo put it, "We, by our arts may be called the grandsons of God." In this field, you get to make any kind of figure you want.

And cartoonists do the same. From Superheroes to the Simpsons to Anime, each world relies on its own set of proportions. And that's related to the wide range of human proportions we see in nature. To point to some extremes, runway models, sumo wrestlers, ballerinas, NBA players, and jockeys each evince widely different sets of proportions. While less extreme, it's also true of any random group of people you see at the supermarket or on the subway.

In the early 1500s, Dürer became very interested in human proportions. He wrote, "I know of no one who has written about a system of human proportion, except a man, Jacobus, a native of Venice." That would be the Italian Jacopo de Barbari. Dürer went on, "He showed me how to construct a man and a woman based on measurements. I was greatly fascinated by his skill and decided to master it." And master it he did. He made hundreds of drawings playing through myriad variations on human proportion while experimenting with different methods of figure construction.

This culminated in a lengthy volume on the subject. Published in 1528, it was titled, *Four Books on Human Proportion*. Like his other book on drawing, it's all about measure. He investigated dozens of different body types, from male, very thin; to female, as he titled her stout; to small children and just about everything else in between. So coming back to the question about correct proportions, there's no one answer—not in art, not in the world in which we live in. There are endless combinations. But following in Dürer's footsteps, we can start with one set and then play variations.

Before we get into the drawing itself, I want to return to some of the procedures introduced in one of the very first lectures. We found that we could draw complex still life objects more easily by breaking them down to simple constituent shapes—rectangles, trapezoids, hemispheres, etc.—each shape drawn with a single contour. Worked well for still life objects and it will work well with figures, too. Dürer points the way.

So grab a pen or pencil and some paper and draw along with me here. We can conceive of the body as consisting of 10 primary parts or shapes. With repetitions for the arms, legs, hands, and feet, 16 shapes in all. Let's start with the largest bone mass. Our first shape, a trapezoid for the rib cage and upper torso. Our second, a smaller, inverted trapezoid for the pelvis and lower torso, about half the size of the upper torso. Then the lower appendages; the legs and feet. Our third shape, a longer thinner trapezoid, one for each thigh. Our fourth, a narrower one for the lower legs. A fifth, a trapezoid or wedge for the feet. Number six, a subtle trapezoid for the neck. Number seven, a trapezoid for the head. Now, the upper appendages of the arms. Number eight, another thin trapezoid for the upper arm. Number nine, another for the lower arm. And number 10, a small trapezoid for the palm of the hand. We could add two more lines for the shoulders and others for the fingers. Some people prefer to use ovoids instead of trapezoids, but same idea. In any case, 10 simple shapes, you get a figure.

Each shape represents a body part that moves independently. You can move your upper torso without moving your hips. And you can move your lower arm without moving your upper arm. Internally, though, within each of these shapes, with the exception of the head, hands, and feet, there's not a lot of movement because these shapes correlate with inflexible bone. The forearm, pelvis, or thigh can't fold or bend, at least, not unless the bone's broken.

For our first figure project, we'll adopt the method Dürer used in his 1528 book. We'll draw three views of the same figure. In the center of the page a front, or anterior, view, to one side, a side, or lateral, view, and to the other, a rear, or posterior, view. After completing this drawing, you'll have a ready method for inflating, compressing, lengthening, or shortening any of the pieces you want and with practice, create figures with the kinds of proportions you want to draw.

In the still life example, we used a vertical centerline. It made sense because many of our objects were bilaterally symmetrical. Dürer does the same for his figure studies, not surprising. While not as symmetrical as bottles, were enough so that using a centerline helps. And I should mention, we're going back to line, now—no value, no shading, no mark making, and no color, just like Dürer. That's because we want to define proportions. Using value, mark making, or color will at least for now just complicate things.

Let me take you through the steps. First, we'll establish height proportions. You'll notice that Dürer has horizontal lines dividing his vertical centerline into segments. These vertical measures mark locations for anatomical events, top of the shoulders, bottom of the chest, that kind of thing. The second step is to establish width measurements. These are the distances right and left from the centerline. They'll define the width of the shoulders or the width at the top of the pelvis. Once we have these measures plotted, we'll draw 16 shapes, blocking-in the figure's proportions. Next, we'll talk about male/female variations and introduce contrapposto. And you'll be able to make modifications so that your figure feels less robotic, more natural.

At this point, the figure will still look pretty flat. Not surprising, we've only been using contour. Step four is to make your figure begin to feel 3D by introducing cross contours and geometric volumes. Our final step in this part of the drawing, step five, will be to integrate the cross contours with the contours to give us a more naturalistic figure.

So, let's start with a fresh sheet of 18 × 24-inch paper in the landscape position. Draw two horizontal lines across the page, the first two inches from the top of the page, the second two inches from the bottom. These are construction lines so draw light and thin. A well-sharpened 2H pencil or a mechanical pencil with a similar lead would work well.

Next, three vertical centerlines—one for each view of the figure. The first, for the anterior or front view, will go in the center at the 12-inch mark. Then six inches to the right, we'll put another for the lateral view. And six inches to the left, a third, for the posterior view. Now we're ready to create our measures along the vertical axis.

You'll remember that in one of the lectures on proportion we introduced the idea of a standard unit of measure, something in the drawing that we use to measure everything else. It's very common in figure drawing to use the head as the standard unit of measure. In fact, Dürer titles or annotates his figure studies with just such descriptions. Like this drawing titled *Strong, handsome man of eight headlengths*. Like Dürer, we'll construct a figure of eight head lengths. This means the length of this figure's body will be equal to eight heads stacked-up.

We'll start with the front view. Try this by eye first. Divide the line in two with a light thin horizontal line, oh, about four inches wide. Next, divide the upper half in two, then the lower half. Eyeball it then make any corrections necessary. Once again, divide each section in two. You should have eight equal divisions. Take some time to adjust, as needed. It's very good eye training. When you're done check with a ruler. Each unit should be an inch and three-quarters. Then number your head heights. The bottom of the first is one, the bottom of the second two, and so on.

Let's take another look at the Dürer to see what occurs at each head height. The first head ends at the bottom of the chin. The second takes us just about to the nipples. The third's the navel and waist. The fourth's the figure's vertical center, just about the crotch and bottom of the pelvis. More or less clear landmarks for the upper part of the body, the next three are a little less tidy. Number five is about mid-thigh. Number six falls below the knee at the top of the calf. Seven leaves us just below the calf muscle. And the chin of head number eight falls in line with the soles of the feet meeting the ground plane.

So let's map something similar on our armature. At the bottom of head one, we'll note chin; at two, nipples; at three, navel; at four, center, bottom of pelvis, and crotch; at five, mid-thigh; at six, bottom of knee and top of calf; at seven, below calf; and at eight, soles of feet.

We've got a good start mapping proportions. But to locate our 16 body-part shapes, a couple other measures will be useful. Let's create a location for the shoulders about a quarter to one-third of a head below the chin. Next, bottom of the rib cage, a similar measure above the navel. Then, the top of the pelvis just below the navel. Then, the center of the knees. About a quarter head above head six. And the ankles between one-third and one-half head above the soles of the feet.

Now, we need some widths. We'll start with the width of the head itself. Let's make that three-quarter of a head length. Make two vertical lines on either side of the centerline to mark the distance. For a width at the shoulders, imagine two head heights flipped horizontal, one head in each direction out from the center, from the sternum. We'll add widths at the bottom of the rib cage and top of the pelvis. The first, a bit less than two-thirds of a head height turned horizontal in either direction from the centerline, the second just a bit wider. The base of the pelvis will be wider, but not as wide as the shoulders, something less than a full head height in either direction.

We're ready to begin to block in the figure. We'll start with the largest shape, encompassing the shoulders and rib cage. Draw a trapezoid. Next, the lower torso, another trapezoid, and we can add a line on either side of the torso to connect the upper with the lower part. Then the thighs, trapezoids to the knee. Now two more, offset just a bit for the lower legs. And another two for the feet. Then another trapezoid for the head. Let's take a look at the neck. Here, an anatomical model will be helpful. When we're looking at the neck straight on it can be deceptive. If you were to outline the figure in this position, the neck would appear to be rather short, about a quarter of a head height.

But if we look from the side, we see the true extent of the neck. It's like a cylinder that meets the back of the skull in the rear and terminates at the clavicle in the front. Feel those two points on your own neck. Touch one with one hand, the other with the other. You'll get a sense of the distance. Take the finger that's touching the point of intersection with the back of the skull and pull it around your head, past your ear, to the front plane of your face. The top of the back of the neck is at about the same height as the cheekbone and about the center of the nose. Also of note, the top of the neck in the front is lower than in the back, same with the bottom of the neck so the full extent of the neck can be a half a head or so.

Coming back to our drawing, we'll draw the shape of the neck as a subtle trapezoid, as if we could see through the head. Starting near the half-measure of the head and extending to a bit above the shoulder line. We can conceive of the cylinder of the neck as inserted between one of the major muscles of the back, the trapezius, and a mass of bone in the front, the clavicles, and sternum. Again, put one hand around your neck, and with the other touch the top of the trapezius. It's actually a very large muscle and extends from the neck all the way down to the mid-back.

To see the clavicles and sternum, let's take a look at a skeleton. And to get a feel for what's going on here, run your hand over your clavicle starting at your left shoulder. You'll notice first that it doesn't go all the way to the far left end of your shoulder and arm. This bone has a bit of a subtle s-curve to it as we follow it toward the breastbone or sternum. That's where it ends. And on the other side of the sternum, we get a second, mirror-image clavicle going out to the right. Traces of the clavicles are often visible on the surface of the body. So we'll put these in our drawing but before we do let's erase the section of the neck that's overlapped by the head as well as the bottom horizontal. It will make the section read better.

Now for the clavicles, draw a line from the center, a bit below the top of the trapezoid and extending up at a diagonal, about three-quarters of the distance to the trapezoid's corner. Do this on both sides. Then from a point along the right side of the neck, a bit below the level of the chin, draw a diagonal down toward the clavicle but don't let the two lines meet. Then do the same thing on the left. Basically, we're setting up a recession of space here using overlap. The clavicles sit in front of the neck. The neck inserts in front of the trapezius and the neck is then overlapped by the chin and jaw.

Let's add two more lines at the termination of the trapezius on either side, curved line segments to represent the deltoid or lateral extension of the shoulder, and a diagonal line on either side to represent the deltoid overlapping the pectoral muscle of the chest. Then erase the parts of the upper trapezoid you no longer need.

Let's hold-off on the arms. Instead, we'll look at connecting the legs to the pelvis. Here, once again, consulting the skeleton will prove useful. The shape of the pelvis including the ball joint of the femur, the large bone of the upper leg, is like a trapezoid with the long edge at the base. But the pelvis itself is trapezoidal with the long edge at the top.

To make a better connection here in our drawing, it'll help to imitate this structure. So if we modify the mini-skirt shape we have into a bikini bottom shape we'll begin to see the true length of the legs and erase the unneeded horizontal at the fourth head.

This is a good time to review how measure's stacking-up in our figure. The figure's eight heads tall. The width of the head is about three-quarters of its height. The upper torso's about two heads in height. And at the widest point, the shoulders are about two head heights turned horizontally or a bit less than three heads in their upright position. At the bottom of the ribcage, at the abdomen, and at the top of the pelvis, the width is less than the shoulders. Less than two heads. The lower torso's about one head tall. And the width at the base is about two wide. The thigh, measured from the hip to the bottom of the knee, is about three heads. The lower leg's a bit less than two heads in length. And from the ankle to the bottom of the foot's about half a head.

Our figure's like the Dürer's an eight-head figure, but the proportions are a bit different. Overall, the figure we've constructed is broader in the chest and shoulders. The takeaway is that by adjusting widths to heights we can get different kinds of figures. Earlier, I'd mentioned that Dürer knew of only one person, Jacopo de Barbari, who was working on a system of human proportions. He was unaware of the work of Jacopo's countryman, Leonardo da Vinci, who from about 1490–1516 was making scores of highly detailed notebook entries on the subject. His *Vitruvian Man* is perhaps the most famous example. The figure's a similar number of heads, seven and a half to Dürer's eight. Yet, he feels a bit taller because he's slimmer in the waist and hips. Botticelli's Primavera is also eight heads. Yet her proportions feel very different than either the Dürer or the Leonardo. Less width to height and, of course, she's female. And in that regard, it's worth taking a look at the kinds of proportionate differences artists have routinely used to differentiate male and female.

This is a drawing by Jean-Auguste-Dominique Ingres, the great French Neo-Classicist. He was looking back to the artists of the Renaissance like Raphael, who in turn were looking back to the artists of Ancient Greece. And there's continuity in that long lineage in the way they were conceiving of the proportions of the human figure and differences between male and female. You'll note that both the male and female upper torsos are trapezoidal in shape, wider at the shoulder, smaller at the waist. The lower torso an inverted trapezoid, that mini-skirt shape, with a bikini bottom triangle inside the mini-skirt that reveals the true length of the thigh. Legs and arms on both figures taper. But there're several conventions adopted to distinguish male from female. Of course, we have the obvious, breasts and sexual organs, but significantly, there are differences of measure that affect overall shape. The male's shoulder width is much greater than that of the woman while her hips are wider than his. When we look at the relationship between shoulders and hips, the male has wide shoulders to narrower hips. The woman's shoulders and hips are more equal in measure. While both figures taper at the waist, her waist is considerably more cinched.

The pelvic bones are different, too, and they are in nature. The male's has a greater height to width ratio, the female, greater width to height. The opening in the male pelvis is more constricted, in the female less so. And the male pubic arch is more angular and acute, the female more curved and obtuse. Because her waist is more cinched and her hips wider, the angle from waist to the hip is more dramatic. Overall, she's more curved, he more angular. And her torso and limbs are all slimmer in relation to their height. And, of course, she's drawn to be shorter than him.

We see many of these same differences in the Leonardo and the Botticelli. So take this into consideration. Look at the proportions in your drawing and personalize them a bit.

I'd like you to leave the heights and limb positions the same but play with the widths and the degree of tapering. Retain the shape vocabulary we're using, trapezoids. Straight lines only, no curved lines yet. We'll get to those but if you curve things now it'll make some of our next steps more difficult like transferring the proportions from the central figure to the other two views. For now, play with the widths. You'll feel the personality of your figure change as you do.

Now, there's something else you may have noticed about Dürer's and Leonardo's figures in contrast to Botticelli's and Ingres's. Both the Dürer and Leonardo are studies on proportion. The figures, like the one we've been drawing, are in static positions, straight forward, everything lining up horizontal and vertical. It makes sense. It brings out the measure of each section or limb. But we don't generally stand like this. Try it. It's much more relaxing to put the weight on one foot like the Primavera and the couple in the Ingres. We call this contrapposto. Now the shoulders, which had lined-up horizontally line-up on a diagonal, same with the hips, the knees, and the ankles.

Let's look at the male figure in the Ingres. His left leg takes the weight. His opposite hip, his right hip, moves down. There's not enough room for the length of his leg in the contracted space, so it goes out to the side. So the hip taking the weight goes high, hip, no weight, low. The bottom of the pelvis follows suit. The knees follow suit. The shoulders move opposite to the hips and thighs. Hips and knees, one direction, shoulders the other. The woman puts her weight on the right leg. And everything happens the same way as in the male but in mirror image. Good composition. If she stood with the same contrapposto, much less balance.

It's important to remember that it's not just the top of the shoulders or the top of the hips that are moving, it's a large mass of bone. When we tilt the shoulders, the mass of the ribcage moves. When we tilt the top of the pelvis, the whole pelvis and femur move. So I'd like you to apply this idea in your drawing.

First, using your kneaded eraser, erase back, significantly lightening the upper and lower torso, and then the left leg. You want to just be able to see them. Then redraw the trapezoid of the pelvis tilting down from left to right. Add the triangular bikini bottoms inside. It should be the same shape, but rotated.

Next, redraw the trapezoid of the upper torso tilting up, from left to right. Then add lines for the sternum, clavicles, deltoids, and pectoral muscle. Then erase the parts of the trapezoid you no longer need. Repeating this will help you cement this construction. The shapes don't change much, only the angle of the shapes. The whole assemblage rotates together.

Next, some line to connect the upper and lower torsos, and a bit more to connect the lower torso to the right thigh. Let's take the left leg out at a diagonal, a trapezoid for the upper leg, another for the lower leg. And a modified wedge shape for the foot. The left knee should be tilting below the right. The left ankle tilting up and make sure the big toe of the left foot lines-up along a horizontal with the right foot.

Now, let's add the arms. We'll draw them extending out at an angle, palms forward. Starting with the right arm, draw a tapering trapezoid from the shoulder. It should be about one head length. The upper arm's total length including the shoulder or deltoid should be about one and a half to one and three-quarter head lengths. Make its width go with whatever choices you've made when you altered your figure. Next, another trapezoid for the lower arm, again, about one head length and the hand, about three-quarters of a head in length. Repeat these steps on the other side to draw the remaining arm and hand. And let's erase the portion of the upper arm that's overlapped by the chest. Then the line separating the shoulder from the upper arm and, finally, any of the non-contrapposto figure you no longer need.

You've now seen how we can use a canon of proportions to draw a figure. You've also seen how small changes in proportion and position can influence the feel of the figure. We'll continue this drawing in the next lecture. We'll add two more views, posterior and lateral, direct some attention to the head, hands, and feet, and learn how to make the figure feel more three-dimensional.

# The Figure: The Head, Hands, and Feet
## Lecture 32

In this lecture, we'll continue with the figure drawing we began in the previous lecture. We'll start by blocking in the side (lateral) and back (posterior) views. In general, the procedure will be to carry over the measures from the frontal figure, then more or less retrace the steps we took in the last lecture. We'll start with a straightforward figure without contrapposto, then erase and adjust lines for a more natural stance. After completing all views of the figure, we'll look in detail at drawing the head, hands, and feet.

**The Head**
After walking through a drawing of the anterior, lateral, and posterior views of a figure, let's turn our attention to the head. Individual heads, like individual bodies, vary in their proportions and their degrees of symmetricality. But there are a couple formulas, or canons, that are widely used as starting points.

In the anterior view, we used the proportion of 3 to 4 for the head's width to height. Start the head by drawing a 3-by-4-inch rectangle for this view, followed by vertical and horizontal centerlines and an egg shape or ovoid. Divide the horizontal into fifths, then do the same with the lower vertical half. Next, follow these generic steps to fill in the features:

- The eyes ride the horizontal half, so place the irises on top of the centerline, in the center of the second and fourth horizontal fifths. Draw the upper and lower lids of each eye to extend across each eye measure.

- Place the tip of the nose on the second fifth of the vertical and the center of the lips at the third. Carry a vertical down from each eye's center. Let the length of the lips extend from one of these verticals to the other.

- For the eyebrow, measure one eye's width straight up from the lower lid and make a mark. Draw the eyebrow.

- Place the top of the ears above the top of the eyelid but below the eyebrow. The bottom of the ears should be in line with the tip of the nose. The ears can extend beyond the rectangle.

- Make the nose one eye wide, wings included. Locate the top of the nasal bone—where the plane of the nose begins to project forward from the face—at about the top of the eyelid.

- To describe the planar structure of the head, add verticals at the temples. You might also indicate that the jaw overlaps the ears, and the ears overlap the side plane of the head.

- Then, draw the neck, indicating that it is overlapped by the jaw.

- Place a couple lines for the cheekbones and, perhaps, a mark or two to create a front plane of the chin.

Of course, many people have narrower heads, wider noses, or longer ears, but these general steps give you a template from which you can create endless variations.

Also, when using these fairly flat linear systems, it's important to remind yourself that the head is three-dimensional. In the anterior position, the tip of the nose is closest to the viewer; the eyes, farther away; and the ears, at a distance behind. The front plane of the head can exhibit curvature, as well.

### Hands and Feet

Hands have the reputation of being difficult to draw—and for good reason. Hands are quite complex, with more than 25 bones and more than 30 muscles. The number of possible configurations of the hand is much larger compared to other parts of the body, such as the head. And unlike the head, ribcage, arms, or legs, the hand is much less symmetrical. Add to that all the different points of view from which the hand is seen—from above, from below, and foreshortened—and the result is a great deal of visual complexity.

To begin to make some sense of the hand, we start with measure and shape. As with the figure and head, actual hands may be thinner, stubbier, or different in myriad other ways, but these general steps will get you started:

- It's easiest to conceive of the hand in three parts: the large shape encompassing the palm or back of the hand minus the fingers, a shape for the fingers, and a final shape for the thumb.

- Start with a tilted rectangle for the palm, a bit taller than it is wide. Above that, draw a trapezoid, just a bit shorter than the rectangle below it and wider on the right. That's a rough shape for the four fingers. The upper shape is a little shorter than the bottom shape because the longest finger—the middle finger—is not usually as long as the palm.

- The fingers attach along a curve, with the pinky attaching at the lowest point on the right. Draw an arc from where the second finger will be. Rise above the dividing line at the middle finger and down below for the location of the pinky.

- You'll notice that the top of your fingers follow an arc, as well. Draw a second arc for the fingertips.

- Divide the top of the palm in four. Because the hand is in a relaxed position, there will be a slight bit of web between the fingers. The more the fingers spread, the larger this gets.

- Then, draw four tapering shapes for the fingers. The middle finger should be longest. The second and fourth fingers should be about the same length; the pinkie should be considerably shorter and can fall partially outside the guide shape.

- Add the two creases at the joints that divide the fingers, more or less, into thirds along an arc.

- We'll approach the thumb in parts: (1) Draw a triangular shape from the top of the palm on the left to a point out to the left at about a quarter to a third of the palm's height. This will approximate the base of the first joint of the thumb. (2) Add a diagonal down into the rectangle. Following that diagonal, draw a curving, blade-like shape for the thumb. It should register close to the top of the palm, although this measure changes as the thumb moves. (3) Draw a curving line from the base of the thumb to the palm.

Now, we'll round and edit the construction shape.

- The wrist is thinner than the hand itself—about three fingers wide. Make this adjustment on both the thumb and pinky sides.

- Add some cross-contours to the thumb and others to the fingers.

- The interior of the palm has three groups of pads and several prominent creases. We can use further cross-contours to describe some of these forms. And we can include a cross-contour at the wrist.

- As a last step, look at your own hand and modify your drawing with the goal of making it closer to what you observe.

Other points to note about drawing hands include the following:

- If you hold your hand laterally, you'll see that the creases where the fingers meet the palm are higher than the knuckle on the back. This makes the fingers look longer from the back. And the body of the back of the hand can appear shorter than the palm side.

- Block out the large shapes first. Start with simple shapes. A trapezoid, rectangle, or ovoid can often be used for the body of the hand.

- When it makes sense, use an aggregate shape or shapes for the fingers. When an aggregate shape doesn't make sense, use an individual shape or shapes for one or more fingers.

- Next, block out the three-dimensional structure using geometric solids. Each finger can be constructed using three hinged, tapering solids, either blocks or cylinders. Then, naturalize what you've drawn.

- In relating the hand to the figure, you can conceive of it as about two-thirds to three-quarters of a head in length.

- Notice that if you relax your hand, the inside is concave (bowl-like), while the outside is convex (ball-like). The fingers naturally bend in toward the center of the palm.

- For additional practice, draw your hands in all the typical positions in which you find them, such as holding a pen or texting.

Feet are generally easier to deal with than hands because they're more unified in shape and volume. The toes are shorter and have a more limited range of motion than the fingers. Again, we can construct a general template for drawing feet; using that, you can practice drawing your own feet in many different positions.

## Volume

What we've been doing here with the figure is, in some ways, similar to what we did in some of the first lectures as we started to tackle still-life objects: Start with a centerline and place simple, flat shapes in relation to measure. The next step was to use geometric solids and turn the flat shapes into volumes. We'll do the same thing here with the figure.

In his *Master Class in Figure Drawing*, Robert Beverly Hale wrote, "Beginners in figure drawing should spend a lot of time drawing simple geometric forms ... like the cube, sphere, cylinder, or ovoid form." Elsewhere in the same work, Hale wrote, "When drawing the ribcage the experienced artist doesn't start his drawing with a detail, such as the nipple or the navel, as a beginner usually does. Instead, he first visualizes the ribcage in the simplest form he can—a box. ... He has learned to visualize all complex forms in terms of very simple masses."

To begin to add dimension to our figures, we'll combine rectilinear solids with elliptical cross-sections. This will help us define planes and capture the rounded quality of many of the figure's forms. For this exercise, make some photocopies of your figure drawing so that you can easily draw over and alter your original image. It's best to make light copies. Once you've finished adding volume to all three views, make 5 to 10 additional copies for use in the next lecture, where we'll learn how we can make the figures we've drawn feel more naturalistic.

## Suggested Reading

Loomis, *Figure Drawing for All It's Worth*, "The Heads, Hands and Feet," pp. 171–188, and "Planes," pp. 76–77.

Reed, *The Figure*, "Heads and Hands," pp. 75–115, and "Construction," pp. 20–45.

Winslow, *Classic Human Anatomy*, "The Proportions of the Whole Figure," pp. 249–261.

# The Figure: The Head, Hands, and Feet
## Lecture 32—Transcript

In this lecture we'll continue with the figure drawing we began in the last lecture. We'll start by blocking-in the side, or lateral, and the back, or posterior, views.

The first step is to carry over the measures from the central figure. To get started, use your T-square. Line it up with the horizontals in the anterior view and transfer the heights to the posterior and lateral views at the same time. These should be light, thin construction lines.

You could start with the eight head measures. You could also add the number and note for each height. Then, carry over the remaining horizontal measures and any notes you think will be useful.

On the posterior view, give yourself width measures like the ones you used in the anterior views. I'd suggested you vary these from the ones I initially gave you. You want to have measures that agree with your anterior view for width at the head, shoulders, bottom of rib cage, top of pelvis, and the crotch.

Now you're ready to tackle the posterior view. You have height and width measures from the front view. In terms of shape, this will be similar to what you've already drawn. We'll more or less, retrace the steps we took in the last lecture, starting with a simple figure without contrapposto. It will be good practice to play through these steps. And we'll add a couple new pieces to reflect the rear view.

Start with a trapezoid for the upper torso. Then, another for the lower torso— the mini-skirt shape. Then the bikini bottom shape. Now connecting lines between the upper and lower torsos. Then the legs and feet. And erase the horizontal at the fourth head.

Let's make some refinements to our basic shapes. We'll start with the upper torso at the shoulders. We'll draw two diagonals for the top of the trapezius muscle. This time we're seeing it from the rear so it'll appear larger. That means longer diagonals than in the front. Then, a subtle trapezoid for the neck, and, erase what's overlapped by the traps. Then, the head shape, and, erase what's overlapped by the neck. Next, a couple curving lines for the shoulder muscles, the deltoids. Make sure they're overlapped by the trapezius. Next, we'll go to the butt or glutes, and add another two curving lines, cross-contours, where the legs join the trunk of the body. And finally, we'll create planes in the feet. Start with two diagonals to define back and side planes, and a small triangle for the toes.

Now we'll convert the figure stance to reflect contrapposto. Using your kneaded eraser lighten the upper torso, lower torso and left leg. Now, redraw the lower torso in contrapposto. Correlate the angle and height of the high hip with the anterior view. Of course, the posterior view should be a mirror image. And do the same with the upper torso. Then add lines to connect the upper and lower torsos and to connect the lower torso to the right thigh.

Now, add a three-sided trapezoid for the left thigh, then a trapezoid for the lower leg, and a slightly rounded trapezoid for the foot. Next two intersecting diagonals for the heel and a final one to clarify the planar structure of the foot.

Now to the arms. Start with two trapezoids for the upper arms. Two more for the lower arms. And two more for the hands. We can erase the portions of the upper arm that won't be seen, as well as the upper portion of the larger trapezoid representing the upper back. And then any of the non-contrapposto torso and leg you no longer need.

Let's turn to the lateral view. It combines aspects of both the anterior and posterior views. I asked you to make modifications in the widths in your figure from the ones I initially gave in the last lecture. And you'll want to be consistent with those choices moving forward in the lateral view. But, let's look at some general widths as a point of reference.

The head seen laterally is wider than in the front view, about a full head-height in width. The neck is about one anterior head width. The width at the shoulders is about one head height. This increases as the chest and spine protrude, front and back, and decreases as the spine curves in at the abdomen. The pelvis is, again, about one head height wide. The thigh, at its widest point, is less than a head, about 80% of one. At the knee about half a head, swells at the calf and tapers at the ankle. And the foot is about a head and a third to a head and a half.

Seen laterally, the shapes of the body are also a bit different from the front view.

So, take out a sketchpad and let's rehearse this. The profile head can be thought of as fitting into a rectangle that's just about square, with a smaller internal square for the back of the skull, a rectangle for the front plane of the face, a triangle for the jaw, and, another for the nose. For the neck the tilted rectangle. For the upper torso, we could use an elongated hexagon. For the lower torso another tilted rectangle. For the upper leg a tapering trapezoid. For the lower leg another. For the foot, a wedge shape. We can use similar shapes to what we used in the anterior view for the arm and hand.

Another common way to block in the shapes of the body is to use ovoids. Here, we'd use a circle for the back of the skull and a vertical ovoid for the front. Another for the neck. And for the upper and lower torso. And others of appropriate measure for the extremities.

There's another factor we need to take into account. And that's the angular alignment. The neck angles back. The upper torso, forward. The pelvis, back so we get this zig-zag motion. The legs, like the pelvis, also angle back but less so.

So, give this a try. Draw a centerline like this one. Let's start with the largest mass, the rib cage and upper torso. We'll draw a directional line. Then the elongated hexagon. Now another directional line for the pelvis and the angled rectangle. And a long directional line for the legs. Then the shapes for the leg and foot. Then a directional line for the neck, and draw the neck. Then the head. And adjust as needed.

Once you've got the idea, move back to the three-view figure drawing. Follow the same, steps starting with the rib cage. Then the pelvis. And connect the two with a line in front. And another in back. Then, the leg and foot.

In this view, we won't add a second leg and foot, or the arms and hands. To finish-up add the neck and head. Stick to simple shapes either rectilinear or ovoid. Keep it very simple for now. Just block the figure in. Make sure that your widths agree with the body type in your two other views.

As another check, let's look at some vertical alignments. These will of course, differ by body type and stance. But, I'd like you to be aware of alignments as a factor in your figure. In this anatomical model, the swell of the spine and butt line up along a vertical, far to one side, the back of the neck, the back of the knee and the ankle line up, too. Next, the top of the sternum and the knee. And, the cheekbone lines-up with the swell of the chest and abdomen. Take this factor into account. Check to make sure your lateral view isn't tipping forward or back.

People always have questions about drawing heads, hands, and feet. So, let's start with the head. Individual heads, like individual bodies, vary in their proportions. They also vary in degree of symmetricality. But there're a couple formulas, or canons, that are widely used as starting points. Especially, when drawing from the imagination. And, this kind of reference can be useful when drawing from observation, too. It helps you see actual proportions in relation to a set of given measures.

In the anterior view, we've used the proportion of 3:4 for the head's width to height. So draw a 3 × 4 inch rectangle for this view. Then vertical and horizontal centerlines. Divide the horizontal into fifths. Then do the same with the lower vertical half.

Next, draw an egg-shape or ovoid into the rectangle. You can draw a 4 × 4 inch rectangle next to this for a lateral view. And then the interior shapes for this view.

Let's start with the anterior view. The eyes ride the horizontal half. So, place the irises on top of the centerline, in the center of the second and fourth fifth. Draw the upper and lower lids of each eye to extend across each eye measure. Place the tip of the nose on the second fifth of the vertical, center of the lips at the third. Carry a vertical down from each eye's center. Let the length of the lips extend from about one to the other.

For the eyebrow, take the eye's width, measure one eye's width straight up from the lower lid. Make a mark and draw the eyebrow. Place the top of the ears above the top of the eyelid, but below the eyebrow. The bottom of the ears should be in line with the tip of the nose. The ears can extend beyond the rectangle.

We'll make the nose one eye wide, wings included. And, locate the top of the nasal bone, that's where the plane of the nose begins to project forward from the face, at about the top of the eyelid.

To describe the planar structure of the head we could add verticals at the temples. We could indicate that the jaw overlaps the ears, the ears the side plane of the head. Then draw the neck, indicating it's overlapped by the jaw. Then place a couple lines for the cheekbones. And, perhaps a mark or two to create a front plane of the chin. And any other refinements you'd like. Now, carry over your measurements to draw the lateral view.

Of course, this is all very generic. Many people have narrower heads, or wider heads, or noses, or longer ears. But, like with the figure, it gives you a template. You can play endless variations on it just like nature herself.

Also, when using these fairly flat linear systems, it's important to remind yourself that the head is three-dimensional. In the anterior position, the tip of the nose is closest to the viewer, the eyes farther away, and the ears, at a distance behind. And, the front plane of the head can exhibit curvature, too.

Hands have the rep of being difficult to draw. And there are good reasons why. First, they're complex. They have lots of movable parts. Four fingers each with three movable joints, a thumb with two, over 25 bones and over 30 muscles. So, the number of possible configurations of the hand compared to, say, the head, well, is much larger. And, unlike the head, ribcage, arms, or legs, the hand is much less symmetrical. Add to that all the different points of view we'll see the hand from, above, below, foreshortened, well, it adds up to a lot of visual complexity.

To begin to make some sense of this, we'll start with measure and shape. As with the figure, actual hands may be thinner or stubbier, or different in myriad ways. But, this will get you started. We'll draw a view of the palm, or planter, side of a left hand as if it's held up with the fingers slightly spread like this. It's easiest to conceive of the hand in three parts—first, the large shape encompassing the palm or back of the hand minus the fingers, then, a shape for the fingers, and, others for the thumb.

Start with a tilted rectangle for the palm, a bit taller than it's wide, then a rough shape for the four fingers above it, a modified trapezoid like this one— wider on the right and a bit shorter than the rectangle below it. The upper shape's a little shorter than the bottom shape because the longest finger, the middle finger, is not usually as long as the palm.

The fingers attach along a curve, not a straight line, with the pinky attaching at the lowest point on the right. So, draw an arc from where the second finger will be. Rise above the dividing line at the middle finger and down below for the location of the pinkie. The tops of the fingers follow an arc as well. So, draw a second arc for the fingertips.

Divide the top of the palm in four for the fingers, there'll be some web between them. The more the fingers spread, the larger this gets. Then, draw four tapering shapes for the fingers. The pinkie will fall partially outside the guide shape. The middle finger should be longest, the second and fourth fingers about the same, though the fourth is often a bit longer and the pinkie considerably shorter. Make any adjustments needed to their relative proportions and shapes. The two creases at the joints divide the fingers, more or less, into thirds along an arc. So, we'll add these, too.

We'll approach the thumb in several pieces. First, a triangular shape from the top of the palm on the left to a point out to the left at about the quarter to a third of the palm's height. This will approximate the base of first joint of the thumb, then a diagonal down to the rectangle. Following that diagonal a curving blade-like shape for the thumb, it should register close to the top of the palm. The height of the palm changes as it moves. As you pull it in towards the palm, it registers higher. Now a curving line for the base of the thumb to the palm.

Now we'll round and edit the construction shape. The wrist is thinner than the hand itself, about two fingers wide, so we'll adjust on both the thumb and pinkie side. Next, we'll add some cross contours to the thumb. We can add others to the other fingers.

The interior of the palm has three groups of pads and several prominent creases. We can use further cross contours to describe some of these forms. And we can include a cross contour at the wrist. Use what we've just drawn as a rough scaffolding and edit as needed. Look at your own hand and modify your drawing with the goal of making it more naturalistic based on what you observe.

Try drawing a dorsal, or back, view of a hand using the same method. Here's an example from Dürer. He not only made hundreds of drawings of figure proportions, but, like Leonardo, assiduously worked out systems of measure for individual body parts.

There are a couple things to note here. If you hold your hand laterally, you'll see that the creases where the fingers meet the palm are higher than the knuckle. This makes the fingers look longer from the back. And the body of the back of the hand can appear shorter than the palm side. Also, note, the base of the fingernails extend to about the halfway point of the top joint. Block out the large shapes first. Make sure the fingertips and joints conform to an arc. And use your own hand as a model. Analyze the distances and measure as you draw.

Take a look at the inside of your hand. If you relax your hand, the inside's concave, bowl-like, from the outside, convex, ball-like. The fingers naturally bend in towards the center of the palm. Once you've drawn the back a good next step would be a concave and convex view.

Then, draw your hands in all the typical positions you find them. It's a very common assignment in figure drawing classes. And, in fact, you'll find scores of hand studies by many famous artists. This page is from the 19th-century French artist, Jean Francois Millet. Like Millet, try a drawing of your hand holding a bowl, then a cup or a glass, holding a pen, texting. Then make a study of your hand turning on a faucet. It's great to look at your actual 3D hand when drawing, but photos can be useful, too.

Start with simple shape. A trapezoid, rectangle, or ovoid can often be used for the body of the hand. When it makes sense, an aggregate shape or shapes for the fingers. When an aggregate shape doesn't make sense, use an individual shape or shapes for one or more fingers. Next, block out the 3D structure using geometric solids. Each finger can be constructed using three hinged tapering solids, either blocks or cylinders. And, then, naturalize what you've drawn. In relating the hand to the figure, you can conceive of it as about two-thirds to three-quarters of a head in length.

Let's take a look at the foot. The foot or footprint is a little over one head in length. Dürer also measured feet. Here we have three correlated views. In both the lateral and top view, he divides the foot into thirds. First, the toes, they also conform to a rectangle that's a third of the foot's height. Then the central wedge shape. And, last, the rear section containing the ankle and the heel.

Feet are generally easier to deal with than hands. They're more unified in shape and volume. The toes are shorter and have a more limited range of motion than the fingers. So, the foot can't morph into so many seemingly different forms.

The problem in drawing feet relates to the fact that we see them most often in foreshortened views, like, Dürer's heel view. Note how he deals with this. Instead of outlining, he moves from contour to cross contour, making sure the lines describing the closer parts of the foot overlap those behind.

Let's follow Dürer's method here for a lateral and posterior view of the foot. Rule out a rectangle that's one and a half by six inches and divide it in horizontal and vertical thirds. An inch or so to the right lay out another rectangle one and a half by 2 and an eighth. Add the horizontals thirds, the two vertical, and one horizontal construction lines that Dürer adds for the heel. In the lateral view, give yourself a point where the Achilles tendon meets the top horizontal line and draw the tendon and heel. The negative shapes can help you gauge accuracy. Then five more points. The first where the top of the body of the foot meets your second vertical line, the second where the top edge of the foot traverses the second horizontal line, the third it intersects the third vertical line, the fourth where it traverses the third horizontal, and the last where the top of the big toe intersects the final vertical. Using these points as guides, draw the top edge of the foot.

Now for the toes. As Dürer has done, give yourself a vertical mark along the bottom horizontal for the tip of each of the small toes. Then position similar points of origin for the tops of the toes. Then draw the toes.

For the posterior view, we'll start by drawing the Achilles tendon and heel, then the ankles, inside higher, outside lower. And follow the remaining overlaps so the foot recedes in space.

Let's also draw an anterior view. Here, the foot's foreshortened. Start with a trapezoid for the body of the foot. The toes attach along a curve or diagonal. So we'll modify the first shape. The front of the toes follow a curve, too. Now we'll add a volumetric front plane. Above we'll indicate the lower leg and ankles, the latter, higher inside, lower outside.

In a foreshortened view, cross contours and line overlaps are all but essential. We'll add a curve at the top to capture the planar quality of the foot. And we'll redraw both right and left sides using overlap. The tendon of the big toe often suggests a plane change in the body of the foot. We'll add a line that more-or-less corresponds with this.

We'll divide the toe shape into thirds. The big toe gets the first third. The others we'll divide in two for the small toes.

Next, we'll convert the two top plane smiling curves into individual frowning curves to capture the volume of the individual toes. Then, work into each toe. The toenails are a great opportunity for more cross contours. With this beginning, the best way to proceed is to draw your own feet in many different positions.

What we've been doing here with the figure's like retracing what we did in some of the first lectures as we started to tackle still-life objects. Start with a centerline, then place simple flat shapes in relation to measure. The next step we took was to turn the flat shapes into geometric volumes. And that's just what we'll do here.

Robert Beverly Hale wrote, "Beginners in figure drawing should spend a lot of time drawing simple geometric forms, like the cube, sphere, cylinder, or ovoid form." "When drawing the ribcage the experienced artist doesn't start his drawing with a detail, such as the nipple or the navel, as a beginner usually does. Instead, he first visualizes the ribcage in the simplest form he can—a box. He has learned to visualize all complex forms in terms of very simple masses."

Here's a preparatory drawing for a Last Supper by Luca Cambiaso that we've looked at several times before. His studies typify this approach.

He's able to attend to everything in a similar way. Architectural elements, furniture, and figures, everything's approached through measure, shape, and volume.

His figures lack all the details that beginners can't resist starting with— no hair, no eyes, no noses, or lips. Yet the figures feel very real, three-dimensional. They have attitude, position, and sit in space. When he does get to details, like facial features, they'll sit securely on those planes because he's taken the time to understand the underlying architecture of the form.

The other great benefit of this approach is that applying directional light becomes pretty obvious. Because we understand the form in terms of plane, it's clear which plane is facing the light and which away.

So, let's move into volume. But, before we do, I think you'll find it useful to have a couple copies of your drawing to experiment with. You could either take a picture of your drawing and print it out at home, or, go to a photocopy shop that has a large format printer. The kind used for architectural plans. They easily accommodate an 18 × 24 or even a 22 × 30 inch sheet of paper. In either case, print out on the light side, so you can easily draw over and alter the image. Another option's to get some tracing paper and trace on top of your drawing.

To add dimension to our figures we'll use an approach that combines Cambiaso's rectilinear solids with elliptical cross-sections. This will help us define planes and capture the rounded quality of many of the figure's forms. If you've made copies, try this on one of the copies. Or, use tracing paper on top of your drawing.

First off, we have to decide on our position relative to the figure. This will define what kinds of planes and ellipses we see. So, let's imagine we're looking pretty-much straight-on and we're standing-up. Our eyelevel will be the same as the figure's. That means we're seeing most of the figure below eyelevel.

You'll remember, at eyelevel a circular cross section appears as a straight line. Just above or below it will begin to appear as an ellipse. At first, a slight one, but, getting progressively fatter as we move farther away from eyelevel in either direction. Above eyelevel, the front of the ellipse appears as a frown, below, as a smile.

So, let's start with the anterior view. First, we'll draw a light horizontal line for the figure's eyelevel at about the vertical half of the head. Next, we'll create side planes in the head. Then the neck. Then the chest and abdomen. Now the pelvis. Then the legs. And feet. Then the ankles, inside high, outside low. Then a front plane for the toes. And, last the arms.

We've now created planes in the figure. Next are the cross contours and cross-sections. This will give us a real three-dimensional feel for the body. You'll want to manage your line weights in the cross sections, greater line weight on the surfaces than in the interior. This will help the form read convincingly.

Let's start down at the ankles. Here, we're far below eyelevel. So, these should be fat cross-sections. We'll draw a cross contour moving from the side of the leg to the front, then back to the other side. Now, with a lighter line weight, we'll move into the interior of the form. Then the other foot, same idea. Now, we'll move to the top of the head. Here, we're just above eyelevel. So, the cross contour will appear as a slight frown. Now just below the horizon, the top of the neck where it meets the back of the skull, then, the base of the neck, then, the top plane between the trapezius and the clavicles, an oval of sorts.

Let's take a look at the connection of the arms and shoulders to the torso. It's useful to conceive of this as happening on a diagonal. You'll likely be able to feel this on your own body—just a bit in from the end of the clavicle, moving down between the pectoral muscle and the deltoid above it. Let's draw a cross section ellipse here. Now drawing through, an ellipse at the bottom of the ribcage. We can adapt the ellipse slightly to capture a concavity at the spine, and, another at the top of the pelvis. Remember, we're moving down, away from eyelevel, so the ellipses should be getting a bit fatter as we progress.

We'll approach the legs connecting to the lower torso similarly to the way we conceived of the arms attaching to the upper torso, diagonal ellipses. Down to the knees, again, we can adapt the ellipses slightly to help capture what we know of the form. Then the feet, we'll add a slightly curving top plane. Like a half cylinder. We'll go back up to the elbow and draw through here, then to the wrist.

We'll divide the hand shape in half with an ellipse. That's about where the fingers protrude from the palm, and slightly curve the flat end of the shape to capture the quality of diverse finger lengths, and a shape or two for the thumbs.

Take the same procedures and apply them to the posterior and lateral views. It'd be a good idea to try this a couple times on your copies before working into the original drawing. Once you've finished adding volume to your three views, print out some more copies, five or ten would be ideal. We'll use them in the next lecture. Again, print them on the light side. The goal's to draw on top of them using the underlying structure you've created.

Next we'll see how we can make the figures we've drawn feel more naturalistic. We'll also discuss the skeletal system and the major muscles. Some anatomical knowledge will help you draw figures both from your imagination and from observation.

# The Figure: Artistic Anatomy
## Lecture 33

S uch artists as Leonardo, Michelangelo, Raphael, Rubens, and many others studied human anatomy, and many artists do so to this day. The reason for this is that knowledge of what's going on below the surface can be a great aid in drawing what's visible on the surface. In this lecture, we'll discuss the skeletal system and major muscles and draw these systems into our figure views.

**Naturalizing the Figure**

At the beginning of the course, we discussed the interplay of contour and cross-contour lines and saw how their skillful integration could create volume. Using the copies you made of your drawing from the last lecture, try experimenting with different ways of moving from contour to cross-contour and compare the results.

Make use of the measure, contour, and cross-contour lines you've already created to bring out a more naturalistic, less mannequin-like figure. You'll find that, in fact, you have to change very little to make this happen. A slight rounding of a line does a great deal in this regard. After doing several variations with line, you can also try adding value to your figures.

Once you've made some experiments, naturalize the figure in your original drawing, using line alone, without adding any hatching or value.

**The Skeletal System**

There are more than 200 bones in the human body, but many repeat left and right, and about half are in our hands and feet. Let's take a tour of the major bones from top to bottom.

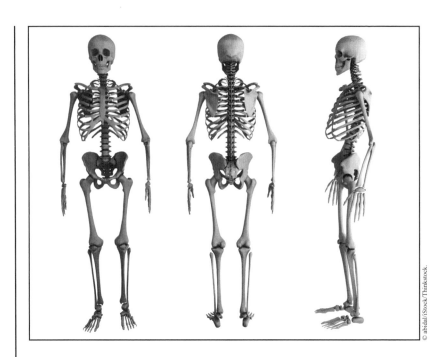

© abidal/iStock/Thinkstock.

The skull has a front plane, right and left side planes, a top plane, a rear plane, and a split-level underside. The bottom of the back of the skull is higher than the under-plane of the chin. In drawing, it's crucial to pay attention to this structure. The large frontal bone of the forehead in relation to the temporal fossae on either side signals the change of plane from front to side. The zygomatic bone, or cheekbone, reiterates this. All the joints in the skull are rigid, with the exception of the mandible, or jaw, which can move both up and down and from side to side.

Attached to the base of the skull is the spinal column. This is the longest section of bone in the body. The vertebrae are similarly shaped and are separated by intervertebral discs. Below the spinal column are the sacrum and coccyx. The upper 24 vertebrae are divided into three sections (cervical, thoracic, and lumbar), each curving in a different direction, which lends the spine its snakelike undulations. The curving shape of the spine is easily visible in the lateral view. It accounts, in part, for the zigzagging spatial thrusts of the neck, ribcage, and pelvis, respectively.

These three vertebral sections are followed by the sacrum, attaching to the pelvis, and the smaller coccyx, projecting to a point. Once again, the assembly of the sacrum and coccyx curves away from the preceding section, the lumbar vertebrae. Depending on an individual's build and body fat, we may see traces of the vertebrae in a rear or partial-rear view. The sacrum can also be a visible landmark through the soft tissue.

The next bone mass is referred to as the *shoulder girdle*, which includes the clavicles; scapulae; and the sternum, or breast bone. Skeletal elements of the front and rear connect in this assembly, and it provides the housing where the head of the humerus (the bone of the upper arm) connects. Studying the scapula and its connection to the clavicle and humerus from multiple points of view will help you understand how the arms connect to the torso.

The sternum is tie-shaped and is located at the front and center of the ribcage. As we know, there are 24 ribs, 12 on each side. All attach to the sternum via cartilage and directly to the spinal column in the rear. The ribcage curves around the body from back to front, with the ribs sloping diagonally downward. The mass of the ribcage defines the three-dimensional structure of the upper torso.

Along with the ribcage, the pelvis is another crucial structure in figure drawing. It's the second largest bone mass. Again, remember that it's three-dimensional, something like an upside-down helmet. The top edge of the pelvis is called the *iliac crest*. This coincides with the top of the mini-skirt shape we drew. The wide bottom of the mini-skirt shape is defined by the top portion of the femur.

In both the arms and legs, the section of the limb closest to the trunk has one bone; the next section, two; and the feet and hands come in at more than 25 each. In the arm, the large upper bone is the humerus. The two smaller bones of the lower arm are the ulna and radius.

The large upper bone of the leg is the femur. On the front of the femur at the knee is the patella. In the lower leg, we find the larger tibia and the much thinner fibula. The bottoms of these bones contribute to form the ankles.

As already noted, both the hands and feet have numerous bones, but these can be grouped into three main sections. In the hand, the first section consists of eight carpal bones. The next section contains the five metacarpals in the palm, followed by the phalanges in the fingers, with two joints in the thumb and three in the other fingers. This structure is more or less repeated in the foot: seven tarsals, followed by metatarsals and phalanges, or toes. At the heel end, the bone of the heel is the calcaneus.

Having a mental picture of the comparative lengths of the major bones and bone groups helps when thinking about proportions. Using the skull's height as a metric, we find that the clavicle, scapula, sternum, sacrum, and hand are somewhat smaller. The ulna, radius, pelvis, and foot are a bit longer. Next in size are the ribcage, humerus, tibia, and fibula—all about one and a half skull heights. The femur is about two skull heights, and the spine is about three.

Not all the bones are equally visible on the surface. The major landmarks include the following:

- Frontal bone of the forehead

- Temporal fossae

- Zygomatic bone

- 7th cervical vertebra

- Jugular notch and sternum

- Front and top of both clavicles

- Scapulae

- Bottom of the 10th rib

- In the arm, the elbow—the meeting of the humerus, radius, and ulna; at the wrist, the ulna on the pinky side and the radius on the thumb side

- In the pelvis, the iliac spine and the anterior superior iliac crest

- In the rear, traces of the sacrum

- In the leg, the great trochanter of the femur; at the knee, the patella; on the outside, both the bottom of the femur and the top of the fibula; on the inside, the top of the tibia; in the mid-lower leg, the front of the tibia; and the ankles.

## The Major Muscles

The muscles, which are much more numerous than the bones, are divided into two main types: voluntary and involuntary. The voluntary muscles are attached to the skeletal structure and are the ones we consciously move. In drawing, these are the muscles in which we're interested. Let's begin by looking at the 13 most prominent muscles of the torso. For most, we'll consider their shape, where they attach to the bone, and their function. Then, we'll chart the major muscles of the legs and arms.

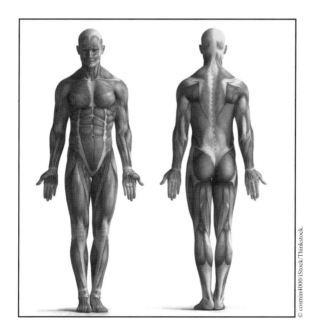

© cosmin4000/iStock/Thinkstock.

Although bones have fixed shapes, muscles don't; they change shape as they relax or contract. When body builders compete, they flex and pose in positions to maximize the visual expression of a muscle or muscle group.

Although we can discuss the nominal shapes of the muscles, it's important to remember that the actual shape is the result of a combination of factors, including the state of the muscle (relaxed, contracted, or in between), the body type of the individual, and the point of view.

Muscle attaches to bone via tendons. Anatomists make a distinction between two types of muscle-to-bone attachment: origin and insertion. Bones of origin tend to remain fixed. The bones that receive insertions are the ones that tend to move when the muscle is contracted.

Starting at the neck, the most prominent muscles of the upper torso include the following:

- Trapezius: large diamond-shaped muscle of the back

- Sternomastoid, or sternocleidomastoid: located on either side of the neck

- Deltoid: originates along the outer half of the clavicle and along the top spine of the scapula

- Pectoralis major: central muscle of the chest

- Serratus: any of three muscles that originate along the sides of the first eight or nine ribs and collect and insert under the scapula on each side

- Rectus abdominis: abdominal muscle

- External obliques: curve around to the side of the abdomen

- Latissimus dorsi: large triangular muscle of the back

- Rhomboid: group of muscles sandwiched between the trapezius and deltoids above and the latissimus dorsi below

- Infraspinatus, teres minor, and teres major: three muscles that cover the back of the scapula

- Erector spinae (sacrospinalis): deep muscle of the back.

The major muscles of the legs include the following:

- Sartorius: crosses from the outside of the hip to the inside of the knee

- Quadriceps: set of four muscles in the front of the thighs

- Adductors: set of five muscles of the inner thigh originating on the pelvis

- Glutes (gluteus): set of three muscles in the buttocks.

## Suggested Reading

Brown and McLean, *Drawing from Life*.

Visiblebody.com, SkeletonPremium and MusclePremium.

Winslow, *Classic Human Anatomy*.

# The Figure: Artistic Anatomy
## Lecture 33—Transcript

In this lecture, you'll make the figure you've drawn more naturalistic. Then we'll discuss the skeletal system and the major muscles. At the end of the last lecture, I'd suggested printing copies of your drawings. We'll use them now.

At the very beginning of the course, we discussed the interplay of cross contour and contour. We saw how their skillful integration could create volume, like in the Holbein. Using the copies, I'd like you to experiment with different ways of moving from contour to cross contour and then compare results.

Start with line alone. Make as much use of the measure, contours and cross contours you've carefully created to bring out a more naturalistic, less mannequin-like, figure. You'll find that you have to change very little to make this happen. A slight rounding of a line does a lot in this regard. And, if you'd like, try some value, hatching or other mark making, follow the planar structure.

You'll find, like Cambiaso that having this structure makes imaging the play of light a straightforward matter. You could also try other variations. For instance, if your figure's male, try a female, or vice versa. Then play with relative proportions. You can make the shoulders smaller, or the pelvis bigger, or, change the positions of the arms, legs, or head and neck.

Once you've made some experiments, naturalize the figure in your original drawing. Use line alone. Don't add any hatching or value. And leave the arms and legs as they are. That's because we'll be adding bone and muscle to our three views. You're likely aware that artists like Leonardo, Michelangelo, Raphael, Rubens and many others studied human anatomy. Many artists do so to this day. Knowledge of what's going on below the surface can really help you draw what's visible on the surface.

We'll start with the skeletal system. The goal's to draw the skeleton into your three views.

Let's take a look at a couple examples. Here, a female, and here, using the same basic proportions, a male. In both cases, we still have the underlying sense of shape and volume. And, the internal skeletal structure has been related to the proportions of the existing figure. There are over 200 bones in our bodies. Different texts quote different numbers. Some interpret a section as a single bone while others define the same section as two or more bones. The number of bones in the body also changes over our lives. We have more separate bones at birth. For instance, the bones of the sacrum and those of the coccyx don't fully fuse until adolescence. And, there's also some variation from individual to individual. For instance, a small percentage of individuals, fewer than 1%, may have an extra cervical rib.

While there are over 200 bones in the body, many repeat left and right. And, about half are in our hands and feet. So that cuts down what we need to study to understand the large masses of the body. Let's take a tour from top to bottom.

We'll start with the skull or cranium. Many people think of this area as being the face. The skull reminds us that the features occupy a fraction of the multi-planar terrain of the head. The skull has a front plane, right and left side planes, a top plane, a rear plane, and a split-level underside. The bottom of the back of the skull is higher up than the under-plane of the chin. In drawing, it's crucial to pay attention to this structure. The large frontal bone of the forehead in relation to the temporal fossae on either side signals the change of plane from front to side. The zygomatic bone, or cheekbone, reiterates this. All the joints in the skull are rigid, with the exception of the mandible, or jaw, which can move both up and down and from side to side.

Attached to the base of the skull we find the spinal or vertebral column. It's the longest section of bone in the body consisting of the upper twenty-four vertebra. These are similarly shaped and separated by intervertebral discs, then the sacrum and coccyx. The upper twenty-four vertebrae are divided into three sections, each curving in a different direction, lending the spine its snake-like undulations. The top seven vertebrae are termed cervical, here meaning neck, so part one is the neck section of the spine. That seventh vertebra is often a visible landmark in the both the posterior and lateral views. The next section, consisting of twelve vertebrae, is termed thoracic, meaning the general area containing the clavicles, sternum, ribcage, and the scapulae, what we've been referring to as the upper torso. The third section consists of five vertebrae. These are termed lumbar, referring to the section of the body below the ribs, and extending to the pelvis.

These three vertebral sections are followed by the sacrum, attaching to the pelvis, and the smaller coccyx projecting to a point. The assembly of the sacrum and coccyx curves, once again, away from the direction preceding section, the lumbar vertebrae. Depending on an individual's build and body fat, we may see traces of the vertebrae in a rear or partial-rear view. The sacrum can also be a visible landmark through the soft tissue. The curving shape of the spine is easily visible in the lateral view. It accounts, in part, for the zigzagging spatial thrusts of the neck, ribcage, and pelvis, respectively. What many people forget is that these same planar shifts are occurring when we view the figure in the anterior and posterior positions. So, it's a good idea to keep this in mind when drawing these views.

The next bone mass is referred to as the shoulder girdle. The main bones concerned are the clavicles, scapulae, and the sternum or breastbone. It's an assembly where skeletal elements of front and rear connect. And it provides the housing where the head of the humerus, the bone of the upper arm, will connect. Feel out along your collarbone from the center of your body. You start at a dip, that's the jugular notch at the top of the sternum, then a slight rise onto the collarbone. Then, perhaps, a slight curving dip and, you're also moving back in space. Then as you've almost reached your arm, a slight drop-off. Here, you're no longer on the collarbone, but on the top plane of the scapula, the acromion. The collarbone's often among the most visible on the surface of the body. Many people draw it extending too far. So that it covers the humerus. It shouldn't. It's actually the complex scapula that we see here.

Neither the clavicles nor scapulae are fixed. We can move a shoulder forward or back because this assembly moves together. With the scapula gliding across the rounded back of the ribcage. The scapula too is often visible through the flesh in many views. While basically triangular in shape its planar structure's complex. Studying the scapula and its connection to the clavicle and humerus, from multiple points of view will really help you understand how the arms connect to the torso.

The sternum's tie-shaped with a hexagonal shorter top section, called the manubrium, and a dagger-like, longer, bottom. It's referred to as the body of the sternum. It ends in a short pointed section called the xiphoid process. The sternum is at the front and center of the ribcage. There are 24 ribs, 12 on each side. All attach to the sternum via cartilage and, directly to the spinal column in the rear. The first 5 pairs of ribs attach singly and directly to the sternum. Though, the top pair's the only one that attaches to the manubrium. It's partially overlapped by the clavicles in the front. And in the rear attaches to the seventh cervical vertebra. The next four pairs attach to the longer body of the sternum.

The following two pairs, six and seven, attach to the angled edge of the sternum. They're also interconnected by web-like cartilage. That cartilage splays like antlers, allowing pairs eight, nine, and ten to attach through this web. The eleventh and twelfth pairs don't connect in the front and are referred to as floating ribs—eleven is longer, twelve, the shortest. The full ribs curve around the body from back to front sloping diagonally down as they curve. Like the skull to the head, the ribcage defines the three-dimensional structure of the upper torso. It's a classic mix of anatomical rectilinearity and curvilinearity. We can think of it like a block or spheroid. Either way, we want to feel the front plane, side planes and back plane. The ribs can serve as cross contours, making volume in this part of the figure palpable. A slight indication of the final full rib, number ten, can often help in this regard.

As long as we're in the region, I note that beginning students often misplace the nipples on both men and women. It's essential to remember that the front plane of the body isn't flat. Let's look at Dürer's cross sections, at the chest-level in particular. Just as the ribcage has a degree of curvature to it, the muscle and soft tissue follow the curve of the armature. It gets a bit cut-off so I've recreated it. You can see that the right side of the chest faces to the right, the left, to the left. The nipples and women's breasts will tend to follow, angling out.

Along with the ribcage, the pelvis is another crucial structure to remember when drawing the figure. It's the second largest bone mass. Again, we want to remember it's 3D, bowl-like. Or like an upside down helmet, of sorts. We'll often see the top edge of the pelvis, the iliac crest. This coincides with the top of the miniskirt shape we drew. Traces of the iliac spine may also be visible. The wide bottom of the miniskirt shape is defined by the top portion of the femur, the great trochanter.

In both the arms and legs, the section of the limb closest to the trunk has one bone, the next section two. And the feet and hands come in at over twenty-five each. In the arm, the large upper bone is the humerus. The two smaller bones of the lower arm are the ulna and radius. Both have a wider and a narrower end. The ulna is wide at the connection with the humerus and narrow at the wrist, the radius the opposite. We'll often see evidence of both at the wrist. In our anterior view, the ulna will be on the inside, the radius on the outside, in the posterior the opposite.

The large upper bone of the leg is the femur. If you stand up straight with your toes together the femur angles in. On the front of the femur at the knee is the patella. This is another often-visible landmark. In the lower leg, we find the larger tibia and the much thinner fibula. The former sits directly below, really centered, on the femur. The fibula attaches to the outside, and a bit below, the top of the tibia. It also extends past the end of the tibia. The bottom of these bones produces the landmarks of the ankles. Since the fibula goes down lower, the outside of ankle appears lower than the inside—inside high, outside low.

As already noted, both hands and feet are bone rich. Thankfully, they group into three main sections. I'll go over them briefly. I don't require my students to draw them. It's difficult at the scale we're drawing at here. In the hand, the first section consists of eight carpal bones, the next the five metacarpals in the palm, then, the phalanges in the fingers with two joints in the thumb and three in the other fingers. The structure is more or less repeated in the foot. Start out with seven tarsals instead of eight carpals, then metatarsals and phalanges or toes. At the heel end, the bone of the heel is the calcaneus.

Let's take a look at comparative lengths of the major bones and bone groups we've discussed, having a mental picture of this helps when thinking about proportions. Using the skull's height as a metric, we find that the clavicle, scapula, sternum, sacrum, and hand are somewhat smaller. The ulna, radius, pelvis, and foot are a bit longer. Next in size are the humerus, ribcage, fibula, tibia, and femur, all about one and two skull heights, and the spine, at close to three.

Not all the bones are equally visible on the surface. Let's review the major landmarks. They include: the frontal bone of the forehead; the temporal fossae; the zygomatic bone; the seventh cervical vertebra; the jugular notch and sternum; the front and top of both clavicles; the scapulae; the bottom of the tenth rib; in the arm, the elbow, the meeting of the humerus, radius and ulna; and at the wrist, the ulna on the pinky-side and the radius, thumb-side; in the pelvis, the iliac spine and the anterior superior iliac crest; and in the rear, traces of the sacrum; moving into the leg, the great trochanter of the femur; at the knee, front and center, the patella; on the outside, both the bottom of the femur and the top of the fibula; on the inside the top of the tibia; in the mid-lower leg, the front of the tibia, the shin bone; and the bottom of the tibia and fibula, the ankles. Next time you're drawing a figure look for these landmarks. If you're drawing from your imagination, you may want to reference them.

To help you see how the skeleton relates to the exterior shapes you've drawn I'd like you to draw a skeleton into each of your figures. An image search will turn up many excellent illustrations online, both of the entire skeletons in different views, as well as individual bones and close-ups of specific sections. Investing in a study skeleton can be a real aid. While life-size is ideal, there are many smaller models that help give a sense of how the parts relate three-dimensionally.

While the number of bones gets pegged in the two hundreds, the muscles are much more numerous. There are two main types of muscles—voluntary and involuntary. The voluntary muscles are attached to the skeletal structure. They're the ones we consciously move. In drawing, these are the ones we're interested in. As with bones, people disagree about what constitutes a single muscle. So, the numbers you see vary from the six hundreds into the eight hundreds. Many sources quote a number around 650. The good news is that our interest in muscles is pretty much aligned with body builders. We're primarily concerned with muscles that can be seen on the surface. That chips away at the number. And because we're bilaterally symmetrical, many get counted twice. That knocks it down, too. But, that still leaves a lot of material to cover. This lecture will constitute an introduction.

The goal here, once you've drawn the skeleton into your three views, is to draw the muscles we'll discuss into half of your anterior and posterior views and fully into the lateral view. You can use graphite pencils for this project. Or, you could use color. When I do with this project with my undergrads at the University of Washington, we use erasable colored pencils. I've found the Col-Erase brand works well. If you'd like to try this, I'd suggest getting eight pencils: yellow, orange, red, blue, brown, gray, black, and white. Imagine the light coming from a single direction. Where the muscle swells toward the light, make it lighter, where the muscles taper, where they're overlapped, and away from the light go darker and into the darker browns, blues and blacks.

We'll look at the thirteen most prominent muscles of the torso in some detail. For most, we'll consider their shape, where they attach to the bone, and their function. Then we'll chart the major muscles of the legs and arms. That will bring us up to about fifty-five muscles, a good start. While bones have fixed shapes, muscles don't. They change shape as they relax or contract. And, that adds a level of complexity.

When body builders compete, they flex and pose in positions to maximize the visual expression of a muscle or muscle group. That's an example of muscle changing shape. While I'll be pointing out the nominal shapes of the muscles, it's important to remember that the actual shape will be the result of the combination of multiple factors. One, the state of the muscle—relaxed, contracted, or in between, the body type of the individual, and of course, the point of view.

Muscle attaches to bone via tendons. That's fibrous connective tissue. Anatomists make a distinction between two types of muscle to bone attachment—origin and insertion. Bones of origin tend to remain fixed. The bones that get the insertion are the ones that tend to move when the muscle is contracted.

So, let's start at the neck. We've already noted the large diamond-shaped muscle of the back, the trapezius, traps in gym parlance. Leonardo makes a study of the muscle here. Its sites of origin are all along the center of the muscle and the body. The top of the diamond attaches to the base of the skull. And, continues down along the twelve vertebra of the ribcage. It inserts, extending out at a diagonal, right and left, into the spines of the scapulae and the far ends of the clavicles. This muscle moves both the scapulae and the neck.

It really helps in understanding the muscles to feel them at work in your own body. You can learn a lot by working out. If you become acquainted with the standard exercises for different muscle groups, you begin to develop an experiential sense of how each muscle moves.

One of the standard exercises for the traps is the shrug. You hold a heavy weight, dumbbells, or a barbell, and pull the muscle up to your ears and hold. Try it with me. If you have some weights around the house that's great, you'll feel the muscle more readily. But even if you don't try it anyway—isolate the muscle, pull up in a shrug. You can feel it lift the scapulae.

The other main visible muscle of the neck is the sternomastoid, also called the sternocleidomastoid. There's one on either side of the neck. It's often seen on the surface. It inserts along the bottom rear of the cranium, behind the jaw and travels at a diagonal to find its origin on the manubrium of the sternum and along the first third or so, of the clavicles. The negative shape between the two sternomastoids creates the V-shape we often see in the neck right above the sternum. This muscle allows the head to swivel right and left, move side to side as well as up and down.

Let's take a look at the shoulders. There are two main muscles responsible for the form we see here. The first are the trapezius or traps, which we've already covered, the other, the deltoids, or delts. Seen in the anterior or posterior view I think of it as being like a half-circle shape, or in volume like a skullcap that's been rotated a couple degrees. Though, it's generally thought of as triangular in shape. Then word deltoid comes to us from the Greek. Delta is the letter d in the Greek alphabet, which is triangular in shape. Each deltoid originates along the outer half of the clavicle and along the top spine of the scapula. It inserts onto the side of the humerus. Leonardo studied this muscle from the front, side, and rear. It's involved in several of the arm's movements, principal among them rotation. If I lift my arm straight up that's the deltoid at work. And, as the top of the muscle contracts, it lifts my arm up from my side. A common deltoid exercise is the straight-arm raise. You extend your arm and raise it along an arc. Do it a couple of times you'll begin to feel the muscle.

On to the chest, the pectoralis major, the pecs. In the anterior view this muscle's like a kid's drawing of a house shape flipped ninety degrees. The point of the house inserts onto the humerus, underneath the deltoid as Leonardo illustrates here. The house's base accounts for its origin along the sternum and the cartilage of the first six or seven ribs. It also has origin sites along the first half of the clavicle. It's the muscle you work when you do a push-up or bench press, or if you're rock climber, pulling yourself up a cliff.

Moving around to the side of the ribcage, we find the serratus, no monosyllabic name here. But it sounds like serrated. It comes from the same Latin root, meaning saw. And, I think you can see why. These muscles have their origins along the sides of the first eight or nine ribs, and collect and insert under the scapula on each side. Their major function is to move the scapula. They're not particularly visible on most people's bodies, though you'll see them on bodybuilders.

Next, the rectus abdominis, or abs, this has its origin along the pubic bone of the pelvis. And inserts onto the costal cartilage of the fifth, sixth and seventh ribs and onto the xiphoid process, or bottom point, of the sternum. The top three sections of the muscle, above the navel, account for the six-pack. If you think about common ab exercises, well, they describe the main movement of this muscle. Sit-ups involve muscle contraction and an accompanying flexion of the spine.

On either side of the abs and below the serratus, we get the external obliques. They curve around to the side of the abdomen. This muscle attaches above, to ribs five through twelve, and below to the pelvis. This, like the abs, is involved when you bend your spine. It also comes into play when you flex to the right or left. So, you're using this muscle when you do twist crunches.

Like the serratus, these are generally only visible on people who've worked-out a lot and have little body fat. The external oblique's appear higher toward the back and slant lower toward the front, like the ribs. Jacopo Pontormo depicts both the serratus and external obliques in this standing figure.

Let's move around to the back. We've already talked about the trapezius and deltoids, which we'll also see from the back. The other really large muscle of the back is the latissimus dorsi, or lats. It's triangular in shape. Has its origin along the protruding spines of the bottom six thoracic vertebrae—that's the bottom six vertebrae of the ribcage—as well as the next five lumbar vertebrae. It has further origins along the spine of the sacrum and along the iliac crest of the pelvis. It has its insertion on the inside of the humerus near the top. It extends to cover the triangular points of the scapulae. This serves to hold them against the ribcage. It really defines the shape of the posterior view of the back. Standard lat exercises are wide-grip chin-ups and wide-grip lat pull-downs. In both, you hold your arms up over the head widely apart. If you just hold your arms up in this position, you can begin to feel the muscle. Not surprisingly, it's used for pulling and climbing. Rowing machines also work the lats.

Zooming-out a bit, you'll see that the lats get overlapped by the trapezius. If someone's well-muscled and doesn't have much body fat we may see some of the external oblique's on either side of the lats. Here, Leonardo's studying the latissimus dorsi in a lateral view. You'll also note the deltoid, serratus, and external oblique.

You'll notice a group of muscles sandwiched-in between the traps and delts above and the lats below. We don't have time here to give them more than a mention. What we're seeing here is a bit of the rhomboid. And then three muscles that cover the back of the scapula, the infraspinatus, the teres minor and the teres major. And, since we're digging down into layers of muscle, there's one more back muscle we should mention. That's the erector spinae. It's a fairly deep muscle. And, as the name implies it's responsible for holding the spine up straight. It's also referred to as the sacrospinalis. It goes all the way from the neck down to the sacrum in two vertical columns. You can often see evidence of the two columns on either side of the spine above the sacrum. It's what you're seeing here in the lower back, both in Leonardo's study and in the photo.

That's our lightening tour of the trunk of the body. As we get into the limbs, the muscles multiply. Let's start with the thigh. In the anterior view, you'll notice that most of the muscles are like vertical strips. And, most attach at the pelvis or near the top of the femur. And, many extend to the area around the knee. The muscle that flamboyantly crosses over from the outside of the hip to the inside of the knee is the sartorius. It's the longest muscle in the body. The name comes from the Latin "sartor" meaning "tailor." Some suggest this muscle got its name because ancient tailors sat in a cross-legged position and the muscle was prominently visible as they did their work. Not sure I buy that. You have to be in pretty athletic shape for the muscle to be visible.

Next, we have the quadriceps or quads. As the name implies there are four of these. Though, we only see three on the surface. If I lift my leg from the hip, I'm using my quads. The center quad is the rectus femoris. On the outside of the thigh we get the vastus lateralis, and on the inside the vastus medialis. The fourth quad is the vastus intermedius. As its name implies it's in the middle, hidden underneath the rectus femoris and sandwiched between the lateralis and the medialis.

The next group is the adductors. Adduction is to move away or toward the center of the body. When I lift my leg out to the side, like this, I'm using my adductors. There are five muscles in this group. They all have their origins on the pelvis. The first four have their insertions along the femur. The final one, on the inside of thigh, inserts onto the tibia. The first is the pectineus, next, the adductor brevis, then the adductor longus, followed by the adductor magnus, and finally, the gracilis. You can clearly see the sartorious and elements of the quads and adductors here.

Moving around to the back, we get the glutes. When you move your thigh backward or climb a set of stairs, you're using your glutes. We have the large gluteus maximus, which overlaps the smaller gluteus medius. The larger muscle has its origins along the iliac crest of the pelvis and on the side edges of the sacrum and coccyx. The insertion is on the femur below the great trochanter. The smaller glute also has its origin on the pelvis, but below the crest, on the ilium and has its insertion on the great trochanter.

Let's take a look from the side because there're a couple other pieces that connect here. The big glute connects with a smaller muscle, the tensor fascia lata. And, both, in turn connect with the long iliotibial tract, which functions as a tendon of the glute and terminates at the tibia. Leonardo's noting much of what we've just studied in this drawing. In the leg on the left, he includes the sartorious, the quads, and the adductors. In the leg on the right, he shows the glutes and the tensor fascia lata.

That's all we can cover in this lecture. We'll pick-up in the next lecture with a conclusion of our discussion of human anatomy.

# The Figure: Drawing Projects
## Lecture 34

In the first part of this lecture, we'll finish our discussion of human anatomy. In the second, we'll review the steps involved in figure construction and highlight a few tips that will help you avoid common pitfalls in figure drawing. We'll then discuss a range of projects: drawing a standing self-portrait, using stick figures, melding figure drawing with linear perspective, and drawing foreshortened figures.

## Continuing with the Major Muscles

In the last lecture, we left off with the glutes. Continuing our inventory, additional major muscles in the legs include the following:

- Hamstrings: group of muscles in the upper leg, below the glutes

- Extensors: group of muscles in the front lower leg; involved in the motion of the foot and toes

- Gastrocnemius: calf muscle; attaches to the Achilles tendon and heel bone

- Soleus: partially overlapped by the calf

- Peroneus longus and peroneus brevis: involved in the motion of the feet.

Major muscles in the arms include the following:

- Biceps: main muscles in the front of the upper arm

- Triceps: main muscles along the back of the upper arm

- Anconeus: muscle directly below the triceps, at the elbow

- Flexors: group of muscles in the front of the lower arm; involved with moving the wrist and fingers

- Extensors: group of muscles in the back of the lower arm; involved with moving the wrist, hand, and fingers.

The best way to begin to absorb all the bones and muscles we've covered is, of course, to draw them. Look online for illustrations to follow and take your time as you continue this study. You could easily spend 15 to 25 hours on the figure in three views—setting up the initial vertical and horizontal measures, drawing basic shapes, constructing the three figures, inserting the skeletons, and adding the muscles—but it will be time well spent.

Once you've completed this investigation, you'll have a much fuller awareness of how bone and muscle relate to the figure, but remember, with many figures, you won't see much of either. Bodybuilders and athletes aside, fat and skin obscure the view. Overall, fat collects most around the center of the body, in the chest, abdomen, buttocks, and hips, followed by the thighs and upper arms. We see less fat on the lower legs and arms and the least on the hands and feet.

### Review of Figure Construction Steps

Before we begin our figure-drawing projects, let's review the construction steps we took in this last drawing:

- Start with linear measure—two horizontal and three vertical lines defining the figure's height in the format shape.

- Divide the vertical measures into head-height units and relate anatomical events to this scale. Using the same scale, establish widths.

- Using this scaffolding, draw 10 simple shapes to represent the ribcage and upper torso, pelvis and lower torso, thighs, lower legs, feet, upper arms, lower arms, hands, neck, and head.

- Introduce contrapposto.

- Add volume through cross-contour. First, draw lines in the long axes to create planes or facets, then draw ellipses or ovoids to further the illusion.

- Integrate contour and cross-contour lines to create a greater sense of naturalism.

Here are a few more general tips to help you avoid common pitfalls in figure drawing:

- Start with the whole, meaning some kind of linear measure or aggregate shape placed on the page. This lets you control composition and helps you avoid the beginner's problem of running out of room.

- Work from the general to the specific. It's difficult to keep the proportions and composition together if you start with details.

- Remember that the figure is three-dimensional. Everything has $x$, $y$, and $z$ coordinates.

- Regarding anatomical knowledge, use it as an aid in drawing your figures, but keep in mind the intent of your drawing. In other words, showing more bone and muscle isn't always better.

Practice drawing all these muscles into half of the anterior and posterior views of your figure and fully into the lateral view. If you want to use colored pencils for this project, get a set of eight: yellow, orange, red, blue, brown, gray, black, and white. Imagine the light coming from a single direction. Where the muscles swell toward the light, make them lighter. Where the muscles taper, where they're overlapped, and where they're away from the light, go darker.

**Project: Self-Portrait in Three Views**
For additional practice with figure proportion, try a standing, full-length self-portrait in three views. The goal here is to analyze a figure observationally in terms of measure and to note actual, as opposed to canonical, proportions. To complete this project, follow these steps:

- Set up the page as you did for the drawing of the figure in three views.

- In order to see your proportions clearly, wear a bathing suit, a leotard, or shorts and a tank top.

- Choose an expressive posture and decide on the positions of your arms and legs.

- Start with the anterior view. Take the measure of your head with your pencil. Then, measure your body height in heads and calibrate the central vertical axis according to this number. Number the head heights.

- Note what landmarks occur at each head height. For example, the nipples might be located at the second head, the naval at the third head, and so on. When important landmarks don't coincide with a head height, make a line where the landmark occurs and an accompanying notation.

- Once you have the heights established, plot the widths.

- With the anterior view plotted, carry the measures to the posterior and lateral views. Then, turning your head, add any other measures you need for these views. If there's something you can't see, have someone take a picture and use the photo to clarify.

- Draw the basic shapes in relation to your measure marks. Check the proportions and adjust.

- Add volume and integrate contour and cross-contour lines to arrive at a more naturalistic figure.

As a second project, use a model to draw another standing figure. Working on this project with a number of different body types will help you develop a sense of the range of human proportions. It also makes you aware of the three-dimensional structure of the body and how structures in the front, side, and rear relate.

Another good project is to invent your own set of proportions. Such a drawing might consist of a subtle variation on the proportions you used in the initial drawing of three figural views, or it could be something more extreme. You might try drawing a child, a weight lifter, or a runway model. Given the body type you're imagining, consider what you might see of the underlying anatomy on the surface.

**Project: Stick Figures**
The humble stick figure can be a useful starting point in figure drawing because it can capture the figure in a specific position that might otherwise seem difficult. Stick figures also enable you to capture movement that you can build on later. Starting with a simple stick figure, you can add a trapezoid or ovoid for the ribcage and another for the pelvis. Then, follow with the other eight body shapes. If you add tapering cylinders for the body parts, you'll have volume.

In an earlier lecture, we saw how we can apply gestural drawing to linear perspective—by roughing in some planes and finding the vanishing point and the horizon. If you combine stick figures with linear perspective and a gestural approach, you have a ready method for quickly drawing complex figures in environments.

**Project: Figures in Perspectival Space and Foreshortened Figures**
The last projects in this lecture are focused on constructing figures in perspectival space. We start with a figure using line in one-point perspective, followed by two-point perspective, followed by the addition of value and color.

Now that you've had a good introduction to figure drawing, you might also try drawing a foreshortened figure. Use a model and your grid for this project. Remember, it's all about measure and a conscientious use of cross-contour and overlap. If you stick to outline, the figure will be flat, not volumetric.

## Suggested Reading

Brown and McLean, *Drawing from Life*, "Foreshortened Figures," pp. 48–60.

Hamm, *Drawing the Head and Figure*.

Loomis, *Successful Drawing*, "Projection of Figures (in Perspective)," pp. 67–77.

# The Figure: Drawing Projects
## Lecture 34—Transcript

In the first part of this lecture, we'll finish our discussion of human anatomy. In the second, we'll discuss a range of figure drawing projects.

We left off with the glutes. Underneath the glutes, we find the tops of the three hamstring muscles. When you lift your lower leg backward, toward the glutes, you're using your hamstrings. Like the quads in front, they form a vertical column in the back. On the outside is the biceps femoris. Then the semitendinosus and, overlapped by the first two, the semimembranosus. Michelangelo's studies the hamstring group here.

We've counted 17 muscles in the upper leg. In the lower leg, we get another 7. We'll start in front with the three muscles of the extensor group. They're involved in the motion of the foot and toes. First, the tibialis anterior, next, the extensor hallucis longus, largely obscured by the tibialis anterior, and the extensor digitorum longus. In the rear, we have two muscles, the gastrocnemius or calf muscle, it attaches to the Achilles tendon and heel bone, and the soleus, partially overlapped by the calf.

From the side, we see two more muscles. The peroneus longus and the peroneus brevis, these muscles are also involved in the motion of the feet and come into play when walking and running. Michelangelo's also studying many of these lower-leg muscles in this drawing.

Let's turn to the muscles of the arm. The muscles of the upper arm feed underneath the deltoid. The main muscles here are the biceps in front and the triceps along the back of the arm. The anatomical terms are biceps brachii and triceps brachii. Brachii means arms. The modern Italian is similar, braccio. We'll get variations on this root in a number of the arm muscles' names. Cep means head. So the bicep brachii is the two-headed arm muscle, the tricep, the three-headed one.

In the front, we'll see the two heads of the biceps. The biceps flex the elbow joint. The motion involved in doing curls. Underneath the biceps is the brachialis and extending below the elbow, the brachioradialis. It has its origin on the humerus and its insertion at the end of the radius.

We'll see the word radialis again. It means the muscle attaches on, or near, the radius. We'll also see ulnaris. As you likely guessed, it means the muscle attaches on or near the ulna. Both the brachialis and the brachioradialis work with the biceps to flex the elbow joint.

At the back of the arm are the triceps. They're involved in straightening the arm. Many tricep exercises, like pulley-push-downs, involve repetitions of this action. The triceps have three heads and a tendon. Directly below the triceps, at the elbow, is the anconeus. This works with the triceps to extend the arm.

In this study of the muscles of the arm, Leonardo shows the deltoid overlapping the biceps and triceps and also depicts the brachioradialis and anconeus.

Let's take a look at the lower arm, anterior view palm facing forward. Our first group of muscles is the flexor group. It's mostly involved with moving the wrist and fingers. It's comprised of four muscles: the pronator teres, the flexor carpi radialis, the palmaris longus, and the flexor carpi ulnaris.

Moving to the back of the arm, we get the extensor group with a final nine muscles. This group's involved in the movement of the wrist, hands, and fingers. It's comprised of the extensor carpi ulnaris, the extensor digiti minimi, the extensor digitorum, the extensor carpi radialis brevis, and the extensor carpi radialis longus. Then sandwiched-in below we get three more: the abductor pollicis longus, the extensor pollicis brevis, the extensor pollicis longus, and the extensor indicis. Leonardo studies the extensor group above and the flexor group below with elegant clarity.

That concludes our review of the major muscles. The best way to begin to absorb all this is to follow Leonardo's example and draw them. The good news is that it's never been easier. There are hundreds of great illustrations and examples online. You can image search each muscle or muscle group by name. Take it slow. It takes time to work through all the stages of this project, from setting up the initial vertical and horizontal measures, to drawing the basic shapes, to constructing the three figures, to inserting the skeletons and finally adding the muscles. Students report spending from 15–25 hours to complete this project but it's time well spent.

Once you've completed this investigation you'll have a much fuller awareness of how bone and muscle relate to the figure. But remember, with many figures we won't see much of either. Bodybuilders and athletes aside, fat and skin obscure the view. And there are places where fat especially collects and forms shapes and bulges of its own, women's breasts are one example. Overall, fat collects most around the center of the body, chest, abdomen, butt, and hips, next, the thighs and upper arms, less again on the lower legs and arms, and least on the hands and feet. These early figurines exemplify the tendency.

So let's talk about some figure drawing projects. The first three involve variations on what we've just done. Let's go over the steps. We started with linear measure. Two horizontal and three vertical lines defining the figure's height in the format shape. Next, we divided the vertical measures into head-height units and related anatomical events to this scale. Then using the same scale, we established widths. Next, using this scaffolding, we drew 10 simple shapes to represent the ribcage and upper torso, the pelvis and lower torso, the thigh, the lower legs, the foot, the upper arm, the lower arm, the hand, the neck, and the head. Then, we introduced contrapposto.

The fourth step involved adding volume through cross contour—first, lines in the long axes to create planes or facets, then ellipses or ovoids to further the illusion. The fifth step involved integrating contour and cross contour to create a greater sense of naturalism.

The first variation to try is a standing, full-length, self-portrait in three views. You'll need a tallish mirror for this. The goal's to analyze a figure observationally in terms of measure and to note actual, as opposed to canonical proportions. Worth noting that proportion and shape carry a lot of information. We routinely recognize people at a distance without seeing their features.

Set up the page as you did in the last drawing. Best to do this without elaborate drapery. You want to be able to see your proportions, so a bathing suit, leotard, shorts, or tank top are all good choices. Next, decide how you want to stand. Think about how posture can be expressive. Are you posing aggressively, timidly, rakishly? Is there contrapposto? Legs together or apart, and where will the arms go?

Start with the anterior view. Take the measure of your head with your pencil. Then measure your body height in heads. Next, calibrate the central vertical axis according to this number and number the head heights. An individual who measures out at eight heads would divide the vertical axis in eight equal segments. Someone five and a quarter head heights, into five and a quarter intervals.

Note what occurs at each head height. For example, second head nipples, third head navel, etc. Some individuals measure out evenly, they have an easy time, and some of us don't. The navel could be somewhat above or below the third head. So when important landmarks don't coincide with a head height, make a line where the landmark occurs with an accompanying annotation.

If you're posing with contrapposto, you could include two height markings for the shoulders, hips, and knees. Or you could indicate both the upper and lower height with a diagonal line.

Once you have your heights established, plot the widths. With the anterior view plotted, carry the measures to your posterior and lateral views. Then turning your head, add any other measures you need from these views. If there's something you can't see, have someone take a picture and use the photo to clarify. Now draw your basic shapes in relation to your measure marks. Check the proportions and adjust. Next, volume. Use the same method we used in the last drawing. Remember to draw the ellipses or ovoids relative to eye level. Then integrate the contour and cross contour to arrive at a more naturalistic figure.

Let's look at a couple examples of this project at different stages. Here, the proportions have been established through shape. And the measure's been carried across the three views. By drawing through, we really begin to get a sense of volume in the figure.

In this example, you can still feel the linear measure, shape, and volumes. All still present in a whispered line weight. But we're well along in moving beyond the mannequin-like beginning to something much more naturalistic, some very good choices here in moving from contour to cross contour. In the anterior view, on the left, note how the shoulder, the deltoid muscle, is described by a contour. The same line becomes the clavicle and is now a cross contour, overlapping the trapezius, behind. You'll note a similar overlap, the trapezius overlapping the neck, in the posterior view. Again, in the front view, the ovoid at the top of the hips conveys the slight swell of the abdomen projecting forward in space.

In this next example, a lot of the pieces are coming together. The three views all feel similarly proportionate. The stance and posture are carried along as well. Note the back of the legs at the knee in the posterior view. The three short overlaps rising from the calves really cement the sensation of volume here. The drapery's also being used as cross contour to describe the underlying form. In the lateral view, note the strap moving from the back and disappearing over the shoulder, adds volume. Last, note how the hair has been analyzed in terms of shape and overlap, creates form.

Let's look at one more. You can still see the vestiges of the under-drawing and how they poke through, supporting the drawing. In the lateral view, the line that rises up along the ridge of the shoulder and through the center of the neck gives it planar structure. In the same view, at the wrist, note the small bit of cross contour related to the ellipse that was drawn there. This now becomes the projection of the bottom of the ulna.

If you belong to a life-drawing group, or have access to a model, try this same project with as many body types as possible. You'll begin to develop a sense of ranges of proportions. It also makes you aware of the three-dimensional structure of the body, and how structures in the front, side, and rear relate.

I mentioned earlier that many people draw the rib cage and pelvis in both front and rear views as if there was no spatial movement, as if the ribcage and pelvis were parallel to the picture plane. The lateral view tells us that this is rarely so. The ribcage tilts forward in space. The pelvis tilts back.

Another great project is to invent your own set of proportions. Think about age, sex, body type, etc. The drawing could consist of a subtle variation on the proportions you used in the initial three-views drawing or it could be something more extreme. Use line—contour and cross contour, in varying line weights, to create space and volume. This will allow you to concentrate on measure. Given the body type, consider what we might see of the underlying anatomy on the surface. We might see a lot or relatively little. And give the pose some thought. Is there contrapposto? What are the arms and legs doing? Let's take a look at a couple examples. I think they'll stimulate your imagination.

Some students stick with the nude and really lean-into the proportions. Here, the hips are wide while both the wrists and ankles really taper. There's strong contrapposto and, in the lateral view, a lot of thrust to both the ribcage and the pelvis.

Some students tackle age. Here, a boy, a toddler, about five heads, still with a fair amount of baby fat. In the anterior view, note how the top of the diaper serves as cross contour creating the swell of the toddler's abdomen. And here, a little girl also about five heads, but much slimmer.

For kids, four to five head heights will feel like a one- to three-year-old. Six heads about five to eight. Seven heads gets us into adolescent and adult proportions. In many adults, the vertical center is at about the groin. In toddlers, it's closer to the navel. As we grow the center, point shifts downward. In other words, the legs grow more than the head or upper body. Some students go for a type, like a ballerina, or runway model, or biker chick.

I ask students to research anything they need, to find costume or accessories that make sense for the drawing. Actual three-dimensional objects are best, but photographs can help. Many artists have used them. Degas, Eakins, and Chuck Close, to name a few. Here's my advice. Don't depend on one picture of a motorcycle helmet or stiletto heel and copy it. Find multiple examples and take bits from each. Conceive of the object in shape and volume then draw it as if seen from three different points of view. It's an excellent visual exercise that helps you imagine the photographed image as real and three-dimensional. Some students create fantastic figures. I really liked this one. It's wonderful, all the wrapping and cross contours. So much form gets brought out. Check out the knees in each view; great management of line overlap. As Dürer did, this is the kind of project you can do over and over, each time investigating a new set of proportions.

There are many ways to approach the figure. And the humble stick figure can be a useful starting point because it can capture the figure in a specific position as well as a set of proportions. Many artists have used stick figures from the 16th-century artists in Dürer's workshop to the 20th century Alberto Giacometti. This method can help you draw figures in many positions that might seem otherwise difficult.

Starting with a simple stick figure you can add a trapezoid or ovoid for the ribcage, then another for the pelvis, and then follow with your other eight body shapes. And if you add tapering cylinders for the body parts, you'll have volume to. So let's try this out.

Let's try some stick figures. We'll start with one standing like in the Giacometti. We'll just start with a stick figure. We'll draw a little line for the shoulders, one for the upper torso, and one for the lower torso. We'll get a leg coming out, lower leg, foot. Get some neck, head, just a little ovoid. And, of course, an arm, and another arm, lower arm. And then we can begin to associate our shapes with this. So we'll start over here with a trapezoid, the upper body, another trapezoid for the lower, and the pelvis. Associate another trapezoid with the line we have for our leg and another one for the lower. And we can associate the trapezoid for our foot and we can do the same thing on the other side. We'll do the same thing for the arm and, of course, a shape for our neck and for the top of the trapezius, the shoulders.

This time, we'll try a crawling figure. So have a line for the spine or backbone, another for the shoulders, and another at the pelvis. You'll have an arm coming out, a lower arm, and a hand. The leg coming down to the knee and we'll get the other arm coming out. And we'll get the other leg going back. And we don't have to use those trapezoids we could use more like ovoids if we wanted to, one for the rib cage, another loosely for the pelvis, something coming down for the leg, another gestural ovoid for the leg and foot. Get that arm coming out, the lower arm down to the hand. We'll get some neck in there.

Let's do a figure walking. We'll start with shoulders, moving down to the hips. We'll have one leg going back, another leg going forward. Maybe we'll put the rib cage in now. You don't have to follow any kind of specific order here. Again, we can work gesturally if we want. Get that other leg going out, foot going forward, a little connector here. Come up to the neck, the shoulders. Now we'll take that arm back, another one moving forward. And if we wanted, of course, we can refine all of our shapes.

Let's do a final figure sitting down. I'll start with the pelvis, just a line, a leg coming out this way, lower leg and foot, same thing over here. We'll come up here to the shoulders, the upper torso shape, and the lower torso shape. We'll build some legs here. And we can go back to our stick over here. Get the arms folding over the chest, a neck going up to our head. And we have a figure seated.

Try drawing this way at the theater or a sporting event, or while watching a video or TV show. People move. There's rarely time to get details. But if you use this kind of shorthand, you can often capture enough so that you can build on the visual note.

In an earlier lecture, I spoke about how you could apply gestural drawing to linear perspective. I showed you how you could rough-in some planes, a room. Find the vanishing point and horizon, and sketch through many complex ideas. If you combine stick figures with linear perspective and a gestural approach, you have a ready method for quickly drawing complex figures in environments, both from observation, and from your imagination.

That's just what Giacometti's doing here. The three figures read in scale and in space because they're drawn in relation to a vanishing point. The space itself, a street flanked by buildings, is a classic box. Same as the room in Leonardo's *Last Supper*.

So try this, too. Try drawing figures in an environment using stick figures with a gestural approach supported by linear perspective. Try it both from your imagination and from observation.

This next group of projects centers on constructing figures in perspectival space. First, using line in one-point perspective, then in two-point perspective, then with value, and finally, using color. We'll start with a figure in one-point perspective using line.

Take out a new sheet of 18 × 24-inch paper. Place it in the portrait orientation. Centered in the page, draw a 16-inch vertical construction line. That means there should be four inches below it and four inches above. We'll be drawing an eight-head figure. At the top of the vertical, draw a horizontal, that's the top of the head; at the bottom, another, for the feet. Now divide the vertical line into eight equal units. At the center mark, make a notation for the crotch. Then decide on your proportions and locate all the vertical and horizontal measures you'll need to draw the 10 basic body shapes. The canon of proportions we used for the figure in three views can serve as the basis for variation.

We'll be drawing a figure in an interior. So while considering proportions consider who this is: sex, body type, age, posture, and pose. Begin to imagine the person as someone particular. Take your drawing to the point where you've blocked in the shapes but don't move to volume yet because I want you to bring in linear perspective before you do. Imagine that your figure's standing centered on a rug or carpet. The goal's to determine point of view, and the carpet, once drawn, will give us eye level, the horizon, and a central vanishing point. And those ingredients will allow you to construct the interior in relation to the figure.

Also, once you've established eye level, you can add volume to the figure. You'll be able to correlate the curvature of the cross-section ellipses and ovoids with height. So the choice about the carpet's shape is important. A lot will follow from it.

Given this, I'd suggest making a number of quick stick figure perspective sketches with different points of view. One, let's say where the carpet is quite oblique—that represents a low eye level—and others where the eye level's higher. This isn't just a technical choice. Eye level establishes whether we're looking up at someone, or down at them, or looking them straight in the eye. It's a meaningful decision. So you could place the horizon first and then draw the carpet based on that.

Here's an example of a drawing just past this stage. The carpet's been placed, volume's been brought into the figure, and a room with a sofa's under construction.

This is the seminal point. You want to take some time to look everything over carefully. Make sure you're satisfied with the way the major planes sit in your composition. The next part requires your invention. What kind of room is it? What's in the room? What's the figure doing?

In this example, the rug's been turned into a yoga mat with a figure to match, another a runway model, another a nude in an ornate home. All the objects in the room, the plants, the fireplace, the divan with the cylindrical pillow, are constructed using volumes related to a vanishing point, as is the figure itself. Find examples of the kinds of things you want to draw, windows, chairs, clothing. If you're using photographic sources really use them. Let the photograph suggest how you could construct the given object using geometric solids, then build them from the appropriate point of view related to the vanishing point and horizon. That's not copying a photo. It's analyzing the visual data in a photo.

After completing this project, try it again but this time starting with stick figures and gestural studies to work out an original composition from scratch. Here are some examples.

Many people would likely think a drawing like this of a girl sitting in a library staring out a window would have had to have been drawn from observation. It has obvious hallmarks of naturalism but with the appropriate knowledge, you can draw things like this from your imagination. This is a wonderful example, great control of line weight and detail. Both make the couple the focal point. Also, great use of cross contour in the figures giving us lots of volume. The floor pattern really makes that plane lie down. And note the window and shoes reflecting into the floor giving it a sheen. This example takes us in a more fantastic direction. One of the things I really like about this drawing is the specificity of the environment, the underside of the highway and the piping running along the slanted surface. And this goes in a more cartoonish direction. The same set of principles can be applied in many different ways.

This is when drawing really gets to be a good bit of fun when you can begin to draw the things you want, the way you want. This brings me back to this Eakins. You likely see how many different things he had to consider in making a drawing like this. And at this point, you're able to wrestle with many of these same pieces to make the drawings you want to make.

That leads us to a couple variations on this project. It wasn't at all uncommon for Eakins and many other artists to build things up in steps. There's an excellent 2001 book on Eakins. It included several essays including one titled "The Camera Artist" by W. Douglass Paschall. Paschall writes:

> From his training at the École des Beaux-Arts, Eakins had learned to see paintings as accretions, as collections of parts to be worked up in succession from sketches, memory, and life study. … For these projects, the camera and its products were merely tools like any other, a compliment to the perspective drawings, costume sketches, sculptures, oil studies, and handwritten notes that contributed their respective parts…

The essential idea is that a painting or a drawing can be built up in steps using a variety of sources. A figure study, a photograph, a perspective drawing, and that the drawing is arrived at through a process of making several drawings.

So, here's the variation. Take a figure study you've done from observation, a self-portrait, or something from the model, a full-length figure is best. Think about how you could use it as a basis for a new drawing of a figure in a specific environment. Use the figure drawing, any other objects, and any photos you need, combined with what you know about composition and perspective to make a wholly new drawing. And you could do the inverse. Do a study of a place from observation, a landscape, a kitchen, a parking lot, the inside of a mall. Then use that as source material. Ask yourself what's going on there. Then invent your figures. You may find that to do the drawing you have to make a series of drawings to discover what you need to know about all the pieces. Many artists have done just that.

Once you've done a figure in one-point perspective, try it in two-point. Start with small gesture studies. It's often easiest to start with the corner of the room first. Place your horizon and vanishing points then rough-in the major planes. Next, draw enhanced stick figures in relation to the large planes. Remember to think compositionally. It's best to do your small sketches in a smaller format shape within a larger page because, in two-point, the vanishing points need to be spaced relatively far apart. It's common for one, or both, to be located outside the drawing's format. The small drawings will help you set this up in the larger drawing.

Here's an example. The drawing's a vertical rectangle. But the page is in the landscape position. This allows for the vanishing points to be placed far right and left, almost at the edges of the page. Let's take a look at a couple other examples. Some of the engaging things to experiment with include the type of figure and type of place. Making things specific, like the girl's age, hairstyle, and the windows, lends believability.

Narrative is something else to explore. Many drawings with figures are, in some sense, telling a story, so ask what's going on. What's the person doing? Here trying on clothing in front of a mirror that's outside the drawing, here a couple at an outdoor café. This is a more elaborate narrative. We get the skis and the guy with the broken leg, then, the wife or girlfriend helping out, stretching to get a book from the high shelf. And you can embroider on reality, here girls with tails and pointy ears living an otherwise middle-class life in the burbs. Or the figures and the place can both be inventions. You'll likely remember this figure from earlier. Many people who draw begin to find figures, places, and situations that they want to investigate and repeat, and that's a great thing. That's why and how artists develop bodies of work, groups of works that are related. It's all about finding things that compel you to play through their possibilities.

Remember, a room's like a block or a box seen from the inside. All the things we find in rooms, including the figures, can be conceived of abstractly built on permutations of blocks, spheres, cylinders, cones, and the like.

Next, try this using value. One idea is to take one of the drawings you've done in line and use it as a model. The utility in this is that you've already solved a whole set of problems—subject matter, composition, proportion, etc.—so you can really concentrate on the new challenge, value.

Remember, shading is just one small part of what value does. Think mood and hierarchy first. In terms of contrast, you'll likely want the most important figure to get the highest contrast, the walls the least. Let the shading happen within that. And when applying the effects of light, remember to imagine a direction for your light source. The specifics of the place can contribute an enormous amount to a drawing. As can the handling of the material, the texture.

Then try color. Consult the color studies you did. Imagine how this last drawing would look in this palette, or alternately in this one. And you'll find out a lot about color by trying the same drawing in multiple palettes, like Monet. Keep everything else the same, change one variable. You find out the meaning of that variable. It works in the sciences and it works in art.

There are all kinds of interesting problems pertaining to drawing the figure from observation. The foreshortened figure is one of them. Now that you've had this introduction to the figure, if you have access to a model, pull out your grid and try what we see Dürer demonstrating in this woodcut. You'll be able to pull on your knowledge of this methodology as well as your new knowledge of figure, itself. I use a version of this method with my students and they get dependably good results. Remember, it's all about measure and a conscientious use of cross contour and overlap. If you stick to outline, the figure will be flat, not volumetric.

When drawing the figure there are a couple things that help you avoid common pitfalls. First, start with the whole. Some kind of linear measure or aggregate shape placed in the page. This lets you control composition and lets you avoid the beginner's problem of running out of room, falling off the page. And work from the general to the specific.

The other way to say this is, at least most of the time, starting with details invites problems, hard to keep the proportions and composition, together. Also, remember, the figure is three-dimensional. Everything has x, y, and z coordinates. Regarding anatomical knowledge, use it as an aid in drawing your figures but showing more bone and muscle isn't always better. Ask yourself what kind of figure you're drawing. What's the intent?

Toward the end of this lecture, in discussing some of my students' drawings, I've foreshadowed where we're going in the final two lectures. Now that you have a number of tools at your disposal, the question becomes what do you want to draw and how do you want to draw it? So we'll take a look at these questions and some options in the final lectures. I hope they'll give you a sense of some possible directions after all the hard work you've done.

# Advanced Concepts: Pictorial Space
## Lecture 35

After working diligently through the many projects in this course, you have some real knowledge and ability at your disposal. You'll likely want to put it to use to make drawings that speak to your own concerns and ambitions. In developing your work, it's useful to be aware of the range of traditions and subjects that have been important in the history of drawing, as well as trends in contemporary art. In this lecture, we'll trace a broad outline of that history, starting back where we began in the first lecture in the Blombos Cave and moving into the present.

### Pictorial Space from Earliest Art

We can chart the whole history of art from the perspective of pictorial space. Going back to the 80,000-year-old drawing incised on a piece of ochre that we saw in Lecture 1, we noted line, shape, value, and pattern. Fast-forward 50,000 years to the drawings in Chauvet Cave, and we get line, value, and overlap. Move forward another 27,000 years to Egypt, and we get line, shape, value, pattern, color, and a clear embrace of spatial illusion, although the world was still depicted as fairly flat.

About 2,000 years later, in Song dynasty China, we have line, shape, value, pattern, color, overlap, and shapes that tilt back into space. By this time, human beings had clearly discovered a great deal about the compositional uses of color and value, using high-contrast events to bring out figures and much more muted value and color contrasts in the ground.

Move ahead another 200 years to northern Italy, and the list of artistic techniques and discoveries becomes longer. We have line, shape, value, pattern, color, overlap, oblique shapes, and three-dimensionality. We have space constructed out of planes: rooms with articulated walls, floors, and ceilings. And we see the effects of light, with more light on the top planes and less on the side planes.

A brief 175 years later, in his *Last Supper*, Leonardo presents a unified theory of line, shape, value, pattern, color, overlap, oblique shape, and value as light creating volume in space. We also see a lifelike and predictable spatial recession that includes both linear and atmospheric perspective.

Artists and their clients or patrons, at least in Europe, were fairly happy with this accumulation of riches. They spent the next 400 years or so playing with this idea of pictorial space. A drawing or painting was essentially like the inside of a box. Even in a landscape, the box metaphor held. Eakins's watercolor was done about 375 years after Leonardo's *The Last Supper* but shares many of the same hallmarks.

### Pictorial Space in Later Art

In the late 19th century, things began to change. Van Gogh painted *The Night Café* in 1888, 15 years after Eakins did his watercolor. Although he was respectful of linear perspective, Van Gogh seems to have kicked and squashed the tidy Renaissance box. The planes were now bent and mangled.

The color was pumped up to levels far beyond unnamable, and even though we see the lights and the cast shadow of the pool table, we don't really see the effects of light on form—the figures, furniture, or wall planes. The surface is animated and the space is partially flattened by all the excited mark-making and texture that sits on the surface, not in it.

With later artists, such as Monet and Cézanne, volume and symmetricality lost further ground. As you recall, the fundamental Renaissance discoveries that led to naturalistic drawing were based on an apparent contradiction. Renaissance artists found that if you closed one eye—always the same one—measured carefully, and tabulated the results on the page, the result resembled the way we think we see with two eyes. But what if we actually looked at the subject with two eyes and tabulated those results? Or what if we paid attention to the way one eye was seeing, then switched to the other?

As we walk around, we think we're seeing a clear, steady, single photographic image. Of course, the reality is that we're constantly seeing two distinct images at the same time, representing two distinct points of view that are actually several inches apart. You'd think this view would make life extremely difficult, but our "software" straightens the world out for us. *Our* reality is that we're seeing one image, though *the* reality is different.

Artists in the late 19th century, Cézanne prominently among them, began to draw and paint while embracing a binocular view of the world. In the early 20th century, Picasso went even further; he wasn't just looking with two eyes but moving his head as he looked, taking in views from straight on, from the side, upwards, and downwards. He was making a mash-up of points of view, which have their similarity with both Egyptian and pre-Renaissance works. For Picasso and many of his contemporaries, the Renaissance tradition of depicting a receding space along a ground plane seen from a fixed viewpoint imposed severe limitations on drawing. Indeed, one way of understanding drawing and painting of the late 19th century and throughout the 20th is as an exploration of the many possibilities that exist in pictorial space. A complex world exists between flatness or two-dimensions and the Renaissance version of the illusion of three-dimensions.

Piet Mondrian's trajectory and body of work are compelling in this regard. He was born in 1872, a year before Eakins did the *Biglin* watercolor. He studied at the Academy of Fine Arts in Amsterdam and, by age 28, was an accomplished artist. Many of his early works were landscapes, and he clearly absorbed many of the same things we've studied in this course, particularly those relating to composition and spatial illusion.

Mondrian died in 1944 at age 71, and his later work might seem completely removed from the early landscapes. But there's a clear evolution to be discovered. If we compare some of Mondrian's landscapes, such as *Row of Eight Young Willows Reflected in Water*, to his later work, we begin to see that the underlying structure of the landscape is based primarily on horizontals intersecting verticals—essentially, a grid.

As we've said, in painting and drawing, what's most important is not what you're looking *at* but what you're looking *for*. What Mondrian was looking for in his mid-30s were landscapes that would sit on the format's surface and have a grid-like aspect: vertical trees and a horizon reflected straight down into water. What he eventually found was that he could do away with the objects and retain the grid-like structure. Along the way, he also found that he could get rid of the structure of the Renaissance box itself.

Van Gogh kicked the box in. Monet pushed it up against the picture plane. Cézanne mangled it. And Picasso and Braque shattered it like glass. But Mondrian eliminated it altogether. The drawn or painted world was pushed up against the picture plane.

## Ambiguous Space

If you spend some time studying Mondrian's later works, such as *Broadway Boogie Woogie*, you'll find that he uses many of the principles we've learned regarding the manipulation of illusionistic space. But rather than using them to reinforce one message, as he did in his earlier paintings, he uses them to contradict one another, producing what we refer to as *ambiguous space*.

Starting in the late 19th century, many artists were, in one way or another, interested in the idea of ambiguous space—configurations that can be read in multiple ways, as two-dimensional, three-dimensional, or somewhere in between. These ways of thinking—the questioning of the kind of space codified in the Renaissance—resulted in both a change in the way many artists thought about representation and in many forays into abstraction.

From the first lecture in this course, we've said that learning to draw is really about learning to see, and you're probably seeing much more now than when we began. Two questions to ask yourself as you move forward are: What do you want to draw? How do you want to draw it?

In the final lecture, we'll talk about a number of projects that will let you build on what you've learned and help you experiment with a range of approaches, with the goal of helping you answer these questions and find areas that are of particular interest to you.

## Suggested Reading

Enstice and Peters, *Drawing*, chapter 1, "The Three-Dimensional Space of a Drawing," pp. 20–46, and chapter 2, "The Two-Dimensional Space of a Drawing," pp. 47–58.

Hockney, David. *I Am a Space Freak*.

Rockman, *Drawing Essentials*, "Different Kinds of Space," pp. 50.

Sale and Betti, *Drawing*, "Categories of Space," pp. 80–98, and "Organizing the Picture Plane," pp. 273–297.

Shan, Ben, *The Shape of Content*.

# Advanced Concepts: Pictorial Space
## Lecture 35—Transcript

After working diligently through these many exercises and assignments, you have some real knowledge and ability at your disposal. You'll likely want to put it to use to make drawings that speak to your own concerns and ambitions. In developing your work, it's useful to be aware of the range of traditions and subjects that have been important in drawing's history and what contemporary artists are drawing as well. So continually looking at a range of diverse drawing and related art is a great long-term project.

Ben Shahn, in his Norton Lectures at Harvard, said that there were two questions for the aspiring artist. "What shall I paint?" And, "How shall I paint it?" We can paraphrase for our purposes, "What shall I draw? How shall I draw it?"

Having to ask these kinds of questions hasn't always been so much the case. In fact, for most of time and in most cultures artists have worked with subject matter, taken an approach, and used materials that were shared by other artists of the same period and geographical area. That's not to say that all art before relatively recent times was geographically homogeneous, but it was much more so than what we find today in most places and there are good reasons for this.

Most societies were more homogenous, religiously, culturally, and, importantly, visually. At the click of my mouse, I can look at examples of art from any place and any time period. From prehistoric cave drawings to what's going on in the galleries in New York or Berlin. Even on my phone, I have access to more images of every kind imaginable than I could consume in a lifetime.

Leonardo, or the Yuan Dynasty ZhàoMèngfǔ, or even a relatively recent figure like Picasso had nothing remotely similar. So we live in a time of great visual plenty and great visual diversity.

Another very important factor is that many artists in many cultures made a kind of art for an existing marketplace. In Europe, during the Renaissance, the Catholic Church was a wealthy and powerful client that needed imagery. So artists contracted to paint madonnas and crucifixions. Or they contracted with kings, queens, and princes to paint their portraits. These artists were business people. They were making products for purchase by clients. And so, the question wasn't so much what kind of art do I want to make, but instead, what does my client want? It's very different from the romantic idea of the bohemian artist, or the artist as a counter-culture figure, someone critical of hierarchical institutions. In Renaissance Europe, successful artists were at least nominally aligned with church and state.

And if we think of the carvings on a Mayan temple, or Indian temple, or on a Native North American totem, this is all art that's related to a culture's particular visual language and related to a broader religious and/or historical context and narrative.

The point is that the model of the artist making his or her own art on spec is a relatively new phenomenon. And because so many recent artists have made whatever they wanted, many have made very different looking things, and many have made different kinds of things at different times in their lives. Like Picasso, or Matisse, or Mondrian, or Philip Guston, and that's a pretty recent phenomena, too.

Another factor particular to the relatively recent present is the lack of any even general agreed-upon standards about what's good and bad in the arts, and by extension, drawing. That's not to say that individuals don't have their own standards and firmly held beliefs. It's just that there's no real agreement among artists, professors, critics, curators, collectors, etc. regarding what they are or should be.

Though it takes time to tease out the truth, at least in medicine, the test is somewhat simpler. Do repeated large double-blind studies on diverse populations and tally the statistical results. Based on hard data researchers can begin to make reasonable conclusions about what might work. Not perfect, but no one has come up with anything even remotely similar to test if a drawing or artwork is worthwhile or worthless.

Perhaps, the only real test is time itself. If successive generations and cultures care about and take pains to preserve certain artworks it suggests they're broadly meaningful to human beings.

Alfred Barr, the founding director of New York's Museum of Modern Art was well aware of this. He wrote, "The historical museum has to be very conservative and careful in its choices. The modern museum, on the other hand, has to be audacious, to take chances. It has to consider the probability that it would be wrong in a good many cases and take the consequences later."

Put a bit more succinctly, the 20th-century American artist Larry Rivers quoted Clement Greenberg, one of the dominant critics of his generation, as saying, "As far as art is concerned, I just prefer good art to bad art, if I can tell the difference."

So how you apply everything you've learned is really up to you. You have to form opinions about what you like and realize other people may disagree with you. This isn't a field where things can be proven in the short-term. It's subjective. Well-meaning individuals disagree vehemently about what constitutes good art and even about what constitutes proper training.

Georges Braque, along with Picasso, one of the developers of Cubism, was quoted as saying, "The whole Renaissance tradition is repugnant to me. The hard and fast rules of perspective which it succeeded in imposing on art were a ghastly mistake, which it has taken us four centuries to redress."

And Robert Beverly Hale, the anatomist I quoted in the section on figure drawing, told the story how the abstract expressionist, Willem de Kooning, scolded him. I'm quoting Hale here, "One day in East Hampton de Kooning came up to my little studio there and said I was ruining any number of people by telling them about anatomy,"

So intelligent, well-intentioned people can disagree and, in fact, today there are university art departments that offer no instruction in either linear perspective or artistic anatomy while others do.

But let me share with you the words of three different writers on art.

The first, Craig Raine, describing the work of the Australian sculptor, Ron Mueck, wrote, "The magic is nothing but hard work and the application of ultra-rigorous standards—who was it said that genius is only the infinite capacity for taking pains?"

The second, Julian Barnes, also in Modern Painters, wrote, "What counts is the surviving object and our living response to it. The tests are simple: does it interest the eye, excite the brain, move the mind, and involve the heart; further, is an apparent level of skill involved?"

And the last by the late critic Robert Hughes, "in art people love rarity, singularity, fully realized handicraft, fine materials, and interesting content."

My own advice is simple. Look at a lot of art. Read about art. See what you love and what you don't. Make judgments. And know that they may change over time. And, of course, have a sense of humor about it.

The great Kurt Vonnegut, perhaps said it best in Palm Sunday, "I have long felt that any reviewer who expresses rage and loathing for a novel or a play or a poem is preposterous. He or she is like a person who has put on full armor and attacked a hot fudge sundae or a banana split."

It's difficult to understand why some people get so worked up. One of the great things about art is that the consequences are generally only experienced on the upside. A bad drawing can't really hurt anybody.

In trying to understand drawing and painting, it's been useful to me to take a broad historical perspective. And I'd like to trace back to where we began in the first lecture, to the Blombos Cave, and bring us forward to the present considering some of the major changes in this field.

Many people are surprised to learn that artists, at least the artists I've known, and I've known many, both personally and through their writings, don't think about style. I've never had a discussion with another artist about this. It's not a concept we use. It tends to be something art historians talk about.

And often, when I meet someone who's not an artist, after they've asked me what I do, the second question is, what style do you do?

While I haven't met artists who talk about style, many talk about pictorial space. On this subject, I've had hours and hours of discussion because considerations and differentiations of approach in regard to pictorial space is really at the core of so much drawing and painting. And it's at the heart of Braque's complaint. He's not railing against a style, but against a system for configuring space in a drawing, linear perspective, so that's telling.

And we can really chart the whole history of art from this perspective.

Going back to that 80,000-year-old drawing incised on a piece of ochre, we noted line, shape, value, and pattern. And if you know what to look for, there's even a bit of volumetric illusion, and what we might even argue, is the first optical illusion or spatial ambiguity.

You could consider it a pattern of flat lines or as a drawing of prisms seen from the right, or contradicting this, a drawing of prisms seen from the left. But I have no idea, and no way of knowing, if the person who made this perceived the illusion of volume here.

Fast-forward 50,000 years and we get line and value, and we even get overlap. But again, I have no idea if the person or persons who drew the horse heads was thinking about space in this way.

Forward about another 27,000 years. Now we have line, shape, value, pattern, and color, and we have a clear embrace of spatial illusion. We can say with certainty that overlap is being employed to signal spatial depth. One hand in front of the harp's strings, another behind. But otherwise, the world is pretty flat and everything's a mash-up of points of view. The god's torso is seen straight-on, the legs and feet, profile.

Move forward another 2,000 years and we have line, shape, value, pattern, color, and overlap, and we have shapes that tilt back into space, parallelograms and ellipses. And human beings have clearly discovered a lot about the compositional use of color and value. It boils down to using high contrast events of value and color to bring out the figures and much more muted value and color contrasts in the ground. Do this and we'll pay more attention to the people every time, but like the Egyptian stele, the ground is still flat and the world's made-up of a mash-up of points of view.

Shoot forward another 200 years and the list gets longer. We have line, shape, value, pattern, color, overlap, and oblique shapes, as before, but we get something new. The flat ground's popped 3D. We have space constructed out of planes. We have a back wall, a sidewall, a ceiling. The table has a top plane and related side planes, as does the bench. But there's more. The table and bench show the effects of light. More light on the top planes, less on the side planes. And we get similar, if less confident, modeling in the drapery and in the heads and hands.

A brief 175 years later and we get the unified theory of line, shape, value, pattern, color, overlap, oblique shape, and value as light creating volume in space. Not to mention a life-like and predictable spatial recession, including both linear and atmospheric perspective, and moreover, an embrace of neutral color. Look at the walls, ceiling, and tablecloths. We haven't really seen that yet. That's unnamable color.

Artists and their clients or patrons, at least in Europe, were pretty happy with this accumulation of riches and they spent the next 400 years or so playing with this idea of pictorial space. A drawing or painting was essentially like the inside of a box. Even in the landscape, the box metaphor holds. Eakins' watercolor was done about 375 years after Leonardo painted his Last Supper and shares many of the same hallmarks. And then things began to change.

Van Gogh painted The Night Café 15 years after Eakins did his watercolor. It's now 1888. Now we know that Van Gogh was respectful of linear perspective, but it's as if the tidy Renaissance box had been kicked about, abused. The planes got bent and squashed, mangled.

The color's pumped-up to levels having more in common with Ugolino's Last Supper than with Leonardo's. And look at the figures, furniture, and walls. Even though we see the lights and the dominant cast shadow of the pool table, we don't really see the effects of light on form. Not on the figures, not on the furniture, and not on the wall planes. And the surface is animated, and the space partially flattened, by all the excited mark making and texture that sits on the surface, not in it.

Six years later, 1894, Monet paints this version of the Rouen Cathedral. The world gets flatter yet. The severe cropping pulls the verticals framing the cathedral's door right onto the picture plane. And the limited value range— no chiaroscuro—adds to the flatness.

Another six years to 1900 and Cézanne paints this still life. Look on the right. You'll note that the side edges of the table are more or less parallel. They're not receding to a vanishing point, harkening back to Ugolino and the Court of Emperor Huizong. And the glass is not symmetrical. It looks like it has two sets of vertical edges, out of focus, vibrating. And the pitcher isn't sitting securely on the table. It's about to tip over.

Even the back edge of the table's amiss. Both the left side and right side tilt down towards the center. And the left side is higher than the right, the table's kind of caving in. And this is the guy who said, "Treat nature by the cylinder, the sphere, the cone, everything in proper perspective so that each side of an object or a plane is directed towards a central point."

You'll remember that the fundamental Renaissance discoveries that led to people being able to get things right were based on an apparent contradiction. What these artists found was that if you closed one eye, always the same one, and measured carefully, and tabulated the results on the page, voilà. It looked like the way we think we see with two eyes. But what if you actually looked at your subject with two eyes and tabulated those results? Or what if I paid attention to the way one eye was seeing and then switched to the other?

Do this with me for a moment. Hold a finger about 10–12 inches in front of your nose. Close one eye, then the other, and alternate them rapidly. Looks a lot like Cézanne's glass, doesn't it? And this is rather interesting. As we walk around, we think we're seeing a clear steady single photographic image. Of course, we're not. The reality is that we're constantly seeing two distinct images at the same time representing two distinct points of view, one several inches away from the other. You'd think it would drive us crazy.

The reason why we can spear a piece of food on our plate or drive into the garage instead of into the garage door is that our software is straightening all this out for us. Our reality is that we're seeing one image, though the reality is different.

It's now 1910. Picasso had a great eye, or really two, and a great visually analytic mind. He could see what someone was up to and grasp where it could lead if you followed it the next several steps. Like fine chess players or entrepreneurs, he saw several steps ahead.

This is Cézanne's wine glass on steroids. Picasso wasn't just looking with two eyes, but moving his head as he looked. He looks straight on, then from the side, then upwards and downwards. And you're likely well aware of even more extreme versions of this method in other works by Picasso.

Picasso's friend, the painter Henri Rousseau, is reported to have said to him, "We are the two greatest painters of this era: you in the Egyptian manner and I in the modern." The way I've always understood Rousseau's comment was that Picasso was making a mash-up of points of view, like the Egyptians. In that regard, he also shares a lot with Ugolino and other pre-Renaissance artists.

I want to come back to Braque's judgment. "The whole Renaissance tradition is repugnant to me. The hard and fast rules of perspective which it succeeded on imposing on art were a ghastly mistake, which it has taken us four centuries to redress." The us included him, Picasso, and a couple others. What he was really saying is that it really limits what and how you draw if the only option is a receding space along a ground plane seen with one eye from a fixed viewpoint.

One way of understanding an awful lot of the drawing and painting of the late 19th century and all of the 20th century is as an exploration of many of the possibilities that exist in pictorial space. Between flatness or two-dimensions, and the illusion of three-dimensions. There's a whole and very complex world that exists here.

Piet Mondrian's trajectory and body of work are compelling in this regard. He was born in 1872, a year before Eakins did the Biglin watercolor. He studied at The Academy of Fine Arts in Amsterdam and by age 28, was an accomplished artist. Many of his early works were landscapes. Like this one.

It's clear from his drawings and paintings that he'd absorbed many of the same lessons as Eakins. Many of the same things we've studied in this course, primary among them, things having to do with composition and spatial illusion. Take a rectangle; divide into two sub-rectangles. You get land and water below, the sky above.

Associate the main subject, a windmill, and trees in the Mondrian or a guy rowing a scull in the Eakins, with the vertical half. Move the viewer back through space in the lower rectangle. Use greater saturation and clarity of edge in the foreground, less to recede, atmospheric perspective. And overall, use subtle neutral color and group your color in a reasonable palette. We could view both as examples of double-complementary palettes, in the Mondrian red-green, yellow-violet, in the Eakins red-green, orange-blue.

Mondrian died in 1944 at age 71. We've looked at his painting *Broadway Boogie Woogie* before. It was completed in 1943, a year before his death. Lots of horizontals and verticals, no diagonals to take us back in space, primary colors, a dark cool, and white. It's pumped.

What happened? How do you get from this to this?

Well, in painting and drawing, what's most important is not what you're looking at but what you're looking for. Remember from the first lecture, learning to draw is really about learning to see. So ask yourself as you move forward, what are you looking for?

Here's a pivotal work where we can see just what Mondrian was looking for. It's titled *Row of Eight Young Willows Reflected in Water*. It was painted between 1902–1907. Piet Mondrian would have been between 30–35 years old. He's attuned to what's going on around him and he's quick to pick up on the flattening he sees in the works of other artists of the day, like Monet and others.

This painting shares some aspects with his windmill painting. There's a large horizontal division yielding land and water below, sky above. The palette's muted and there's some depth of space. The water and the trees reflection are closer, the trees themselves, farther away. But it's clearly much flatter than the windmill, little atmospheric perspective, and no receding diagonals.

If we look at the underlying structure, we find that it's built on lots of horizontals, intersecting lots of verticals, basically, a grid. You can't get much flatter than a grid. Add some flat color to the shapes in the grid. Begins to look familiar, no?

Many people I've met, non-artists, have the idea that abstraction and figuration are wholly different things but, in fact, for many artists they're often intimately connected.

What Mondrian was looking for in his mid-30s were landscapes that would sit on the format's surface, landscapes without diagonals. Landscapes where things hued to verticals and horizontals, landscapes that had a grid-like aspect. So vertical trees and the horizon reflected straight down in the water, well, that made perfect sense.

What he eventually found was that he could do away with the objects and retain the grid-like structure and along the way, he found he could get rid of the structure of the box itself.

Van Gogh kicked it in, Monet pushed-it up against the picture plane, Cézanne mangled it, and Picasso and Braque shattered it like glass. But Mondrian got rid of it all together. The drawn or painted world was pushed up against the picture plane.

That's not to say there's no readable space in *Broadway Boogie Woogie*. There is, of a kind, but it's a purely pictorial space, a type of invented space. It doesn't fully match up with the kind of space we experience in nature.

Stare at the red rectangle located near the center of the canvas' bottom edge. Now look up to the right at the similarly shaped red rectangle in the lower right quadrant. Do you feel the space? Do you feel the recession?

If you remember in an earlier lecture, I outlined 12 principles that affect the illusion of space on a two-dimensional surface. The third was position along the pages vertical axis. That's coming into play here. The red located lower along the format's vertical axis feels closer, one higher along the vertical axis, farther away. They also relate along a diagonal. That was the fifth principle. Diagonals create spatial depth. Connecting them, which is just what our eyes do, creates a long block pulling back, somewhat ambiguously, into space.

Let's make another comparison. Compare the blue rectangle in the lower left quadrant with the red one diagonally above it. Can you feel them flipping back and forth? First, the blue one feels forward, then the red.

The blue feels closer because of principles one, three, and five. It's lower along the vertical axis. It relates to the red above it on a diagonal and it appears to overlap the vertical grid while the red occupies the same plane as that grid. But the red fights back. How? It's bigger; scale. And all else being equal, warms advance over cools, principle eleven.

And that's the Boogie Woogie. That's the dance. Everything's in motion. If you spend some time studying this painting, you'll find Mondrian's using many of the principles you learned regarding the manipulation of illusionistic space. But rather than using them to reinforce one message, like he did as a younger man painting the trees and windmill, he uses them to contradict one another. And we refer to this as ambiguous space.

One visual maneuver seems to suggest X is in front, another that it's behind. Put something lower in the format so it appears to be forward, but also put something bigger above in such a way as to contradict that visual assertion.

Starting in the late 19th century, many artists were, in one way or another, interested in the idea of ambiguous space. It's at the core of a lot of abstraction.

As we'd noted earlier when we looked at this Stella we could read it as essentially flat, a bunch of stripes on a surface, and we could also read it as 3D. We could read each vertical half as a room receding into space, or conversely, as if we were looking down at a pyramid, or we could read one side as a room, the other as the pyramid.

And there's another possibility between 2D and 3D. We could read the central diamond and the two half diamonds flanking it, as overlapping a wall of horizontal stripes. Or we could read two hourglasses overlapping a wall of vertical stripes.

These ways of thinking, this questioning of the kind of space codified in the Renaissance, didn't just affect abstraction. They changed the way many artists thought about representation.

Jasper Johns famously drew and painted flags, targets, letters, and numbers. One way of understanding this is that if you want to make a truthful drawing or painting, or one might say, a realistic drawing or painting, it should be flat. Why? Because a piece of paper is really flat, as is a stretched canvas. That's the reality. So paint things that are flat to begin with. Or even invert the Renaissance window by having the flat thing project into the space of the real room. That's just what Johns did in his iconic painting *Three Flags*. This isn't the illusion of space, it's literal space, but he's playing with us too. As the flags get closer, they get smaller. The inverse of what we should reasonably expect by pictorial convention.

While often representational, Johns would not be considered naturalistic. He purposely avoids most spatial illusion. There were other artists, though, who wanted to pursue illusionistic representation, but were also profoundly affected by many of the visual ideas that we see in abstract artists like Mondrian and Stella.

We've seen how Giorgio Morandi, would push and pull space. The negative shapes between the bottles, the ground, swells forward while some of the bottles dematerialize into the ground.

And Richard Diebenkorn also accentuates the negatives. Part of this is the result of his often severe cropping, or near cropping, of the figure; in this instance, the figure on the left at the elbow, head, and foot, and in the figure on the right at the knee and calf. That produces the flat puzzle-shape negatives around the figures. This is reiterated in his treatment of value, little chiaroscuro. That creates volume, more local value to reiterate flat shape.

William Bailey also sends mixed-signals. While the objects are modeled, none of these objects have top planes. There're no ellipses. No curving cross contours. The cross contours are nothing more than horizontal lines. The shapes and cross contours say flat, say 2D. The modeling says 3D.

And we find many of the same ideas I've been discussing at play in this pastel by Norman Lundin. It's both highly abstract and highly representational. You'll notice that just about everything is either horizontal or vertical. A lot like the Mondrian. We even get the reflection of the table in the floor, like Mondrian's trees, more horizontals, and verticals, very grid-like. And like the Johns, we get a rectangle inside a rectangle. And like the Bailey, the object, the table, has almost no visible top plane, robbing it of dimension.

But in deference to the 3D, we get the subtle cast shadow of the table leg diagonally describing the depth of space under the table. And we get the diagonal floorboards receding to a vanishing point, mixed messages. And Chuck Close famously combines naturalistic representation with a grid. Kind of like Eakins meets Mondrian.

In the final lecture, we'll talk about a number of projects that will let you build on what you've learned and help you experiment with a range of approaches with the goal of helping you find areas that are of particular interest to you. And reflecting on this discussion, they'll incorporate a range of spatial approaches.

# Advanced Drawing Projects
## Lecture 36

Thus far, this course has covered the bulk of what students might learn in the first three years of university-level drawing classes. This final lecture will outline some intermediate and advanced projects. Although the lecture itself is about 30 minutes, the projects could take six months or more to realize. Some are directly related to topics discussed in the last lecture. They'll help you expand on what you've learned and try some alternative approaches, guiding you in your search to find your own areas of artistic interest.

### Artistic Approach
In the last lecture, we posed two questions: What do you want to draw? How do you want to draw it? In developing your own drawing, these two questions are pivotal.

Many art classes are organized around such subjects as still lifes, interiors, landscapes, and the figure. In understanding these nominal subjects, it's critical to note the importance of approach. Although one artist might approach a still life with purely formal concerns, another might approach it to explore a particular theme, such as mortality, fertility, or consumerism. For example, most Cézanne still lifes are formal, but many other European still lifes are narrative. For example, the general goal of the sub-genres known as *memento mori* and *vanitas* was to remind European Christians that life here on earth is temporary.

Approach can be partially designated by a term, such as Impressionism, Cubism, Baroque, or Pop Art. Such terms have their uses, but they tend to be imprecise. Degas and Monet are often lumped together as Impressionists, yet their methods and approaches were quite different. Similarly, Van Gogh and Gauguin are considered Post-Impressionists, but their drawings and paintings have distinct concerns.

Overall, it's often more useful to ask what kind of problem an artist was interested in or what the goal of a particular project was. These kinds of questions can be accompanied by those that help us reverse-engineer the work and understand the methodology: What were the materials? What was the procedure?

Often, the reason a drawing looks the way it does is that the artist was tackling a specific problem and, in response, invented or adopted a set of procedures. When you consider these questions, you develop a more profound understanding of what's behind a given work. And understanding things in this way puts you in a better position to understand how you might work on similar problems or on problems that intrigue you.

## Intermediate Projects
The following intermediate projects are designed to help you relate technical and formal considerations—line, shape, space, composition, proportion, value, texture, and color—to your own subject matter and content. They are also meant to prompt you to explore different means for creating drawings, including observation, construction, and abstraction.

## Abstract Drawing Based on a Figurative Painting
Our first intermediate project is an abstract drawing based on a figurative painting. The idea here is to develop a drawing with a spatial structure that has depth but doesn't function like a Renaissance window or box. It's space without gravity.

To begin the project, select a complex naturalistic figurative painting, one with a compelling structure. The goal is to abstract the structure or architecture lying beneath the figurative elements. The resulting drawing should consist of lines and shapes that you will then use to create your drawing. This is where your own invention comes into play.

Begin to use line weight to suggest a hierarchy. Turn the lines and shapes into planes and volumes but without reference to gravity. To aid in this, you might want to rotate the paper every 15 minutes as you draw. Each time, respond as if the bottom edge had gravity. In the end, many of the assertions will contradict one another, but you'll have succeeded in creating a very different kind of visual space than in prior drawings. As a final step, you could take the drawing back into figuration, adding any elements you might want; at the same time, try to avoid the primacy of a floor plane and a single point of view.

A related project entails drawing the rectangle's armature and using this as a jumping-off point to improvise with abstract volumetric structures in space. One essential idea is that abstraction and figuration are not opposites but intimately connected; they exist along a continuum.

## Multiple Points of View and Scale Changes

For another project that will extend your understanding of composition and space, start observationally, but instead of drawing from a fixed point of view, draw from multiple viewpoints. Instead of drawing any of the things you see just once, repeat them as many times as needed. And instead of keeping all the proportions related naturalistically, allow them to vary to serve the composition.

One variant of this project is to minimize the shift of location and retain all proportions accurately. Draw in one location for 15 or 20 minutes, then move a couple of feet to the right. Draw what you see from this view on top of the first. Then, move a couple feet to the left of the first view and repeat. As you draw, see how you can weave the three views together.

## Earlier Drawing as Source Material

Using one drawing you've made as source material for another allows you to have a dialogue with yourself surrounding visual themes. And as we've said, this is the way many artists build a body of work: They let one piece suggest a second, a third, a fourth, and so on.

Start with the drawing you did from multiple viewpoints as a source for a new drawing. You're no longer drawing directly from observation but from a drawing you just made. At this point, you might add some value, say, 10 to 20 percent hatching while the rest of the drawing remains line. Assign the hatching to what should be the focal area and focal point.

## External Source Material

For the next project, continue working with multiple viewpoints and multiple scales, but ask yourself what you'd like the drawing to be about. Define a theme or idea. You can use any of your prior drawings as source material or make new and specific studies for this drawing. To find a theme, look to a wide range of source material, from other artworks, to literature, to something from popular culture.

## Figure Study Combined with Source Material

Next, you could tackle a related project with a more traditional spatial construct. Select a figure drawing you've done and use it as if it had been made as a study for a more complex drawing. The central idea is to imagine a new environment for the figure and create or search out the materials you'll need, such as perspective studies, photographs, and so on, to be able to depict the environment convincingly. As you work, consider the following questions:

- What is the subject?

- What is happening in the drawing?

- Where is the figure located?

- What kind of place is this?

It's a good idea to do some preliminary gestural sketches to work out your composition, then get the source material you'll need to complete the drawing.

## Model in a Narrative Pose

You might also find an opportunity to pose a model in a specific environment with narrative intent. In forming the pose, consider what the person is doing and why. Think about the mood of the scene and the subject being addressed. Also consider the room where you're drawing and how a section of it could be transformed. Will you put the model in the center of the room, in a corner, by a window? What kind of light will you use—strong directional light, candlelight, light from a television or laptop?

You can work through your ideas before meeting with the model by making small sketches to help you visualize what you might want to set up. Once you've set up the scene you intend to draw, take some time to look at it carefully and ask yourself how it could be improved.

## Imaginary Self-Portrait
For this project, draw yourself from direct observation, but complete the rest of the drawing using linear perspective and other constructive methods.

## Advanced Projects
Our last set of projects is more advanced. Although you'll still be dealing with a range of technical issues, your main goal is to locate areas of personal interest and relate these to drawing. Remember that an area of personal interest can be anything, from nature, to the grotesque, to politics, to geometrical pattern, and much more. An area of interest can also be formal, as in Monet's interest in color and light or Mondrian's interest in the relation of two-dimensional to three-dimensional space.

## Locating Subject and Content
The goal of the first advanced project is to locate content or subject matter. Find source material that's meaningful to you, such as a traditional artwork, an element from popular culture, a passage from literature, a piece of music, or even a chart or diagram. Then, ask yourself the following questions about the materials you've gathered:

- What is the subject?

- How is it being presented formally?

- Why do you feel the presentation is successful?

- How do you intend to use the source material you've chosen?

Next, determine what drawing materials you'll use and at what scale. As you continue to think about your drawing, again, ask yourself a few questions:

- Do you intend to make a line drawing, a drawing that's partially line with some or full value, or a drawing that depends on color?

- How will your drawing be composed?

- How will you address space and proportion?

- Will you use mark or texture?

When you've completed your drawing, give yourself a critique. Ask yourself what's working well and what's not. Also consider whether the subject or content is something you might want to pursue. If it is, you might use this drawing as the basis for others. If it isn't, identify a new theme or subject and try the project again.

**Charcoal on Primed Canvas**
As you've discovered, working through all these projects takes time and effort. One way to surprise yourself and get varied results is to use materials in unexpected ways. For example, try a value drawing using charcoal on a piece of unstretched canvas primed with gesso. You'll find that the canvas is very forgiving; it takes a great deal of erasure with little wear and tear.

**Triptych: Line Drawing Using Black and White Acrylic**
Another structure you might use to further develop your subject matter is the triptych, a work made of three separate panels. As a further challenge, you could try this project using black and white acrylic on three sheets of a heavier artist's grade paper. Work with the paint as a drawing medium, using the black to create line and the white to eliminate it.

**Drawing Using Non–Art Store Materials**
This final project brings us back to the Blombos Cave, where we began in Lecture 1. People have been making art for a long while but have had paper for only a fairly short period—and have had the convenience of art stores for even less time. The challenge is to make a drawing without any art store materials. One of the opportunities here is to capitalize on the way materiality relates to a given subject or might even suggest a subject.

## Your Future in Drawing

Drawing, like many other pursuits, returns dividends in proportion to investment. The more you put into it, the more you're likely to get out. And the more you work on areas that are difficult for you, the more you'll advance well beyond what you assumed were your own limitations. Evaluate your skills and be frank about your areas of greatest difficulty. As you zero in on those aspects and practice them repeatedly, the difficulty will diminish. Above all, find what you love to draw. This will motivate you and lead you to your own creative discoveries.

## Suggested Reading

Cembalest, "How Edward Hopper Storyboarded *Nighthawks*."

Enstice and Peters, *Drawing*, chapter 8, "Subject Matter," and chapter 11, "Visualizations."

Rockman, *Drawing Essentials*, chapter 4, "Developing Ideas, Resolving Problems and Evaluating Results."

Sale and Betti, *Drawing*, chapter 10, "Thematic Development," pp. 299–326, and chapter 11, "A Look at Art Today."

Sewell, ed., *Thomas Eakins*, "The Camera Artist," pp. 239–255, and "Photographs and the Making of Paintings," p. 225–238.

Smagula, *Creative Drawing*, chapter 11, "Exploring Themes," and chapter 12, "Image and Idea."

# Advanced Drawing Projects
## Lecture 36—Transcript

What I've presented so far encompasses the bulk of what I cover in my university drawing classes at the first three levels, what someone might typically study from their freshman through junior years. In this final lecture, I'll outline some advanced and senior level projects.

While this lecture is about 30 minutes, the projects could take six months or more to realize. Some are directly related to topics discussed in the last lecture. They'll help you expand on what you've learned and try some alternate approaches. I hope they'll help you locate your own areas of interest. I think you'll find the process enjoyable and stimulating.

At the beginning of the last lecture I paraphrased Ben Shahn, saying that there were two important questions to consider, what shall I draw? And how shall I draw it? In developing your own drawing, these two questions are pivotal.

There are large nominal classes of subjects like still lifes, interiors, landscapes, and the figure. In understanding these nominal subjects it's critical to note the importance of, what I'd call, approach. Here's what I mean. While one artist might approach a still life with purely formal concerns, another might approach it to explore a theme like mortality, or fertility, or consumerism.

For example, most Cézanne still lifes are formal but there are many European still lifes that are narrative. Like the sub-genres of memento mori and vanitas, serving to remind that life here on earth is temporary.

Approach can be partially designated by a term. Many of these end in "ism," like impressionism or cubism and we have other designators like baroque or pop art. And these terms all have their uses but they tend to be imprecise. Degas and Monet are often lumped together as impressionist, yet their methods and approach were quite different. Similarly, Van Gogh and Gauguin are considered post-impressionists, but their drawings and paintings have distinct concerns.

Overall, I've found it more useful to ask what kind of problem an artist was interested in or ask, what the goal of a project was. And I'd accompany these kinds of questions with those that helped me reverse engineer the work and understand the methodology. What were the materials? What was the procedure? The role of problem solving and procedure's significant. Let me offer an example.

A common challenge in drawing is developing eye/hand coordination. There's an exercise called blind contour that's designed to address this. Here's the gist. Draw observationally with line, any subject, but don't look at the page, only look at the subject. Link your eye to your hand. As you trace over the edges of your subject with your eye, the pencil travels across the surface in tandem. Blind contours always have a look to them and that's rooted in the procedure. Try it. I think you'll see what I mean.

If you saw a blind contour and liked it, you might be tempted to copy the look, try to imitate the style. But that would be quite different than making a blind contour with an understanding of the problem and adoption of the methodology. The point is, often the reason why a drawing looks the way it does is because the artist was tackling a specific problem and in response, they invented or adopted a set of procedures.

When you consider these questions, what problem or question the artist was tackling, you develop a more profound understanding of what's behind a given work. And understanding things in this way puts you in a better position to understand how you might work on similar problems or on the problems that intrigue you.

Let's look at a couple examples. Thomas Eakins and Claude Monet were contemporaries. Both born in the 1840s and both studied painting in Paris in the 1860s. But the projects and procedures they adopted couldn't have been more different.

Eakins was interested in verisimilitude, in accuracy and precision. That was his project. How do you get there? What kind of methodology will work? In an earlier lecture, I quoted W. Douglass Paschall on Eakins. He wrote that he saw his work "…as accretions, as collections of parts to be worked up in succession from sketches, memory, and life study." And he used perspective studies and photographs, too.

Monet's interests lay elsewhere. He wasn't interested in naturalistic precision. Among his primary foci, at least for several decades, were light and color. How the play of light at different times of day in different weather conditions could be interpreted in different palettes and how a given subject is transformed materially by atmospheric conditions. Both its mood and its seeming dimensionality

How do you tackle this problem? Well, identify your subject. Go there and set-up. Draw as much as possible from direct observation. As the light and weather change, start a new drawing or painting.

If you engage with Eakins' methodology, constructive, multi-step, synthesizing many pieces of visual data, you end up with one result. Follow Monet's procedure, quite another.

And this is how artists develop bodies of coherent work. It's nothing more than finding a problem to work on and a set of procedures appropriate to that problem. Then it's a matter of playing out the intriguing variations that occur to you. When you do this, you set yourself up to make some interesting discoveries.

So let's get into some projects. My goal for you is that: You relate technical and formal considerations—things like line, shape, space, composition, proportion, value, texture, and color—to your own subject matter and content. And I want you to begin to explore different means for the creation of drawings including observation, construction, and abstraction. And, also, the use of specific source material.

In the lectures on the armature and composition, we learned that drawings have abstract structures. And in the last lecture, we saw how Mondrian's landscape had a particular abstract structure comprised of horizontals and verticals. The first project I'll describe here involves developing a drawing with a spatial structure that has depth but doesn't function like a Renaissance window or box. It's a space without gravity.

There are two ways to set this up. The first involves selecting a complex naturalistic figurative painting, one with a compelling structure. The goal is to abstract the structure, to abstract the architecture lying beneath all the figurative elements. Then use that structure to create your drawing. Best to find a large, high-quality reproduction of the painting you select.

You could start directly on your paper. First, creating a format shape that's proportionate to the original, then lightly drawing the lines that mirror the structure of the painting, the large divisions in the ground, the aggregate figure shapes, and the sub-shapes within both.

You could also start with a piece of tracing paper over the reproduction and trace the lines, horizontals, verticals, and diagonals that reveal the painting's structure. If you're working with a digital image, you could do this in a program like Photoshop.

In either case, the next step is to draw a proportionate format and structure, lightly, on a sheet of paper. The resulting drawing should consist of lines and shapes, pretty flat, parallel to the picture plane. No box. No real planes.

The next step is your own invention. Begin to use line weight to suggest a hierarchy. And no need to follow the painting's structure at this point. Turn your lines and shapes into planes and volumes but without reference to gravity. To aid in this, you might want to rotate the drawing every 15 minutes as you draw, each time responding as if the bottom edge had gravity. In the end, many of the assertions will contradict one another and you'll have succeeded in creating a very different kind of visual space than in prior drawings.

A second way of attacking this is to simply start with some form of armature derived from a given format's shape like we did in the lecture on that subject. This will also give you a fairly flat linear structure. Everything will be parallel to the picture plane and progress the same way. Begin to create a hierarchy using line weight, then planes and volumes.

As a final step, you could take this back into figuration, adding any elements you might want. You could use prior drawings done from observation as source material but avoid the primacy of a floor plane and a single point of view. Here's an example.

So this is a drawing project where we could start with figuration, a reproduction of a figurative painting. Move to abstraction and then back to figuration, all within the same drawing.

Here's another, though the initial structural lines are very light.

A related project entails drawing the rectangle's armature and using this as a jumping-off-point to improvise with abstract volumetric structures in space. The essential idea is that abstraction and figuration are intimately connected. Not opposites. They exist along a continuum.

Here's another project that will extend your understanding of composition and space. Start observationally, but instead of drawing from a fixed point of view, draw from multiple points of view. And instead of drawing a given object once, it can be repeated as many times as needed. In addition, instead of keeping all the proportions related naturalistically, here the proportions can vary to serve the composition.

You could start by using the figure, but this could be done with any subject. And if you are using the figure, anything else in the room can be interpolated from the architecture of the room to any of the other objects you see. You could use your drawing materials that are sitting next to you, or your foot, or the drawing itself.

I'd suggest using line because it'll allow you to concentrate on composing the elements without having to think about value or color. But using value and color would be great variations on this project later on. Let's take a look at a couple examples.

You'll note here that we have a strong aggregate shape. A triangle, that holds the disparate elements together. Composition's one of the challenges in this drawing. You're working additively. The shapes aren't there in front of you for you to see and to be seen all at one time so you have to think strategically as you build the drawing.

If you try this on 18 × 24-inch paper, make the drawing's format anything but 18 × 24-inches. As you build the composition, consciously find the right format shape. Pay attention to the large planes in the room where you're drawing. Consider using them to structure the space. Like the figure, these architectural elements can be sized and repeated as needed.

You'll note on the left we have the corner of the room showing two walls and a ceiling. We get it repeated at a smaller scale in the doorway in the upper right.

Sometimes I'll pose the model sitting on a ladder. This drawing made great use of it. The ladder serves as both a geometric scaffolding and a powerful actor skewering the dismembered figure.

There are many variants on this project. One is to do this in a more limited way by minimizing the shift of location and retaining all proportions accurately.

Here's the procedure. Start drawing in one location. Keep things light. Work for 15–20 minutes. Then move a couple feet to the right. Draw what you see from this view on top of the first. Then move a couple feet to the left of the first view and repeat. Then begin to weave the three views together.

One of the things I'd like you to consider is how one drawing could serve as source material for another. This allows you to have a dialogue with yourself surrounding visual themes. As noted, this has to do with the way many artists build a body of work. They let one piece suggest a second, a third, and a fourth. So try using a drawing you did from multiple viewpoints as a source for a new drawing. You're no longer drawing directly from observation, but from a drawing you just made and at this point, you could include some value.

For instance, you could have 10-20 percent hatching while the rest of the drawing remains line. The goal is to assign the hatching to what should be the focal area and focal point.

The woman who did this drawing used it as the basis for this drawing. You'll note how the hatching supports the drawing's visual hierarchy. It helps to make the central figure dominant.

As Ben Shahn suggests, it's important for aspiring artists to determine what they want to draw. But then, it's important to find the source materials needed to make a given drawing. This project will get you thinking about this. For this project, continue working with multiple viewpoints and multiple scales, but ask yourself what you'd like to draw about. Define a theme or idea.

You can use any of your prior drawings as source material, but you could also make new and specific studies for this drawing like Michelangelo or Eakins often would. These could be perspective studies, studies of specific objects, or places, or rooms.

Look to a wide range of source material, from other artworks to literature, to something from popular culture, or really, anything else you might be interested in.

Here, the theme was food, a contemporary cornucopia. There's a very intricate play between the angular zigzagging structure of the boxes and table and the very organic shapes of the food, itself.

One of the things that begin to happen as you take on these kinds of projects is that your work becomes more individual because you're drawing things that have some greater meaning to you.

Here, we begin to get a mash-up of different types of representation. From the illustrational to characters related to cartooning.

Others individuals go in a more fantastic direction, robotic figures, and ominous creatures. When you begin to find out what you want to draw about, it becomes engrossing. Or menacing hands crawling through an architectural space.

Other individuals go in a more personal and contemplative direction. This is by the same young woman who made the drawing of the figure being skewered by the ladder. That became an important visual theme she carried through a number of drawings. And that's pay dirt. That's what you're looking for; visual themes that mean something to you.

Next, you could tackle a related project with a more traditional spatial construct, very much following Eakins methodology. You could combine figure studies with perspective studies and even use photographs to support the finished work. Select a figure drawing you did and use it as if it had been made as a study for a drawing of your own device.

Once again, consider subject matter and content, and supplement the figure study with any other source material you might need, perspective studies, web research, and the like. I'd encourage you to consider the following questions: What's the subject? What's happening in the drawing? Where's the figure located? What kind of place is it?

It's a good idea to do some preliminary quick gestural sketches to work out your composition. Then get the source material you'll need to complete the drawing.

This drawing uses a standing male figure study. He gets flipped mirror image to serve the composition. The architecture's invented using linear perspective, and visual sources were found for the sphinx, the lion's head, columns, and tree limbs.

Here, again, we start with a standing male. The gallery is created using linear perspective. Visual resources were used for several of the other figures. Andy Warhol on the right, Sargent's Madame X on the left, and Munch's screaming figure behind her.

Here, a study in foreshortening was used. Source material is found for the drape, the wolf, the deer, the basket, and the landscape events.

Here, a similar study was used. A great job imagining and researching the medical equipment and setting, and well composed with the handwriting and doctor on the left balanced by the curtain on the right.

So go through your figure drawings. Could be a self-portrait you did for this course, or if you meet with a figure drawing group periodically you may have a stack of possible drawings to use. Either will work. The central idea is to imagine a new environment for the figure and search out the materials you'll need to be able to do this convincingly.

Incidentally, this drawing by Norman Lundin was made in a similar way. He drew the basics of the figure using a model. Then, after she'd finished posing, he invented the blackboard and the play of light and shadow.

You might also find an opportunity to pose a specific model in an environment with narrative intent. If you have someone who's willing to pose for you or you belong to a figure-drawing group, this is a great project because posing a model can involve much more than just having the person sit or stand in a given way.

I quoted this from earlier, E.L. Doctorow, but it's worth repeating here. He wrote, "After the set is lit, the camera is positioned, the actors have taken their place, costumed, their hair dressed to indicate economic class, education, age, social status, virtue or the lack of it—95 percent of the meaning of a scene is established before anyone says a word."

So, in forming the pose, consider what the person's doing and why. Consider the mood of the scene and the subject being addressed. Think about the room where you're drawing and how a section of it could be transformed. Will you put the model in the center of the room? Against a wall? In a corner? By a window? What kind of light will you use? A strong directional light? Dispersed light? Colored light? A candle? Flashlight? Light from a television or laptop?

It's great if you have access to professional models. This allows you to pose the person nude, costumed, or some mix of the two, but if nude, consider why the figure's nude. In drawing classes, the model's routinely nude but the nudity can take on a kind of banality. It's an accepted fact that there's a naked person in the room and everyone's staring and drawing, it's a figure drawing class, and the drawings generally betray the fact. They look like drawings of a model posing in a classroom.

But if the model's wearing a bra or T-shirt, and nothing else, it can add a narrative quality. Depending on the pose and how the scene is set, it could appear as someone caught in an intimate moment in their home. Similarly, if the model's costumed it's important to ask what they're wearing and why.

And consider the rest of the set-up. What kind of furniture's involved? Are there chairs? Tables? Lamps? A carpet? And what kind? How's it all arranged? This is just the kind of scene setting that Vermeer did so wonderfully. Every carpet, map, chair and pitcher was chosen and posed with exquisite care.

You can work through your ideas before meeting with the model by making small sketches to help you visualize what you might want to set up. Once you've set-up the scene you intend to draw, take some time to look at it carefully and ask yourself if there are ways to improve it.

I routinely ask my students at the University of Washington to pose the model; one proposed blindfolding and binding the model's hands, very dramatic. Another came in with a set of props, a Viking helmet, sunglasses, a fur coat, and a skull. Setting a directional light threw a great horned-cast shadow on the wall. In another class, we set-up a murder scene, replete with a toppled chair, knife and rubber rat, noirishly lit.

We've also taken these kinds of drawings, done directly from observation, and then used them as the basis for another drawing. I remember a variation of this last one that had us in an apartment looking out the window into the window of the building across the street to reveal the murder scene, Hitchcockian.

These kinds of projects allow you to weave observation, imagination, and constructive drawing methods together to create things that you'd be hard-pressed to draw from observation alone.

Here's another project that requires connecting observation and constructive methods. It can also require finding source materials. I call it an imaginary self-portrait. In essence, you draw yourself from direct observation but the rest of the drawing is made using linear perspective and other constructive methods.

You'll notice here that there's a mix of line and hatching. It's used hierarchically to make us pay attention to the figure and tree. The one real bit of solid value occurs in the eye and that predictably becomes the focal point.

This next group of projects is more advanced. While you'll still be dealing with a range of technical issues, your main goal is to locate areas of personal interest and relate these to drawing.

An area of personal interest could be anything. Nature has inspired many artists from visual artists to poets, to composers. So has love. But it could equally be something quite different, more abstract, like measuring. That subject really impelled Dürer, and several 100 years later, Giacometti.

Leonardo had various themes or ideas he returned to repeatedly in his drawings, from human anatomy to the grotesque, to the movement of water, and geometrical pattern.

Michael Gibson, writing in the *International Herald Tribune*, reported on a conversation Picasso had with André Malraux in which he said he believed in themes that, "included such things as 'birth, pregnancy, suffering, murder, the couple, death, revolt, [and] possibly the kiss.'"

Clearly, much 20th- and 21st-century art has revolved around themes associated with war, politics, class, ethnicity, sexual identity, and the environment, among many others. On the flip side, an area of interest could be formal. Mondrian or Morandi were primarily interested in the relation of 2D to 3D space, Monet with color and light.

The first project's goal is to locate content or subject matter. Find source material that's meaningful to you where the subject plays an important role, and is successfully presented, and something you'd like to use as the basis for your own work.

It could be a traditional artwork like a painting, sculpture, or photograph, or something from the web, or from popular culture from a YouTube video, a piece of animation, a film clip, or a video game, or something from TV, could be an ad. Or it could be something else, like a map, a diagram, or a chart. Or it could be textual, something from literature, a poem, a lyric, or a piece of music. Or something related to science, history, politics, or economics. Or related to any of the other interests you have. It could be fashion, sports, food, or gardening.

Gather your source material first, hard copy or digital files. Ask yourself questions about the materials you've gathered, like these: What's the subject? How's it being addressed formally? Why do you feel it's successful? How do you intend to use it?

If you've been working through this course with a friend or family member, having these discussions with someone else can be invaluable, either in person or via email or phone. If not, use writing. Pursue a dialogue with yourself. As we've seen, Leonardo, Dürer, and Van Gogh all write about their studio concerns. Many artists do. It can be an extremely useful tool.

So now, you've selected your source material and have a sense about how you'll use it. The next step is to determine what material you'll use and at what scale. Make some notes about this, too. Then ask yourself how you intend to make your drawing. Will it be a line drawing? Partially line with some value? Or fully in value? Or color? How will it be composed? What about space? And proportion? Will there be mark or texture?

All the things you've painstakingly studied now have to be considered in view of expression as they relate to your theme or idea. When you've completed your drawing, give yourself a critique. Ask yourself what's working well and what's not. Based on this assessment you may want to work back into the drawing and repeat this step.

When you've gone as far as you can, ask yourself if the subject or content is something you want to continue with. If it is, you could use this drawing as the basis for a second, third, or fourth drawing. If this drawing was done with line, you might want to try color. If value, line. If small, try it at a larger scale. Or try recomposing the elements. If this isn't something you'd like to pursue, you could identify a new theme or subject and try again.

Working this way takes time. It's hit or miss. So give yourself multiple opportunities. One way to shake things up is to vary the materials in some unexpected ways. These last three projects do just this.

The first is a value drawing using charcoal on primed canvas. I'd suggest making the drawing at least 32 inches in one direction. That gives it some heft. The other dimension is up to you and should be dictated by compositional considerations.

To do this project you'll need a piece of un-stretched canvas or linen that you'll prime with gesso. Tack the canvas to a wall, large drawing board, or piece of plywood. Make sure you tack at regular intervals so the surface will remain flat. Give the canvas at least two coats, one horizontal, let it dry, then another vertical. Once fully dry, start the drawing with vine charcoal. As your composition becomes clear, you can use compressed and charcoal pencil, too.

One of the great things about charcoal on primed canvas is that it's so forgiving. It takes a great deal of erasure with little wear and tear. You can even wash the charcoal off with mild soap and water to get back to a very white surface. And, of course, you can always fix an area and re-prime to get back to virgin white.

When I do this with my advanced drawing students, after they've completed this project, we have a critique. The central question we ask is this. Is there a theme that's emerging that would suggest a group of works that relate across this theme?

Here's an example of one of these charcoal on canvas drawings, a memorable drawing that emerged from this student's thoughts about how technology is omnipresent and invasive. I think you can see how a drawing like this might well lead to other drawings dealing with our relationship to technology.

Another structure you might use to further develop your subject matter is the triptych. A work made of three separate but related panels. If you haven't seen many triptychs, look up Hieronymus Bosch, Hans Memling, Max Beckmann, and Francis Bacon. This one's by the 19th-century Japanese artist Utagawa Hiroshige, a great proponent of the form.

As a further challenge, you could try this project using black and white acrylic on three sheets of a heavier artist's grade paper. Use the paint as a drawing medium. Use the black to make line, the white to eliminate it.

Start with small notebook drawings to begin to develop your idea. Then collect the source material you'll need to move forward.

This last project brings us back to the Blombos Cave where we began in Lecture 1. People have been making art for a very long time. People have had paper for a pretty short time and the convenience of art stores for even less. This project takes us back to our roots, maybe literally, to roots.

The challenge is to make a drawing without any art store materials. One of the opportunities here is to capitalize on the way materiality relates to a given subject. The way materials might even suggest a subject. Over the years, I've seen many interesting examples spanning drawings made by dripping wax on wood, or drawing with wine on a bed sheet, and even lipstick on a pork belly. These approaches can be evocative and provocative.

Drawing, like many other pursuits, returns dividends in proportion to investment. The more you put in, the more you'll likely get out. And the more you work on areas that are difficult for you, the more you'll advance well beyond what you assumed were your own limitations. Evaluate your skills and be frank about your areas of greatest difficulty. Zero-in on those aspects and practice them repeatedly. The difficulty will diminish.

Find what you love to draw. This will motivate you and lead you to your own creative discoveries.

Thank you.

# Additional Activities

## Lectures 1–3

For those looking for a broad history of art as a companion to help situate what they're learning about drawing, *Janson's History of Art* is one the standards for the Western canon. Another is *The Story of Art* by E. H. Gombrich. For a more inclusive worldview, Stokstad and Cothren's *Art History*, weighing in at a hefty 1,240 pages, is highly regarded. It starts with prehistory and, in addition to the Western canon, covers Asia, Islam, Africa, and the Americas. Though out of print, Daniel Mendelowitz's 1966 book *Drawing* is a good introduction to the history of (mostly) Western drawing from prehistory to the early 20th century.

Quite a few books have good introductory sections on getting to know your materials. The chapter "Media and Materials" in Bernard Chaet's *The Art of Drawing* contains much useful information. Arthur Guptill's books *Rendering in Pencil* and *Rendering in Pen and Ink* have excellent sections, as well. In the first book see, chapter 2, "Equipment and Studio," and chapter 3, "Preliminary Exercises." In the book on pen and ink, see chapters 2 through 5.

## Lectures 4–11

In the lectures, we covered only a fraction of the many artists who use line, shape, volume, and composition in compelling ways. Below are listed a few names, with search terms when applicable, that will bring up many more excellent examples.

Note: Specific sites are listed for some works. If a work is not easily found, its listing includes the name of a book from the bibliography for this course in which it appears.

### Contour and Cross-Contour Line

Alexander Calder drawings
Juan Gris Line drawings
George Grosz drawings
Al Hirschfeld drawings

Jean-Auguste-Dominique Ingres line drawings
Gustav Klimt drawings
Gaston Lachaise drawings
Sol LeWitt drawings
Henri Matisse line drawings, including *Nude in the Studio* (pen and ink, 1935)
Pablo Picasso line drawings

## Line and Volume

Luca Cambiaso, especially his preparatory drawings

## Gestural Line

Honoré Daumier drawings
Willem de Kooning drawings
Frank Gehry drawings
Rembrandt van Rijn drawings

## Shape

Arshile Gorky
Fernand Léger drawings
Henri Matisse cut-outs
Joan Miró drawings
Donald Sultan drawings

## Positive and Negative Shape

Richard Diebenkorn drawings
M. C. Escher
Philip Pearlstein drawings
Fairfield Porter
Euan Uglow

## Composition

Balthus (Balthazar Klossowski de Rola)

Max Beckman
Edgar Degas
Piero della Francesca
Lucian Freud
Edward Hopper
Rembrandt van Rijn drawings

### Lectures 12–14

In his 2001 book *Secret Knowledge*, the artist David Hockney advanced the theory that the great changes evidenced in the Renaissance were traceable to the use of such optical devices as the *camera lucida* and *camera obscura* to project images onto a surface and trace them. As part of this project, he put together what he termed *The Great Wall* of art. It's a compilation of reproductions of art historical works arranged chronologically that shows a distinct change in the 15th century, when artists' ability to portray subjects naturalistically took off. A Google search will turn up a number of images of the wall, as well as articles about his project.

For those interested in the subject of mechanical devices used by Western artists, Martin Kemp's book *The Science of Art* has an excellent chapter on the subject.

Although the thought of drawing or painting a still life of books might not at first seem an exciting proposition, artists have done remarkable things with this idea. For example, the contemporary artist Vincent Desiderio painted a tour-de-force image titled *Cockaigne* that you can view at http://www.hirshhorn.si.edu/collection/vincent-desiderio-cockaigne/.

If you search the subject "still life of books," you'll find works by a number by 17th-century Dutch artists, including Jan Davidszoon de Heem. Many of the works you'll find fall within the larger category of *vanitas*. The idea expressed here is that knowledge is fleeting and, thus, a vain pursuit. Many of these images also contain skulls or snuffed-out candles to further illustrate the point.

Still life can be much more than just a bunch of random objects posed on a table. For additional inspiration, look for *Agnus Dei* by the 17th-century

Spanish artist Francisco de Zurbarán. Next, fast forward a couple hundred years to Frida Kahlo's still lifes of fruit. They're clearly set up and composed to bring out visual references to sexual organs and fertility. Finally, the contemporary artists Audrey Flack, Wayne Thiebaud, and Janet Fish each have a fresh take on the form.

## Lectures 15–19
### Perspective

Robert Bechtle drawings
Jacopo Bellini drawings
Leonardo da Vinci, *Study for the Adoration of the Magi* (c. 1481)
Rackstraw Downes drawings
Thomas Eakins, *Perspective Study for the Biglin Brothers Turning the Stake*, *The Pair Oared Shell*, *Perspective Study for Baseball Players Practicing*
M. C. Escher
Anselm Kiefer
Giovanni Battista Piranesi drawings

### Three-Point Perspective

Charles Sheeler, *Delmonico Building* (lithograph, 1926, http://www.metmuseum.org/toah/works-of-art/68.728)

## Lectures 20–30
As in the earlier section on formal language (Lectures 5–11), there are many excellent examples that could be added to what we looked at in this section of the course. Below are listed a few more individuals who are well worth looking up.

### Value, General

Kent Bellows
Edgar Degas monotypes
Sidney Goodman
Francisco Goya drawings

## Value, Compositional Use of Value

Akira Arita drawings
John Luke, *Self-Portrait* (pencil on paper, Mendelowitz, Faber, and Wakeman, *A Guide to Drawing*, p. 27)
John Singer Sargent, *Study of a Nude Man* (c. 1874–1880, Rockman, *Drawing Essentials*, p. 93)

## Value, Chiaroscuro

Caravaggio
Alfred Leslie drawings
Georges Seurat drawings
Giovanni Battista Tiepolo drawings

## Value, Black and White

Aubrey Beardsley drawings
Honoré Daumier, *Don Quixote and Sancho Panza* (c. 1850,
http://www.metmuseum.org/collection/the-collection-online/search/333888)

## Value, Positive and Negative Shape

Richard Diebenkorn drawings
Emil Nolde, *Harbor* (brush and ink, c. 1900,
http://www.artic.edu/aic/collections/artwork/23101)
*Notan*
A. R. Penck drawings, black and white

## Value, Gesture and Compositional Sketching

Edward Hopper, *Study for East Side Interior* (chalk and charcoal on paper, 9 x 11½ in., 1922, http://whitney.org/WatchAndListen/AudioGuides?play_id=845), *Study for Evening Wind* (1921, Mendelowitz, Faber, and Wakeman, *A Guide to Drawing*, p. 149) drawing for *Morning Sun* (1952, Brown and McLean, *Drawing from Life.* p. 29).

## Planar Head

Planar heads are available from http://www.planesofthehead.com.

## Texture and Mark

Texture and mark are used expressively in a range of drawing types. If you pull up the Charles Schulz characters Charlie Brown and Pigpen, you get a very clear illustration of how potently mark affects the character of the subject portrayed.

## Texture and Mark, General

Pieter Bruegel, *The Beekeepers* (pen and brown ink, 1568)
Honoré Daumier drawings
Jean Dubuffet drawings
Alberto Giacometti drawings
Philip Guston drawings
William Kentridge drawings and animations
Roy Lichtenstein drawings
Henry Moore drawings
Saul Steinberg drawings

## Texture and Mark, Cross-Hatching

Hiëronymus Bosch drawings
Pieter Breughel the Elder drawings
Paul Cadmus drawings
R. Crumb drawings
David Levine drawings
Raphael (Raffaello Sanzio) drawings
Peter Paul Rubens drawings

## Texture and Mark, Simulated Textures

Kent Bellows
Vija Celmins

Audrey Flack

René Magritte, *The Thought Which Sees* (graphite, 1965, http://www.moma.org/collection/object.php?object_id=35714)

Catherine Murphy, *Paint Jacket Pockets* (pencil on paper, 2002, http://www.moma.org/collection/object.php?object_id=96790)

Sylvia Plimack Mangold drawings

Mark Tansey

## Color

Pierre Bonnard

Yvonne Jacquette

Wayne Thiebaud

Édouard Vuillard

In addition, below are listed a number of color websites that may prove interesting:

- *ColorCube*, http://www.colorcube.com/illusions/illusion.htm. This site provides visual illustration of some optical effects.

- *Color Matters*, http://colormatters.com. This site focuses on color in relation to symbolism, marketing, and a number of other related subjects.

- *Color Palette Generator*, http://www.degraeve.com/color-palette/. This site allows you to upload an image and create a set of swatches related to the image.

- *A Breakdown of Color in Film Stills*, http://imgur.com/a/PyRly. Analyzes movie stills in terms of the color palettes used in the shots.

- *Movies in Color*, http://moviesincolor.com/. Like the preceding site, this one also analyzes movie stills in terms of the color palettes used in the shots.

## The Figure, General

Jean-Auguste-Dominique Ingres drawings
Jacopo da Pontormo drawings
Raphael (Raffaello Sanzio) drawings

## The Figure, Anatomy

Bernhard Siegfried Albinus
Andreas Vesalius

## The Figure in Perspectival Space

Henri de Toulouse-Lautrec, *The Laundress* (1888, Mendelowitz, Faber, and Wakeman, *A Guide to Drawing*, p. 41)

## The Figure, Foreshortened

Giovanni Paolo Lomazzo, *Foreshortened Nude Man* (Mendelowitz, Faber, and Wakeman, *A Guide to Drawing*, p. 43)
Andrea Mantegna, *Lamentation of Christ* (http://en.wikipedia.org/wiki/Lamentation_of_Christ_%28Mantegna%29)

Additionally, here is a list of some prominent artists who have done substantial work with the figure over the past 50 years. Their work represents a broad range of approaches.

Steven Assael
Paul Cadmus
George Condo
R. Crumb
John Currin
Richard Diebenkorn
Marlene Dumas
Eric Fischl

Lucian Freud
Gregory Gillespie
David Hockney
John Koch
Alfred Leslie
Loretta Lux
Elizabeth Peyton
Alice Neel
Philip Pearlstein
Jenny Saville
Luc Tuymans
James Valerio

## Lectures 35–36

To figure out where you want to go, it can be helpful to look at a wide array of work and see where you feel some kinship. The following three lists for further research include either contemporary artists who are currently active or artists who were active during the last 100 years. Most are artists who weren't mentioned in the lectures or in these accompanying notes. Needless to say, these lists are far from inclusive, and as you search each individual, you'll come up with 5 or 10 others artists who are or were in some way associated with your initial target.

The first list highlights abstraction because many people who otherwise have a real interest in art find abstraction challenging. However, some of what you've learned about drawing in this course should offer inroads to other work that might at first be difficult to appreciate. If you've kept abstraction at arm's length, here are some artists you might look up:

Willem de Kooning
Arthur Dove
Marsden Hartley
Howard Hodgkin
Franz Kline
Emma Kunz
Kazimir Malevich
Kurt Schwitters

Sean Scully
Terry Winters

Below are a few artists who straddle abstraction and figuration:

Louise Bourgeois
Cecily Brown
Richard Diebenkorn
Philip Guston
Philip Pearlstein
Gerhard Richter
Matthias Weischer

Finally, the following artists span some of the enormous range of figuration we've seen over recent decades:

Jean-Michel Basquiat
William Beckman
Paul Cadmus
James Castle
Vija Celmins
Sue Coe
John Currin
Tacita Dean
Jan De Vliegher
Rackstraw Downes
Marlene Dumas
Eric Fischl
Ann Gale
Gregory Gillespie
Ignacio Ituria
Yvonne Jacquette
William Kentridge
John Koch
Catherine Murphy
Alice Neel
David Park

Ed Paschke
Jenny Saville
James Valerio

A last note: Don't be afraid to change or try new things. Although some artists have been consistent over the decades of their lives, many others have embraced change. A look at the careers of such artists as Edvard Munch, Picasso, Matisse, Mondrian, or Philip Guston can be instructive in this regard.

# Bibliography

**Drawing: Contemporary Sources**

Aristides, Juliette. *Classical Drawing Atelier.* Watson-Guptill, 2006. A solid and well-illustrated introduction to drawing based in post-Renaissance and pre-20th-century practices and techniques in the West.

————. *Classical Painting Atelier.* Watson-Guptill, 2008. A companion to Aristides's drawing book. For the purposes of this course, this volume has useful chapters on composition and value.

————. *Lessons in Classical Drawing.* Watson-Guptill, 2011. A third volume from Aristides that includes a DVD tutorial.

Bothwell, Dorr, and Marlys Mayfield. *Notan: The Dark-Light Principle of Design.* Dover, 1991. A good introduction to *notan*, discussed in Lecture 22.

Boyer, Sheri Lynn. http://www.artinstructionblog.com/drawing-lesson-a-theory-of-light-and-shade. Many of my students have found this site helpful. It provides an overview of value and light and shade.

Chaet, Bernard. *The Art of Drawing.* 3rd ed. Harcourt Brace Jovanovich, 1983. A good, straightforward text. Provides clear explanations and examples of line, value, texture, and figure-ground relationships. Also includes a good chapter on materials.

*Character Design.* http://pinterest.com/characterdesigh/. This site is popular among my students who have an interest in concept art, comics, manga, and video games.

Curtis, Brian. *Drawing from Observation.* McGraw-Hill, 2009. This source contains a great deal of good material, with a focus on observational drawing. The explanations are clear and in-depth. The many illustrations also help the reader understand the topics under discussion.

Eagle, Ellen. *Pastel Painting Atelier*. Watson-Guptill, 2013. Although a number of books in this bibliography have a section or chapter devoted to pastel, this book represents a comprehensive introduction to the subject with many fine illustrations by a range of artists.

Enstice, Wayne, and Melody Peters. *Drawing: Space, Form and Expression*. 2nd ed. Prentice Hall, 1995. This book contains all the materials commonly presented in a college-level drawing course. It's well-organized, with a wealth of reproductions of artists' works, including many contemporary examples.

Faber, David L., and Daniel M. Mendelowitz. *A Concise Guide to Drawing*, 8th ed. Cengage Learning, 2012. Another comprehensive college-level drawing book. Covers all the important formal elements with sections on still life, landscape, and the figure. Also contains many helpful visual examples, including contemporary ones.

Goldstein, Nathan. *The Art of Responsive Drawing*. 3rd ed. Prentice Hall, 1984. A thorough book with much useful information.

Guptill, Arthur L., and Susan E. Meyer, *Rendering in Pencil*. Watson-Guptill, 1977. This is one of my favorite books on drawing. It is thorough and provides clear explanations. Note: Arthur Guptill, Jack Hamm, and Andrew Loomis were all primarily illustrators and were first published in the early to mid-20th century. They each wrote multiple texts on drawing, many of which are listed in this bibliography. Their books are decidedly different in character from books published from the 1970s onward and geared to the college classroom (e.g., those by Enstice, Faber, Goldstein, Mendelowitz, Rockman, Sale, Smagula, and others.). Guptill, Hamm, and Loomis tend to be more prescriptive, with a greater reliance on recipes. Also, some of the drawing examples of female nudes veer toward the pin-up, and some drawings of different "ethnic types" would make most contemporary readers cringe. That said, these men were extremely knowledgeable and wrote in clear and concise terms. There is a wealth of good information in their respective volumes.

———. *Rendering in Pen and Ink*. Watson-Guptill, 1997. Like the book on pencil, an excellent work.

Hamm, Jack. *Drawing Scenery: Landscapes and Seascapes.* Perigee Trade, 1988. Hamm starts out with many basics about composition. He then goes on, in his encyclopedic way, to catalog 38 kinds of trees, many other kinds of rocks, and cloud types charted by altitude.

————. *First Lessons in Drawing and Painting.* Perigee Trade, 1988. Although this book is not comprehensive, it includes plenty of excellent information.

————. *How to Draw Animals.* Perigee Trade, 1983. If you want to draw animals, this is a good place to start. Hamm starts with some anatomical basics. Then, he runs through scores of different animals, pointing out differences among species. For example, he doesn't just give you one bear but contrasts the Kodiak with the polar, grizzly, black, Himalayan, sloth, and Malayan varieties.

The J. Paul Getty Museum. *Formal Analysis.* http://www.getty.edu/education/teachers/building_lessons/formal_analysis.html. This link provides an introduction to formal analysis.

The Kennedy Center. *Formal Visual Analysis.* https://artsedge.kennedy-center.org/educators/how-to/from-theory-to-practice/formal-visual-analysis. This site lists many formal language terms with concise definitions.

Loomis, Andrew. *Fun with a Pencil.* Titan Books, 2013. There's a fair degree of overlap in Loomis's books, but they all have excellent information, including this one. This volume concerns itself a bit more with cartooning than the others.

————. *Successful Drawing.* Titan Books, 2012. An excellent book with good sections on basic forms, form in light, linear perspective, and relating the figure to perspective.

Mendelowitz, Daniel M. *Drawing.* Holt, Rinehart and Winston, 1967. This is not a how-to book but, instead a good introduction to the history of (mostly) Western drawing from prehistory to the early 20th century.

Mendelowitz, Daniel, David L. Faber, and Duane Wakeman. *A Guide to Drawing.* 7th ed. Cengage Learning, 2006. From the same publisher and by some of the same authors as *A Concise Guide to Drawing*, above, this source has many of the same materials.

Pumphrey, Richard. *The Elements of Art.* Prentice Hall College Division, 1996. Though introduced as a book on design, not drawing, this volume provides an excellent introduction to formal language and many important aspects of two-dimensional art.

Rockman, Deborah. *Drawing Essentials.* Oxford University Press, 2009. A well-thought-out book with chapters on all the major topics generally covered in a college-level drawing course.

Sale, Teel, and Claudia Betti. *Drawing: A Contemporary Approach.* 5th ed. Thomson Wadsworth, 2004. A fairly comprehensive book, with many good explanations and illustrations.

Smagula, Howard J. *Creative Drawing.* 2nd ed. McGraw-Hill, 2002. Yet another thorough and well-illustrated book covering the major topics generally discussed in a university drawing course.

Stevens, Peter, S. *A Handbook of Regular Patterns.* MIT Press, 1981. An excellent and comprehensive book on pattern. The text is clear, analytical, and accompanied by a wealth of illustrations.

**Drawing: Historical Sources**

Ackerman, Gerald, and Graydon Parrish. *Charles Bargue and Jean-Leon Gérôme Drawing Course.* ACR, 2011. This is a reprinting of the 19th-century *Cours de Dessin* of Charles Bargue, a French lithogropher, and Jean-Léon Gérôme, the academician known for his orientalist paintings. The method involves copying drawings of plaster casts, starting with line to block out shape, then volume attached to planar structure. This is used as a guide to then apply value. The young Pablo Picasso made copies of a number of these drawings.

Alberti, Leon Battista, and Martin Kemp. *On Painting*. Penguin, 1991. A seminal 15th-century text on drawing and painting.

Cennini, Cennino d'Andrea. *The Craftsman's Handbook*. Dover, 1933. Among the first Western manuals on artistic materials and procedures. Written in 15th-century Italy, it describes many of the methods for making materials and their application.

da Vinci, Leonardo. *A Treatise on Painting*. Dover, 2005. http://www. treatiseonpainting.org. This is a translation of a text based, at least in part, on Leonardo's manuscripts. A number of versions were published in Europe during the 16th and 17th centuries. It is somewhat fragmented but interesting nonetheless. Multiple early editions can be viewed at the link listed above.

———. http://www.universalleonardo.org/. This site, curated by Martin Kemp, has an excellent selection of Leonardo's drawings and manuscript pages.

de Honnecourt, Villard. *The Sketchbook of Villard de Honnecourt*. Edited by Theodore Bowie. Indiana University Press, 1959. A 13th-century sketchbook of drawings with subjects spanning figures, animals, and architecture. This source is noteworthy for our course because it constitutes an early example of a draftsman using simple geometric shapes to draw more complex objects (plates 35 through 38). Plate 35 has the inscription "Here begins the method of representation."

Dürer, Albrecht. *Four Books on Human Proportions*. http://brbl-dl.library. yale.edu/vufind/Record/3783330. The entire 1528 volume containing Dürer's exploration of human proportions is available as a pdf at this site.

———. *Underweysung der Messung*. http://brbl-dl.library.yale.edu/vufind/ Record/3529943. The original German text printed in 1525.

———. *Underweysung der Messung*. http://brbl-dl.library.yale.edu/vufind/ Record/3529943. An additional eight pages published in 1538.

Dürer, Albrecht, and Walter Strauss. *The Human Figure by Albrecht Dürer: The Complete Dresden Sketchbooks*. Dover, 1972. https://archive.org/stream/

Bibliography

bub_gb_1vEEAAAAYAAJ#page/n51/mode/thumb. A collection of many of Dürer's annotated figure studies done in preparation for his 1528 publication *Four Books on Human Proportion*.

———. *The Painter's Manual*. Abaris Books, 1977. An English translation of Dürer's *Underweysung der Messung*.

Eakins, Thomas. *A Drawing Manual*. Philadelphia Museum of Art, 2005. This is an unfinished book written by Eakins based on his teaching at the Pennsylvania Academy of Fine Arts. Though fragmentary, it shows the kind of analytical and quantitative thinking that engaged him.

Koller, E. L. *Light, Shade, and Shadow*. Dover, 2008. This book was originally published in 1914. Though a slim volume, it covers the perspective of shadows in some detail.

Ruskin, John. *The Elements of Drawing*. Dover, 1971. Ruskin was better known as an art critic than an artist, but he was an accomplished draftsman nonetheless. His book, originally published in 1857, is heavier on text and has fewer illustrations than most contemporary books on drawing. That said, much of the information here is relevant.

Speed, Harold. *The Practice and Science of Drawing*. Dover, 1972. Originally published in 1917, this is a well-known text on drawing, much of it dealing with both line and mass.

Vasari, Giorgio. *Vasari on Technique*. Dover, 2011. This 1550 text on methods in architecture, sculpture, painting, and design was written by the well-known author of *Lives of the Artists*. It gives us a contemporary view of the materials, methods, and techniques used by Renaissance artists.

**Linear Perspective**

Auvil, Kenneth W. *Perspective Drawing*. 2nd ed. McGraw-Hill, 1996. A concise and thorough book with clear illustrations.

D'Amelio, Joseph. *Perspective Drawing Handbook*. Dover, 2004. This book was originally published in 1964. It is well-illustrated and covers many of the most important concepts related to one- and two-point perspective.

Montague, John. *Basic Perspective Drawing*. 6th ed. Wiley, 2013. Among the clearest and most thorough books on linear perspective. The newest edition includes a key code that gives you access to a website with instructional videos.

Norling, Ernest R. *Perspective Made Easy*. Dover Publications, 1999. This book was first published in 1939, and its illustrations may look somewhat dated. That said, the subject is well- presented. Both the text and illustrations communicate the essential points in a vivid way.

Robertson, Scott, and Thomas Berling. *How to Draw*. Design Studio Press, 2013. A good recent book on perspective. It covers all the basics and has detailed sections on drawing cars and planes.

Veltman, Kim H. *Linear Perspective and the Visual Dimensions of Science and Art*. Deutscher Kunstverlag, 1986. This is not a how-to book. Instead, it's a historical study of Leonardo's writings on, and use of, perspective and related subjects. Contains a great deal of fascinating material.

**Figure Drawing and Anatomy**

Bridgman, George B. *Bridgman's Complete Guide to Drawing from Life*. Sterling, 1952. Bridgman taught figure drawing and anatomy at The Art Students League in New York City for many years. This book includes his own drawings, accompanied by explanations of the major body parts. There is also a chapter on drapery.

Brown, Clint, and Cheryl McLean. *Drawing from Life*. 2nd ed. Harcourt Brace, 1997. A comprehensive guide to figure drawing. Many of the formal considerations are covered in the first section on fundamentals. This is followed by a section on anatomy and another on composition and expression.

Goldstein, Nathan. *Figure Drawing.* 4th ed. Prentice Hall, 1993. A good overview of figure drawing. Well-illustrated, with chapters on structural, anatomical, and expressive approaches

Hale, Robert Beverly. *Master Class in Figure Drawing.* Watson-Guptill, 1991. This text is distilled from Hale's anatomy classes at The Art Students League in New York. Hale moves through the major structures of muscle and bone in the human body, relating them to choices made in drawings by important artists from Leonardo to Rubens.

————. *Lectures on Artistic Anatomy and Figure Drawing.* http://www.joan.com/art_video.htm. These videos of Hale teaching at The Art Students League in New York provide excellent material. There are 10 talks in all, each covering a section of the body, as follows: Lecture 1, Rib Cage (78 minutes); Lecture 2, Pelvis (81 minutes); Lecture 3, Leg (74 minutes); Lecture 4, Foot (72 minutes); Lecture 5, Shoulder Girdle 1 (77 minutes); Lecture 6, Shoulder Girdle 2 (68 minutes); Lecture 7, Arm (76 minutes); Lecture 8, Hand (80 minutes); Lecture 9, Head and Skull (80 minutes); Lecture 10, Head and Features (97 minutes).

Hale, Robert Beverly, and Jacob Collins. *Drawing Lessons from the Great Masters.* Watson-Guptill, 1989. This book analyzes artists' drawings in relation to the use of line, light, plane, and anatomy.

Hamm, Jack. *Cartooning the Head and Figure.* Perigee Trade, 1986. As the title suggests, this book is all about cartooning. The examples are decidedly early to mid-20th century, but there's a great deal of excellent information here. Hamm had an encyclopedic personality. There are pages devoted to charting scores of cartoon noses, ears, and lips. A wonderful book to leaf through.

————. *Drawing the Head and Figure.* Perigee Trade, 1988. A great introduction to constructive figure drawing. In other words, the approach is not about observation but about using systems of measure and shape to draw figures from your imagination. Concerns itself a bit less with constructing three-dimensional form than either Loomis or Reed.

Loomis, Andrew. *Drawing the Head and Hands.* Titan Books, 2011. An excellent introduction to the subject.

―――. *Figure Drawing for All It's Worth.* Titan Books, 2011. Contains a great deal of good information about measure, anatomy, constructing the figure from blocks, and drawing from observation.

Reed, Walt. *The Figure.* 30th ed. North Light Books, 1984. An excellent book with chapters on figure construction and anatomy.

Thomson, Arthur. *A Handbook of Anatomy for Art Students.* 5th ed. Dover, 2011. This book is primarily text with some illustrations. It contains thorough descriptions of the major anatomical structures of the body.

Vanderpoel, John H. *The Human Figure.* Dover, 1958. Considered one of the early-20th-century classics on the subject, this book was originally published in 1935. Like many books of the period, it has more text than illustration, and some contemporary readers find the prose difficult. That said, there is a wealth of good information to be found here.

Visiblebody.com. SkeletonPremium and MusclePremium. These apps let you move through all the important bones and muscles, which are rendered in three dimensions. You can rotate them and see them in motion, as well. This is one of the best ways to get a clear idea of how the various anatomical structures relate. The apps are compatible with many phones, tablets, and various operating systems.

Winslow, Valerie L. *Classic Human Anatomy.* Watson-Guptill, 2009. Among the most recent and comprehensive books on anatomy for the artist. It does a good job of outlining and illustrating the important bones and muscles.

## Color

Albers, Josef. *Interaction of Color.* Yale University Press, 2006. Albers was a student, and later, a colleague, of Itten's (see below) at the Bauhaus. His book has become one of the standards used in art schools and universities in the United States. The strengths of his approach center on bringing out optical relationships, namely, how color is relative. A single color can be made to appear darker or lighter, warmer or cooler based on the surrounding colors—hence, the *Interaction* in the title.

*A Breakdown of Color in Film Stills*. http://imgur.com/a/PyRly. A good site that breaks down the color palettes in film stills into swatches.

Guptill, Arthur L. *Oil Painting Step-By-Step*. 9th ed. Watson-Guptill, 1978. Though primarily a book on oil painting, this source includes several useful chapters on color.

Guptill, Arthur L., and Susan E. Meyer, *Watercolor Painting Step-By-Step*. 2nd ed. Watson-Guptill, 1968. Similar to the oil painting guide above, this book has several excellent chapters on color.

Itten, Johannes, and Faber Birren. *The Elements of Color*. Van Nostrand Reinhold Company, 1970. Along with Albers's book, Itten's is one of those most used in U.S. academia today. The two approaches are similar.

Loomis, Andrew. *Creative Illustration*. Titan Books, 2012. As with all Loomis's books, there's excellent information here on many aspects of drawing, including line, tone, composition, and perspective. Also includes a useful chapter on color.

Robertson, Jean, and Craig McDaniel. *Painting as a Language*. Cengage Learning, 1999. Although primarily a book on painting, this source includes a good chapter on color, as well chapters on space, the picture plane, and abstraction.

**Drawing and Painting Materials**

Many of the contemporary drawing books listed above have excellent chapters on materials. In addition, several books that deal solely with this subject are listed below.

Chaet, Bernard. *An Artist's Notebook: Techniques and Materials.* Holt, Rinehart and Winston, 1979. This book has a lengthy chapter on drawing materials. Also includes a chapter on color.

Doerner, Max. *The Materials of the Artist.* Mariner Books, 1949. First published in 1921. Before Mayer published *The Artist's Handbook*, this source was among the most thorough and up-to-date texts on the subject. Like Mayer's work, it deals primarily with painting materials.

Eastlake, Sir Charles Lock. *Methods and Materials of Painting of the Great Schools and Masters.* Dover, 2001. This book, by a former president of the British Royal Academy, was originally published in 1847 as *Materials for a History of Oil Painting.* It is a lengthy volume—more than 1,000 pages—covering historical painting methods and techniques in the West.

Gettins, Rutherford J., and George L. Stout. *Painting Materials.* Dover Art Instruction, 2011. Originally published in 1942 and written by two specialists affiliated with the Department of Conservation at Harvard's Fogg Art Museum. This is a technical work with extensive information on pigments, mediums, and supports.

Gottsegen. Mark David. *The Painter's Handbook.* Watson-Guptill, 2006. Among the most recent, useful, and readable of the books listed here. The recipes are clear and concise. There is also a good introductory chapter on common drawing materials and papers.

Mayer, Ralph. *The Artist's Handbook.* 5th ed. Viking, 1991. First published in 1940, this book remains one of the standard references in the field. It is mostly concerned with painting materials but includes chapters on pastel and watercolor.

Speed, Harold. *Oil Painting Techniques and Materials.* Dover, 1987. First published in 1924, this book is regarded by many as a classic, covering traditional oil painting materials and techniques.

Turner, Jacques. *Brushes: A Handbook for Artists.* Design Press, 1992. A fairly comprehensive look at brushes used with a wide range of materials.

**Bibliography**

Van de Wettering, Ernst. *Rembrandt: The Painter at Work.* University of California Press, 2009. An interesting book that examines Rembrandt's materials and painting methods.

**Health and Safety**

McCann, Michael. *Artist Beware.* Lyons Press, 2005. This book has become a standard in the field.

Rossol, Monona. *The Artist's Complete Health and Safety Guide.* Allworth Press, 2001. Along with McCann's book, this is a well-reviewed and highly regarded text on the subject.

**Artists' Writings, Interviews with Artists, and Artist Video Clips**

Along with the more hands-on texts, it's useful to get a sense of what a range of artists actually think about. Below is a modest selection spanning artists' writings, interviews with artists, and clips of artists at work.

Ashton, Dore. *Picasso on Art*, De Capo Press, 1988.

Bacon, Francis. *Fragments of a Portrait*, https://www.youtube.com/watch?v=xoFMH_D6xLk. *Francis Bacon's Last Interview*, https://www.youtube.com/watch?v=p-d9TdRYUaQ. *Francis Bacon Rare Interview, 1971*, https://www.youtube.com/watch?v=aFDiemYxuvA.

Baselitz, Georg. *Georg Baselitz Talks about Farewell Bill*, https://www.youtube.com/watch?v=A6ipu0KzUds.

Cembalest, Robin. "How Edward Hopper Storyboarded *Nighthawks*." http://www.artnews.com/2013/07/25/how-edward-hopper-storyboarded-nighthawks/.

da Vinci, Leonardo. *The Notebooks of Leonardo da Vinci.* 2 vols. Edited by Jean Paul Richeter. Dover, 1970.

Desiderio, Vincent. *LCAD Vincent Desiderio Painting Demo*, https://www.youtube.com/watch?v=GxRN9tcN6pQ&list=PLnCjvdddc6_45 u4kYcwZJCbj_xmWcyfbr.

De Vliegher, Jan. http://www.youtube.com/watch?v=-T4ZW8NZOeA&feature=youtu.be.

Fischl, Eric. *Dive Deep: Eric Fischl and the Process of Painting*. https://www.youtube.com/watch?v=MWpYD4LWpVc.

Freud, Lucian. *An Exclusive Tour of Freud's Studio*, https://www.youtube.com/watch?v=4YMV4EyaPMM. *Lucian Freud's Rarest Interview*, https://www.youtube.com/watch?v=i5KcT4PBh2M.

Gaugain, Paul. *The Writings of a Savage.* Viking, 1978.

Henri, Robert. *The Art Spirit.* Basic Books, 2007.

Hockney, David. *David Hockney by David Hockney.* Abrams, 1977. *I Am a Space Freak*, http://channel.louisiana.dk/video/david-hockney-i-am-space-freak. *Photoshop Is Boring*, https://www.youtube.com/watch?v=oAx_aYGmpoM. *Who Gets to Call It Art*, https://www.youtube.com/watch?v=CjfIKymXMa4.

Kahlo, Frida, with an introduction by Carlos Fuentes. *Diary of Frida Kahlo*. Bloomsbury, 1995.

Katz, Alex. https://www.youtube.com/watch?v=p1bA6Sbk24Y.

Kiefer, Anselm. https://www.youtube.com/watch?v=qmn-w2J68pU.

Klee, Paul. *Diaries of Paul Klee*. University of California Press, 1968.

Kuspit, Donald. *Fischl: An Interview with Eric Fischl.* Vintage, 1987.

Lundin, Norman, and David Brody. *Norman Lundin: Selections from Three Decades of Drawing and Painting*. University of Washington Press, 2006.

Matisse, Henri. *Matisse on Art*. Phaidon, 1973.

Redon, Odilon. *To Myself: Notes on Life, Art, and Artists*. George Braziller, 1996.

Richter, Gerhard. *Gerhard Richter Painting*, http://www.youtube.com/watch?v=yF6EluMNR14. *Gerhard Richter in the Studio*, https://www.youtube.com/watch?v=ExfNJDh4K1g.

Richter, Gerhard, and Hans Ulbrich-Obrist. *The Daily Practice of Painting*. The MIT Press, 1995.

Shan, Ben. *The Shape of Content*. Harvard University Press, 1992. This volume contains six essays by Shahn delivered in 1956–1957 at Harvard University as part of The Charles Eliot Norton Lecture series. Shahn writes clearly and succinctly about art. Students of this course will find the final essay, "The Education of an Artist," of particular interest.

Sylvester, David. *The Brutality of Fact: Interviews with Francis Bacon*. Thames and Hudson, 1990.

Van Gogh, Vincent. *Letters of Vincent Van Gogh*. Penguin, 1998.

Wellington, Hubert. *The Journal of Eugene Delacroix*. Phaidon, 1995.

**Compilations of Artists' Writings**

Chipp, Herschel B. *Theories of Modern Art*. University of California Press, 1984. This volume includes writings by many 19th- and 20th-century artists, from Paul Cézanne to Henry Moore.

Goldwater, Robert, and Marco Treves. *Artists on Art*, Pantheon, 1974. This volume includes artists' writings from the 14th to the 20th centuries.

Harrison, Charles, and Paul Wood. *Art in Theory, 1900–1990.* Blackwell, 1995. As the title indicates, this book covers the period 1900–1990 with writings by many artists and writers, from Gaugain and Freud to Barbara Kruger and Richard Serra.

**Art History and Criticism**

This short list contains texts referenced in the course and a few others that are either comprehensive or will serve as introductions to aspects of art history or criticism.

Davies, Penelope. *Janson's History of Art.* 8th ed. Pearson, 2010. One of the standards used in university art history survey courses covering the Western canon at length.

Fineberg, Jonathan. *Art since 1940.* 3rd ed. Pearson, 2010. As the title indicates, this book covers art since 1940. Though not comprehensive, it's a readable overview that will give the reader a sense of the important individuals and ideas during this period.

Gombrich, Ernst. *The Story of Art.* 16th ed. Phaidon Press, 1995. One of the bestselling introductions to the history of (mostly) Western art. Well written and accessible.

*Grove Dictionary of Art,* Oxford University Press, 1996. This 34-volume work is as comprehensive as anything available. Not something you're likely to buy for your home library, but major libraries will have a copy. It's extremely useful for getting information and references for any topic you might become interested in.

Hickey, Dave. *Air Guitar: Essays on Art and Democracy.* Art Issues Press, 1997. A collection of essays by one of the more witty contemporary critics. It can serve as an introduction to some contemporary thought on art.

Hockney, David. *Secret Knowledge.* Studio, 2006. Artist David Hockney advances the theory that the great changes evidenced in the Renaissance were traceable to the use of such optical devices as the *camera lucida* and *camera obscura.* He argues that artists from Van Eyck to Caravaggio to Ingres used them to project images onto a surface and trace them. There is also a BBC documentary on the same subject that makes for interesting viewing (http://youtu.be/ynrnfBnhWSo).

Hughes, Robert. *Nothing If Not Critical.* Penguin Books, 1992. Hughes was the art critic for *TIME* magazine for many years and one of the most prominent art critics of the late 20th century. This is a collection of his essays on both historical and more contemporary artists. The prose is unusually lucid.

————. *The Shock of the New.* Knopf, 1991. An excellent introduction for anyone interested in beginning to understand what might be termed "modern art."

Kemp, Martin. *The Science of Art.* Yale University Press, 1992. This is a fascinating book for those interested in many of the more quantitative aspects of art. It covers the relationship of science to art in the West from the Renaissance through the 19th century. It includes an interesting chapter on mechanical devices used in drawing and painting. The appendix boasts one of the most lucid and concise descriptions of the principles underlying linear perspective.

Kleiner, Fred S. *Gardner's Art through the Ages: A Global History.* 2 vols. 14th ed. Wadsworth, 2012. Another standard comprehensive text used in university art history courses.

Sewell, Darrel, ed. *Thomas Eakins.* Philadelphia Museum of Art, 2001. Include several excellent articles on Eakins's working methods.

Stokstad, Marilyn, and Michael Cothren. *Art History.* 4th ed. Pearson, 2010. An inclusive world history of art. Starting with prehistory, it covers Asia, Islam, Africa, and the Americas, in addition to the Western canon.

# Notes

# Notes

# Notes

# Notes

# Notes